100% EXTERNSHIP SUCCESS

100% Externship SUCCESS

CAROL SILVIS

DELMAR
CENGAGE Learning

Australia • Brazil • Japan • Korea • Mexico • Singapore • Spain • United Kingdom • United States

100% Externship Success
Carol Silvis

Vice President, Career Education SBU:
Dawn Gerrain

Director of Learning Solutions:
John Fedor

Managing Editor:
Robert L. Serenka, Jr.

Senior Acquisitions Editor:
Martine Edwards

Product Manager:
Anne Orgren

Editorial Assistant:
Michael Spring

Director of Production:
Wendy A. Troeger

Production Manager:
Mark Bernard

Content Project Manager:
Mark Bernard

Art Director:
Dave Arsenault

Technology Project Manager:
Sandy Charette

Director of Marketing:
Wendy E. Mapstone

Channel Manager:
Gerard McAvey

Marketing Coordinator:
Jonathan Sheehan

Cover Design:
David Arsenault

For product information and technology assistance, contact us at
Professional & Career Group Customer Support, 1-800-423-0563
For permission to use material from this text or product,
submit all requests online at **www.cengage.com/permissions**
Further permissions questions can be emailed to
permissionrequest@cengage.com

Library of Congress Control Number: 2007045699

ISBN-13: 978-1-4180-1549-7

ISBN-10: 1-4180-1549-0

Delmar Cengage Learning
5 Maxwell Drive
Clifton Park, NY 12065-2919
USA

Cengage Learning products are represented in Canada by Nelson Education, Ltd.

For your lifelong learning solutions, visit **delmar.cengage.com**

Visit our corporate website at **www.cengage.com**

Printed in the United States
3 4 5 6 XXX 16 15 14 13

Contents

2 HOW TO SUCCEED AT YOUR EXTERNSHIP 103

Preface

Welcome to the 100% Externship Success Kit. It is important for today's graduates to prepare before beginning the search for an externship and/or job. Employers expect prospective applicants to display the proper attitude, have appropriate resumes and portfolios, develop interviewing skills, and research the company to which they are applying.

The Career Readiness Kit equips students and instructors with the tools needed to plan and search for an externship and/or job. In addition, information on turning the externship into a job and being successful in a career is presented.

COVERAGE

The Career Readiness Kit is an informative textbook with a back-of-the-book CD that contains worksheets, games, and hands-on exercises. The text provides advice and guidelines for taking a personal inventory, writing a resume, planning for the interview, finding an externship or job, and achieving success in the workplace. Special features include self-assessments, exercises, reflection questions, summary lists, and case studies. The Personal Data Keeper at the end of the text provides students with an organized format for recording skills, previous employment, and references. This document is designed to be used as a reference for completing employment applications and is also available on the CD.

The Career Readiness Kit is presented in an easy-to-read format, is filled with tips, and offers complete externship guidelines.

KEY FEATURES OF THIS TEXT

- Learning Objectives focus the readers' attention on important content.
- Key Terms alert readers to need-to-know information.
- Self-assessments guide readers in matching themselves to a position in an effort to assure success.
- Summary lists of essential information lead to a clearer understanding of what employers want and what the prospective employee should do to address those wants.
- Concepts guide the reader by providing information on preparing a resume and portfolio, developing interviewing skills, and searching for and working at an externship and/or job.
- Exercises, reflection questions, and tips all contribute valuable information and practice for readers.
- End-of-chapter case studies encourage students to apply the concepts presented in the chapter. The scenarios are intended to encourage analytical and decision-making skills through critical thinking.
- End-of-chapter questions promote memory skills.
- Back-of-the book CD containing activities, games, and practice tests accompanies the text.
- Online Resources are available to the Instructor, including teaching suggestions, chapter tests, and PowerPoint slides.

The 100% Externship Success Kit

1. Provides information necessary to procure a suitable job.
2. Provides students with an assessment of their skills and abilities.
3. Provides students with an assessment of their personal characteristics.
4. Provides information, exercises, case studies, and questionnaires to develop career-enhancing skills and personal traits.

Anyone who is seeking an externship and/or permanent employment can use this text to increase chances for success, including students, adults in retraining, and others who will be doing an externship or conducting a job search.

YOU WILL LEARN HOW TO:

1. Assess your personal assets and determine your personal value system.
2. Assess your skills and abilities, and identify transferable skills.
3. Assess life experiences.
4. Match your skills/abilities to a position.
5. Define the basic components and benefits of an externship.
6. Write an effective resume, reference sheet, and cover letter.
7. Develop interviewing skills and determine proper interview dress.
8. Fill out an application effectively and organize a portfolio.
9. Identify key professional traits and what constitutes a positive work ethic.
10. Research a company and search for an externship position.

HOW TO GET THE MOST OUT OF THIS BOOK

Read the Learning Objectives, text, and summaries to get the most out of the core material. Complete all assessments and assignments to develop your knowledge and skills. Evaluate your progress by completing the activities, reflection questions, case studies, and end-of-the chapter questions.

ACKNOWLEDGEMENTS

A special thanks to Martine Edwards, acquisitions editor, for her vision, suggestions, and assistance with this project; editor Jennifer

Anderson for lending her expertise; editor Barbara Price for her help and guidance; and to all the reviewers for this text.

I would also like to acknowledge my family—Ryan, Niki, and Mikaila—for their encouragement.

ABOUT THE AUTHOR

Carol A. Silvis, M.Ed., is a post-secondary instructor, lecturer, and author of numerous publications. She conducts seminars and workshops on career planning, customer service, telephone techniques, time management/organization, stress management, and written communications for various companies and schools. She has also coordinated writing conferences. Her master's in adult education has prepared her to deal with the special concerns of adult students and individuals in the workplace. Carol lives in Murrysville, Pennsylvania.

Preparing for Your Externship

CHAPTER 1

Determining Your Career Path

1

LEARNING OBJECTIVES

After completing this chapter, you should be able to:

1. Assess your personal assets.
2. Determine your personal value system.
3. Assess your skills and abilities.
4. Identify transferable skills.
5. Assess life experience.
6. Match your skills/abilities to a position.

Chapter 1 helps you identify your personal assets and personality traits in order to use them to your advantage when considering an externship and/or job. The self-assessments will aid in the identification of those characteristics needed for success in the workplace as well as those that should be avoided or improved. In addition, this chapter provides self-assessments that will help you identify your strengths and weaknesses with regard to the skills and abilities you will need for your career.

KEY TERMS

attributes	inventory	self-assessment
career	life experience	transferable skills
career center	life skills	values
competencies	life stages	
evaluate	personal asset	

❯ INTRODUCTION

At any given time, companies and organizations have a variety of job openings in a number of fields. There are those jobs that provide a living, and those that provide a living through a rewarding career. The type of position you obtain depends largely on what you put into your job search and how well you match yourself to a particular opening. Finding a job that you can turn into a successful, rewarding career takes planning. The first step is to complete a **self-assessment** (or evaluation) so you can match your interests, goals, skills, education, and **values** (or beliefs) to a position that is a good fit for you.

● MATCH YOURSELF TO A CAREER

If you have particular interests and abilities, why not use them to create a custom-designed **career** or occupation? A significant number of people find themselves trapped in what they consider dead-end jobs, while others in those same jobs love what they do. How can that be? Perhaps it is because those who are the happiest are a better match for their jobs, or they have a positive attitude toward their tasks or the services they provide.

Too many people spend too many hours at jobs they do not like. If you match yourself to a particular job, you will be aligned with work you will enjoy doing, which in turn will give you a positive experience.

You can match yourself to a job by determining the type of position you would like and considering your personal traits, likes and dislikes, and abilities. Another way to determine if you like a particular type of work or company is to do an externship. Although the externship is a chance to learn skills in a work environment, it is also an opportunity to determine if you like performing specific tasks and/or working in a certain environment.

When you are determining the type of career you want, consider your likes and dislikes with regard to the industry, the type of company environment, the personnel, and the tasks you will perform. Also consider realistically how the position will fit into your lifestyle (i.e., family commitments, travel time, benefits, etc.).

EXERCISE 1-A

In the space provided, describe your ideal job, environment, and specific duties you would like to perform.

- In what field will you work?

  _____

  _____

- In what size and type of company will you work?

  _____

  _____

- What are your specific responsibilities in this position?

  _____

  _____

- What is the perfect work environment for you?

  _____

  _____

- What are the perfect tasks you would enjoy completing?

  _____

  _____

- What is your supervisor like?

  _____

  _____

- What are your coworkers like?

  _____

  _____

1

EXERCISE 1-B

Fill out the match yourself to your career self-assessment in Table 1–1.

Table 1–1   SELF-ASSESSMENT: MATCH YOURSELF TO YOUR CAREER

To match yourself with a job, check the following items that apply to you. You may want to take into consideration other items not listed here that pertain to your specific interests. Add those to the list as well.

I WOULD LIKE TO WORK IN THIS ENVIRONMENT:

☐ A business office	☐ A relaxed atmosphere	☐ A financial institution
☐ An educational setting	☐ A retail store	☐ A hospital
☐ A small company	☐ A large company	☐ A thrilling place
☐ Outdoors	☐ Indoors	☐ A doctor's office

I WOULD LIKE TO WORK UNDER THESE CONDITIONS:

☐ With others	☐ By myself	☐ With tools
☐ With my hands	☐ With equipment	☐ Using my intelligence
☐ With close supervision	☐ With little supervision	☐ Using creativity/ideas
☐ Under pressure	☐ With heavy equipment	☐ With numbers/data

I WOULD LIKE TO WORK IN THIS FIELD:

☐ Television/media	☐ Politics	☐ Illustration/design
☐ Legal	☐ Entrepreneurship	☐ Counseling
☐ Sports	☐ Journalism	☐ Accounting
☐ Technical	☐ Health care	☐ Sales
☐ Science	☐ Advertising	☐ Government
☐ _____	☐ _____	☐ _____
☐ _____	☐ _____	☐ _____
☐ _____	☐ _____	☐ _____

FIND THE CAREER FOR YOU

What type of environment did you choose in Table 1–1? What field(s) did you select? Is it possible to find a job in the combined field and environment you chose? If it is possible, begin your search with the size of the company and the location that you prefer. If it is not possible, you may need to revise your choices.

Check the latest edition of the *Occupational Outlook Handbook* (put out by the United States Department of Labor) at your library for a listing of professions. You may also find information at your school's **career center**, which is a special department that provides assistance in finding a suitable job. In addition, vocational assessment tests are available on the market and on the Internet. They can be helpful tools in deciding the right career path for you.

ASSESS YOUR PERSONAL ASSETS

Your **personal assets** are your special talents, abilities, and character traits. If you hope to be happy and successful in a career, you will want to match yourself to a position not only with your skills, but also with your personality traits and your beliefs or values. Employees who are happy performing their tasks will most likely remain in their positions for many years. On the contrary, if employees are dissatisfied and unhappy, they will likely seek other employment. Increase your chances for a successful career by assessing your skills and personality traits.

VALUES

Certain things, people, and ideals are important to each of us. They make up our core beliefs and determine who we are. Values are individual and diverse; what is valuable to one person may not be to another. We all have our personal needs and wants. Some people want glory and fame; others want anonymity. Some people want an exciting career; others want a paycheck.

What do you value the most? Spend some time thinking about this important question. By aligning your career search with your values, you increase your chances for satisfaction. It is difficult to work for an employer or a company that goes against your values. How can you perform satisfactorily whenever you do not agree with what is going on in the company or with the way you must do the work? It is important to take your values into consideration when you make your final career choice.

Some of your values may change over time as you mature and develop in your job skills. They also change as your personal circumstances change. For instance, when you are single, your career may be your main priority, and you will gladly work overtime to achieve advancement. Later, if you have children, you may not want to put as many hours into your career. You may eventually shift your values and want to spend more time with your family.

EXERCISE 1-C

Fill out the Values Self-Assessment in Table 1–2 to determine what is most important to you.

Table 1–2 **VALUES SELF-ASSESSMENT CHECKLIST**

VALUES SELF-ASSESSMENT

What do you value? Rate the following items by assigning each of them a number. Use a one (1) for the most important, a two (2) for important, and a three (3) for fairly important. At the bottom of the list, you may add anything else not listed here that you feel is important to you.

☐ Family/Relatives	☐ Being Alone	☐ Improving the
☐ Privacy	☐ Helping the World	Environment
☐ Helping Others	☐ Community	☐ Physical Challenges
☐ Being with Others	☐ Creativity	☐ Independence
☐ Being Appreciated	☐ Free Time	☐ Education/Knowledge
☐ Freedom	☐ Owning a Home	☐ Excitement/Adventure
☐ Social Life	☐ Fame	☐ Financial Security
☐ Power/Authority	☐ Recreation	☐ Feeling Good About Self
☐ Honesty	☐ Leading Others	☐ Raising Awareness
☐ Volunteering	☐ Expensive Things	☐ Philanthropy
☐ Wealth	☐ Religion/Spirituality	
☐ Friends	☐ Good Job/Career	

CAREER SATISFACTION

You will spend a lot of hours working at your career, so it makes sense to find a position you will enjoy. When deciding what type of position you want, ask, "Does this job relate to my values?" If it does, proceed with the job self-assessment to determine if it fits your interests and abilities, which will add to your job satisfaction.

EXERCISE 1-D

Fill out the job self-assessment in Table 1–3.

Table 1–3   JOB SELF-ASSESSMENT CHECKLIST

JOB SELF-ASSESSMENT

What do you want from a job? Rate the following items by assigning each of them a number. Use a one (1) for the most important, a two (2) for important, and a three (3) for fairly important. At the bottom of this list, you may also add anything else not listed here that you feel is important to you.

☐ Job Security	☐ High Wages
☐ Advancement/Promotions	☐ Variety
☐ Creativity	☐ Good Working Conditions
☐ Recognition	☐ Being Appreciated
☐ Interesting/Challenging Work	☐ Camaraderie
☐ Working Alone	☐ Working with Others
☐ Set Routine	☐ Physical Challenges
☐ Independence	☐ Empowerment
☐ Good Benefits	☐ Chance to Contribute
☐ Power/Authority	☐ Raises
☐ Excitement/Adventure	☐ Fame
☐ Success	☐ Ethical Environment
☐ Clear Direction	☐ Entertainment
☐ Fair Supervision	☐ Sense of Belonging
☐ Knowledge	☐ Financial Security

Match Your Values

Now that you have determined your value system and what you want from a career, you can look for companies that meet your needs.

Interests

What are your interests? Do you like to read and/or write? If so, perhaps you should look for a position as a reporter or an editor. Are you fascinated by numbers? Maybe a career as an accountant, a payroll clerk, or a tax specialist is for you. Do you have a need to help others who are hurt? Look into a medical career. There are several areas from which to choose—medical assistant, nurse, doctor, dentist, transcriptionist, medical billing clerk, and so on.

Keep asking yourself questions about what you would like to do. Consider your hobbies, what you do for recreation, and the clubs to which you belong. Is there a particular industry that is closely associated with your interests? If so, is it feasible for you to work in that particular field? What skills will you need? Do you have the skills, and if not, can you get them?

Taking a position in a field in which you are interested will seem less like work and more like a fulfilling career.

EXERCISE 1-E

Go to the library or search the Internet to research a career(s) you are interested in pursuing. Write a one-page paper on the career, including the advantages and disadvantages.

ASK YOURSELF THESE QUESTIONS:

- What do you have to offer an employer?
- What sets you apart from the other applicants for this position?
- Do you have the skills to perform the tasks you will be expected to complete?
- Are your skills top notch?
- Do you have the required training for the position you want?
- If you do not have the required training for the position you want, can you obtain it in a reasonable amount of time or can you learn it on the externship?

ASSESS SKILLS AND COMPETENCIES

Consider your **competencies**, which are your particular abilities and areas of expertise. What you are capable of doing and your know-how forms your areas of competency. Once you have decided on an area of interest, you will need to obtain the proper education, training, and skills required to do the work if you do not already have them.

Take Inventory

Take an **inventory** or an account of your abilities, skills, and education. Think about everything you have done at work, learned at school, and used throughout your personal life. On a separate sheet of paper, write down anything you have learned that will help you in a future position.

When evaluating your skills, take nothing for granted. You may feel your skills and experiences are insignificant, but an employer may feel differently. For example, a salesclerk may not think about all the different skills she has acquired. These may include providing customer service, solving problems, resolving complaints, handling money and making change, completing paperwork, using the telephone, arranging displays, inventorying and stocking clothing, running the cash register, following a schedule, and so on. *Everything* you have done in previous jobs is of interest to an employer. Spend some time thinking about what you have done in your past work history. What did you enjoy? What did you dislike? What are your strengths? Your weaknesses?

When stating accomplishments, think in terms of action verbs to describe what you have done. For example, *I supervised three office clerks*. List all work experience and skills, including both paid and unpaid work that will help you get the next job.

EXERCISE 1-F

Use the skills self-assessment in Table 1–4 to stimulate your thinking. Check off the skills that apply to you and add any others that are not listed.

Table 1–4 SKILLS SELF-ASSESSMENT CHECKLIST

SKILLS SELF-ASSESSMENT

Check all that apply to you and add skills you have that are not listed.

☐ Create	☐ Operate Computer	☐ Supervise
☐ Sell	☐ Organize Data	☐ Solve Problems
☐ Record Data	☐ Drive	☐ Invent
☐ Teach/Train	☐ Write Proposals	☐ Speak in Public
☐ Serve Customers	☐ Design Newsletters	☐ Service Computers
☐ Generate Reports	☐ Calculate Figures	☐ Assemble Products
☐ Analyze Data	☐ Handle Money	☐ Build Things
☐ Prepare Budgets	☐ Plan	☐ File
☐ Operate Fax	☐ Coordinate	☐ Operate Copier

(Continued)

EXERCISE 1-F (Continued)

☐ Operate Scanner   ☐ Proficient in Access   ☐ Handle Complaints
☐ Set up Systems   ☐ Proficient in PowerPoint   ☐ Write Grants
☐ Write Reports   ☐ Service Equipment   ☐ Design Brochures
☐ Write Correspondence   ☐ Work with Others   ☐ Design Advertising
☐ Troubleshoot   ☐ Work Independently   Copy
☐ Demonstrate Products   ☐ Operate Multiline   ☐ Locate Information
☐ Verify   Telephone   ☐ Do Accounts Payable/
☐ Repair/Fix   ☐ Operate Postage   Receivable
☐ Transcribe   Machine   ☐ Provide Health Care
☐ Proficient in Word   ☐ Operate Heavy Duty   ☐ Schedule/Run
☐ Proficient in Excel   Equipment   Meetings
☐ _____   ☐ _____   ☐ _____

Check the specialty skills you have and the software programs you can operate that are given in Table 1–5. Add to the list any others that apply to you.

Table 1–5 **SPECIALIZED SKILLS LIST**

SPECIALIZED SKILLS SELF-ASSESSMENT

Check all that apply to you and add skills you have that are not listed.

☐ MS Office   ☐ Peachtree   ☐ PageMaker
☐ CPR   ☐ Transcription   ☐ Windows XP
☐ CPT Coding   ☐ Legal Terminology   ☐ QuickBooks
☐ _____   ☐ _____   ☐ _____
☐ _____   ☐ _____   ☐ _____

Match Your Skills

By taking inventory of your skills, you will know exactly what type
of position you are able to fill. You can look at a job description and
know if it is right for you. You will also be able to determine whether
you should obtain additional skills that will make you more competitive in your chosen career. This competitiveness may lead to a permanent position.

EXERCISE 1-G

Fill out the machines operated self-assessment in Table 1–6.

Table 1–6 **SELF-ASSESSMENT: MACHINES OPERATED CHECKLIST**

MACHINES OPERATED SELF-ASSESSMENT

Look over the following list of business machines, and check all those you can operate with proficiency. Add to the list any other machines you can operate.

☐ Copier	☐ Scanner
☐ Fax	☐ Paging System
☐ Multiline Phone	☐ Calculator
☐ Mailing Machine	☐ Dictaphone
☐ Printer	☐ Credit Card Machine
☐ Cash Register	☐ Computer
☐ CD Burner	☐ Shredder
☐ Digital Camera	☐ Web Camera
☐ Lottery Machine	☐ Laminator
☐ _____	☐ _____
☐ _____	☐ _____
☐ _____	☐ _____

Assess Skills

Assess your skills by evaluating the level of each. Are they top-notch? If not, what can you do to get them to a higher level? Training seminars, workshops, and classes on almost any subject are held in a number of locations. Find the training you need to gain new skills or to improve the ones you have. Identify your weak areas and improve them by practicing your skills. Capitalize on your strengths. Check local libraries, colleges, and high school adult programs for suitable courses and programs that will help you or take an on-line class. Check to see if your company offers training. Employers are often willing either to train you or to send you to seminars or courses.

WHERE CAN YOU GET TRAINING?

▶ Seminars

▶ Workshops

- Company training programs
- College courses
- High school adult programs
- Community adult programs
- Internet courses
- Libraries
- Practice skills on your own

EXERCISE 1-H

Choose a skill you would like to learn or to improve. Conduct research to determine where you can take a class or workshop and gain the skill or improvement. If possible, enroll in the class or seminar.

PERSONAL ATTRIBUTES

Your personal **attributes** include mannerisms and characteristics, such as dependability and loyalty. After taking inventory of your skills and abilities, look at your traits that will be of value to an employer. All employers are looking for honest, hardworking employees who come to work everyday and give their best. Your personal traits tell an employer that you will get along with coworkers, supervisors, and customers.

A great number of people are fired from jobs because they cannot get along with coworkers, customers, and supervisors. Personality conflicts cause turmoil in the workplace and damage morale. Such harm is very costly to employers. Many employers hire inexperienced individuals over experienced ones who they feel may cause problems within the company.

Employers ask specific questions during the interview to gauge a candidate's personality and determine how he or she might complement the personalities of the other employees. Belonging to clubs, organizations, and sporting teams indicates that a person has a team-player attitude and is able to interact with others. Holding an office in an organization displays leadership ability, which is another valuable trait for the workplace.

EXERCISE 1-I

Look over the Personal Attributes given in Table 1–7 to get an idea of characteristics that describe you. Then make a list of your personal attributes on the lines provided.

Table 1–7   PERSONAL ATTRIBUTES REVIEW LIST

Friendly	Organized	Stubborn
Honest/Trustworthy	Disorganized	Humorous
Responsible	Punctual	Athletic
Sincere	Loyal	Detail Oriented
Dependable	Critical Thinker	Problem Solver
Calm	Persistent	Avoids Problems
Efficient/Effective	Team Player	Loner
Creative	Dedicated	Caring/Supportive
Perceptive	Assertive	Energetic
Adaptable	Manages Time	Leadership Abilities
Resourceful	Analytical	Takes Initiative
Self-starter	Self-disciplined	Accepts Criticism
Motivated	Rises to Challenge	Contributes Suggestions
Easygoing	Efficient	Flexible
Discreet	Open-minded	Rational
Outgoing	Intelligent	Skilled
Industrious	Realistic	Self-confident
Tactful	Poised	Confident

_____

_____

_____

_____

_____

_____

_____

_____

_____

Match Your Personality

Think of your personal attributes in relation to the work you will do. For instance, if you are caring/supportive, sincere, and calm, a career in health care or teaching may be for you. If you are a problem solver and a leader, perhaps you would make a good manager. Think about careers that could be right for your personality.

TRANSFERABLE SKILLS

Although you will list basic skills, think beyond them when determining what you have learned during your education and from every job experience. These skills will be helpful whenever you pursue an externship. These extra, useful skills are called **transferable skills**. An example of a transferable skill is customer service. If you provided customer service while at a part-time job, you should be able to provide customer service at an externship. Therefore, the skill of customer service transfers from one position to the other.

Think about the previous example given of the salesclerk and the skills she performed that could transfer to several different positions.

Transferable skills can serve you throughout your career since you can take them from one position to another, bridging your skills from company to company.

Communication skills, time management/organization skills, handling finances, operating basic equipment, solving problems, and interaction with people are all excellent transferable skills for any field of employment. Everyone should procure a working knowledge of computers, telephones, and the Internet to enhance transferable skills.

EXERCISE 1-J

Fill out the transferable skills self-assessment in Table 1–8.

Table 1–8 SELF-ASSESSMENT: TRANSFERABLE SKILLS CHECKLIST

TRANSFERABLE SKILLS SELF-ASSESSMENT

Look over the list of transferable skills below and check all that apply to you. At the bottom of this list, you may add anything not listed here that applies to you.

☐ Providing Customer Service	☐ Managing Time	☐ Supervising
	☐ Being Assertive	☐ Helping Others
☐ Solving Problems	☐ Managing Complaints	☐ Charting Information

(Continued)

EXERCISE 1-J (Continued)

☐ Comparing Data/Items	☐ Inventorying	☐ Processing
☐ Arranging Meetings	☐ Collecting Money	Information
☐ Moving Merchandise	☐ Estimating	☐ Delegating
☐ Distributing Items	☐ Troubleshooting	☐ Arranging Information
☐ Using a Multiline	☐ Budgeting	☐ Locating Information
Phone	☐ Controlling Costs	☐ Repairing Items
☐ Listening	☐ Writing	☐ Displaying
☐ Displaying Creativity	☐ Speaking in Public	Merchandise
☐ Figuring	☐ Spelling	☐ Coordinating Activities
☐ Displaying Poise	☐ Organizing	
☐ Persuasion	☐ Making Decisions	

1

Match Your Skills

Can you think of other transferable skills you have to offer an employer? If so, add them to the list from Table 1–8. How can you use any of the transferable skills checked in Table 1–8 to advantage when searching for an externship? Did this list give you ideas for additional skills you have that were not listed?

TRANSFERABLE SKILLS SUMMARY

▶ Providing customer service
▶ Doing accounts payable/receivable
▶ Writing
▶ Cooking
▶ Organizing
▶ Managing time
▶ Team building
▶ Supervising
▶ Speaking
▶ Interacting with children
▶ Interacting with adults

▶ Operating computers
▶ Using telephones
▶ Searching the Internet
▶ Operating a cash register
▶ Operating a copier
▶ Fund-raising
▶ Chairing meetings
▶ Holding office in an organization
▶ Solving problems
▶ Handling complaints
▶ Planning events
▶ Decorating
▶ Greeting people

EVALUATE

To **evaluate** is to examine and explore all options open to you when considering a career and to take advantage of all available opportunities. Be flexible and willing to adapt to changes.

Focus on your interests, abilities, skills, and education to obtain an interesting, rewarding position. The closer you can match your background and interests to a career, the more satisfied you will be. And satisfied employees are likely to remain on the job.

Through an evaluation of your skills, abilities, interests, and personal traits, you will learn what you have to offer perspective employers. Consequently, you will be able to communicate more effectively whenever you are asked the all-important interview questions.

● ASSESSING LIFE EXPERIENCE

Adults perform a variety of functions, such as parenting, shopping, running a household, cooking, paying bills, getting involved in schools and communities, and so on. This accumulation of **life experience** defines people in unique ways; each person has a different set of circumstances that lead to different ways of handling the circumstances.

Life experiences help people in participation in group discussions and meetings, projects, demonstrations, and teaching other adults. Individuals know how they like to be treated; therefore, they know how to treat others, including coworkers, supervisors, and customers. Because people have dealt with certain problems, they can transfer what they have learned from those problems and subsequent solutions they have applied. The results and consequences of decisions guide them through similar situations. By drawing on life experiences, employees can make the workplace a rewarding experience.

Once hired, employees want to complete their tasks efficiently to keep their jobs and advance in them. It is easier to learn new tasks if employees can incorporate life experiences which they can relate to the tasks. This also makes tasks and duties more meaningful.

Life experiences enable employees to bring diverse backgrounds into the workplace. Dealing with life experiences helps employees handle similar problems and situations that occur in the workplace. For example, they learn to develop better judgment, get along with others, solve problems, assimilate learning, use skills, and draw from their vast storehouse of facts. They have also formed habits like dependability, punctuality, organization, time management, and problem-solving skills.

Various **life stages** bring about different experience and learning. These life stages include childhood, young adulthood, adulthood, parenthood, school/college student, spouse, and employee, among others. Each stage comes with its own set of pluses and minuses that teach us how to live, work, and deal with consequences.

Life skills can transfer to an externship as well. Life skills are those abilities and talents you accumulate through every day living. For instance, if you pay personal bills and balance your checkbook on a regular basis, you should be able to do accounts payable for a business; therefore, it is a transferable skill. If you can cook a variety of meals for your family, you could be a cook or a chef in the workplace. If you keep your family and home organized, you should be able to organize an office. Belonging to an organization or sports team creates a team-player attitude, and companies need and want team players. Did you hold office or organize a fund-raiser? Both activities give you desirable transferable skills. Think about how your life experiences can help you with an externship position.

EXERCISE 1-K

Review the transferable skills you checked in Table 1–8. These are life skills you have learned that might transfer to an externship and/or permanent job. Next, look over the list of life skills in Table 1–9 and check those that pertain to you. Add to the list any other life skills that apply to you.

Table 1–9 SELF-ASSESSMENT: LIFE SKILLS

LIFE SKILLS SELF-ASSESSMENT

Look over the list of transferable skills below and check all that apply to you. At the bottom of this list, you may add anything not listed here that applies to you.

☐ Providing childcare

☐ Teaching children

☐ Balancing a checkbook

☐ Preparing meals

☐ Cleaning a home

☐ Organizing a home

☐ Preparing a budget

☐ Paying bills

☐ Making small repairs

☐ Buying and organizing food, clothing, furniture

☐ Decorating a home

☐ Caring for aging parents

☐ Taking classes/earning a degree

☐ Planning vacations/trips

☐ Booking airline and hotel reservations

☐ Preparing tax returns

☐ Carpooling

☐ Planning parties

☐ Placing phone calls

☐ Making and keeping appointments

☐ Working with community leaders

☐ Volunteering (community, school, church)

☐ Maintaining personal records

☐ Meeting personal deadlines

☐ Studying/Researching

☐ Exercising

END OF CHAPTER WORK

CASE STUDIES

● VALUES CASE STUDY

Omar works in a small electronics repair business. He learned that the company owner has been buying refurbished parts to use for television and DVD repairs, but he has been charging customers for new parts. Omar does not like being involved in the deception; however, he keeps quiet so that he does not jeopardize his job.

Questions to Ask Yourself

1. Does Omar have an obligation to the customers to disclose the truth, or does he have an obligation to his boss to keep quiet?

   _____

   _____

2. Could Omar face legal charges for concealing the information about the parts?

   _____

   _____

Things to Consider

People should be able to align their values with the company's. Otherwise, they will have a difficult time being true to their feelings and loyal to the company. In Omar's case, his values seem to clash with those of his employer. Therefore, he will have a difficult time living with his decision to ignore the employer's unethical behavior. Omar should reassess his situation and decide if it is worth staying with the company.

As far as legalities, if Omar knowingly deceives customers, he is as guilty as the owner and could face prosecution. Law enforcement officials would consider Omar a law breaker.

TRANSFERABLE SKILLS CASE STUDY

After looking for a job for several months, Belinda was getting discouraged. A friend suggested that she update her resume and add transferable skills. Belinda reassessed her background and added these transferable skills: multitasking, time management, organization, providing customer service, and problem-solving skills.

Questions to Ask Yourself

1. Did Belinda choose transferable skills that will enhance her resume?

   _____

   _____

1

2. Explain your answer.

_____

_____

Things to Consider

When listing skills on a resume, be sure to consider everything you have learned throughout your life that could be an asset on the job. Employers want well-organized employees who manage their time well, multitask, organize, and solve problems. Think creatively about the tasks you do every day. Have you handled money, done banking, reconciled a checkbook, held an office, raised money for a cause, worked as part of a team, organized a fundraiser, or chaired a meeting? These are just some of the skills that any employer would appreciate.

● **LIFE EXPERIENCE CASE STUDY**

Maria has been a single mother for eight years. She provided childcare in her home for two neighborhood children while their parents worked. Now that Maria's children are in junior high, she would like to enter the workforce. She does not know what she is qualified to do.

Questions to Ask Yourself

1. Would Maria be qualified to pursue a job at a daycare or preschool?

_____

_____

2. If Maria does not want to be a childcare provider or teacher, what other careers might she pursue where she can use her life experience?

_____

_____

Things to Consider

Maria has several life skills that will help her in seeking employment. If she does want to work in a daycare or preschool, she can certainly transfer the skills she used to provide care for the neighbors' children. However, she may need additional formal training.

If Maria does not want to provide care to children, she could fall back on her organization, time management, teaching, cooking, and general household skills to pursue other types of work. These may include chef, office manager, cleaner, trainer, planner, etc.

END OF CHAPTER QUESTIONS

1. Why do you suppose some people remain in jobs they do not like?

2. Would you remain in a job you disliked?

3. Name two values you consider important to you.

4. Why is it important to take your values into consideration when you make a career choice?

5. Give an example of how your values can change over time.

6. Why consider your hobbies when pursuing a career?

7. What particular industry or field is closely associated with your interests?

8. List four things you could do to gain new skills or improve the ones you have.

9. What two things do you consider to be most important in a job?

10. List five skills you have to offer an employer.

11. How can life experience help you better perform duties for an externship or a job?

12. Name two life skills that would be helpful during an externship or job.

13. How can life experience be helpful when dealing with coworkers?

14. What could belonging to a club or organization indicate about a person?

CHAPTER 2

Finding and Preparing for an Externship

2

After completing this chapter, you should be able to:

1. Define the basic components of an externship.
2. Identify at least three benefits of completing an externship.
3. Define networking.
4. Identify at least three benefits of networking.
5. Write an effective resume.
6. Write an effective reference sheet.
7. Write an effective cover letter.
8. Develop interviewing skills.
9. Determine proper interview dress.
10. Fill out an application effectively.
11. Organize a portfolio.
12. Define job shadow.
13. Identify key professional traits that define a team player.
14. Identify what constitutes a positive work ethic.
15. Research a company.
16. Search for an externship position.

Chapter 2 defines an externship and why it is important to seek one. This chapter also directs you in finding an externship and/or job by providing direction for writing an effective resume, reference sheet, and cover letter. Information is provided on putting together a winning portfolio, dressing for success, and interviewing effectively. In addition, you will be instructed on how to research a company and search for an appropriate externship position.

KEY TERMS

application	Internet site	reference sheet
cover letter	job objective	resume
externship	job shadow	screening interview
group interview	networking	structured interview
illegal question	portfolio	team player
informational interview	professional organization	work ethic
integrity	punctual	

INTRODUCTION

Career development begins with an assessment of your skills, abilities, and education and with the intention of finding the right job for you. This job should fit your personality and interests and afford you the opportunity to grow and develop.

An **externship** allows you to hone your skills and use your education in a position of interest to you. An externship can be a stepping stone to career success. Turning an externship into a successful career requires careful planning on your part. In Chapter 1 you assessed your skills, education, and personal character traits. Review these assessments before making a career choice so you can determine if you have the proper skills and education for the field you want to enter. If you do not have the skills and education needed, can you obtain them?

In addition to being skilled, you will be expected to display positive personal and professional traits in order to advance in your position. Look over the personal assessment of professional traits that you filled out in Chapter 1. If you are lacking traits that will make you a professional, think about how you can obtain them.

PLANNING AN EXTERNSHIP

Before accepting an externship, do some planning in order to get the most out of the experience. Look over the reflection questions and give the answers to them serious consideration. This information will give you the direction in which to proceed.

- What do you hope to gain from your externship?
- What skills do you want to use?
- Do you want to work in a store? A restaurant? A hospital? An office? A hotel?
- What is most important to you (i.e., is location more important than the type of position you will have)?
- Are the hours you will work more important than the skills you will be using?

EXERCISE 2-A

Before taking an externship position, think about these questions. Then, answer them on the lines provided.

1. In what kind of industry do you want to work?

_____

_____

2. What are the responsibilities of the type of position in which you would like to work?

_____

_____

3. Will you use all or most of your skills?

_____

_____

4. Will you gain exposure to a variety of duties?

_____

_____

(Continued)

2

EXERCISE 2-A (Continued)

5. Will you get a chance to interact with professionals in your field
    of study?

    _____

    _____

6. Will you need to learn additional skills for the externship?

    _____

    _____

7. Will you have a paid externship?

    _____

    _____

8. Is there a possibility of placement with the company after your
    externship is completed?

    _____

    _____

9. What is the location of the company?

    _____

    _____

10. How many hours per week will you work during the externship?

    _____

    _____

REQUIREMENTS OF AN EXTERNSHIP

Procedures and protocols for externships vary widely among schools.
Many coordinate their own externships or have a school externship coordinator who will oversee the experience. The coordinator may assist the
extern with finding and coordinating an externship, or the coordinator
may set up the externship, arrange an interview, and select an appropriate student for the position. If a student has a part-time job that he or
she would like to use as an externship, the coordinator must approve it.

The student will be expected to follow externship guidelines.
An example of how one externship program could work includes
requiring that participants work a specific number of hours within a

specified time period and complete weekly time sheets to verify attendance. The student may likely sign a contract, agreeing to school policy regarding the externship and the submission of documentation of attendance and duties completed.

Check with your particular school to determine what you need to do to participate in an externship/internship.

Employers may also be expected to meet externship guidelines and/or sign an agreement with the school in order to ensure a successful externship for the student.

POSSIBLE EXTERNSHIP REQUIREMENTS

▶ follow externship guidelines

▶ sign externship contract agreeing to meet the school policy requirements

▶ work the required number of hours within the required time period

▶ submit timesheets as documentation of hours worked

▶ evaluate the externship experience

EXERCISE 2-B

Work with a friend to practice interviewing for an externship. Have your friend ask you job-related sample questions. Afterwards, the two of you should evaluate the answers you gave. Videotape the interview if possible so you can review it.

FINDING AN EXTERNSHIP

Plan to get the most out of your externship. If you will not be using your skills or performing a variety of tasks on the externship, it may not be a beneficial experience. You may want to look for another one. If you need additional skills to accept an externship, can you obtain them in a timely manner? What about the location? An externship located in close proximity to your home will make getting to work every day easier.

You will also want to know whether or not your school arranges externships, offers credits for them, and/or schedules regular classes along with the externship. Check with your school placement office on externship details. Most schools require students to find their own externships.

If your school does not arrange externships, you will need to find your own. Finding an externship is similar to finding a job. Read the section in this chapter on finding job leads, and prepare a list of companies in Exercise 2-H. Ask yourself if any of these companies are suitable for your externship. Concentrate on places near your school or home.

EXERCISE 2-C

Decide on two companies where you would like to do an externship. Call and ask if they have available opportunities. If the companies you called do not have externships, contact other ones until you secure a suitable position.

You may be required to send a **resume**, or summary of your background information, to the company you have contacted for your externship. If so, follow the instructions given later in this chapter to prepare a resume that best presents your qualifications. Of course, you will want to concentrate on your education and skills. Have a friend or teacher look over your resume.

When you attain an interview for an externship, treat it with as much care and preparation as you would an interview for a regular job. The externship is your first step into the workforce of your chosen career path, and you want to present a good first impression. Tips for handling standard interviews are given in this chapter. Refer to these tips when you are preparing for the externship interview.

FINDING EXTERNSHIP JOB LEADS

Information about job openings can either be visible or hidden. Visible job leads are advertised to the public, while the hidden ones are not. Traditionally, many job seekers will apply for visible jobs and not seek out the hidden ones.

THE VISIBLE JOB MARKET

The visible job market includes positions that are advertised in newspapers, on the Internet, on radio and television, and by employment agencies. Lots of people apply for these advertised jobs, so the competition for them is great. The pay and benefits for these positions are generally near or slightly above the minimum wage. When searching for an externship, you may want to check newspaper and Internet want ads to get a sense of which companies have positions suited to you.

SEARCH THE INTERNET

The Internet provides access to hundreds of newspaper classified ads around the country, which makes job searching quick and efficient. When searching for an externship position, you can access ads from multiple locations without the cost of buying a newspaper or making long-distance telephone calls to locate information.

Thousands of companies, agencies, and educational institutions have their own Web sites. Typical sites provide information about the company, personnel, and available jobs. Many post job titles, job descriptions and requirements, salary ranges, and benefits.

Check the Web sites of companies in which you are interested to determine if they offer externships and how to apply for them.

2

TABLE 2–1

JOB SEEKER INTERNET SITES LIST

INTERNET SITES OF INTEREST TO JOB SEEKERS	
U.S. Dept. of Labor—America's Job Bank	http://www.ajb.dni.us
Career Mosaic	http://www.careermosaic.com
Monster Board	http://www.monster.com
Career Path	http://www.careerpath.com
Job Center	http://www.jobcenter.com
Resume Writing Resources	http://www.golden.net/ archeus/reswri.htm
CareerMart	http://www.careermart.com
USA CityLink	http://www.usacitylink.com
Careers and Jobs	http://www.starthere.com/jobs
Helpwanted.com	http://www.helpwanted.com

Note: Web sites are subject to change.

EXERCISE 2-D

Do an externship search on one or more of the Web sites listed in Table 2–1. Look for companies that are close to your home and that offer positions in your particular field of study.

Write down in Table 2–2 the company name, address, telephone number, and job requirements. Add any other miscellaneous information from the ad that you feel is important to note.

Table 2–2   **LIST OF COMPANIES TO CONTACT FORM**

MY LIST OF POSSIBLE COMPANIES TO CONTACT			
Company Name	Address	Telephone No.	Job Requirements

READ NEWSPAPER WANT ADS

Newspaper want ads are a popular way to locate specific job openings. This allows you to find companies where you can apply for externships. Read the classified section of local daily and Sunday newspapers for suitable employment positions. Sunday papers generally have a comprehensive job listing. However, the disadvantages of using want ads are (1) the majority of jobs are not listed in the want ads, and (2) many people will probably apply for the same positions, thereby increasing competition.

Think in broad terms whenever you are searching for a position. For instance, if you are an accounting major, check under the headings accountant, bookkeeper, accounts payable/receivable, payroll, and similar ones. All job openings that you will be qualified for will not be listed under the heading *accountant*, so be creative.

Ads vary in the amount of information they provide. Some ads do not give locations, types of companies/services, or a company name. They may have a P.O. Box address or may state to send resumes in care of the paper. These are called blind ads. Usually, these employers want to avoid giving a name and having a large number of applicants inundate them.

Some want ads are placed by employers; others are placed by employment agencies. Learn to recognize the difference. Agency ads do not give the hiring company's name, address, or phone number. They do, however, identify their agency's name and phone number in the ad, although it may not be clear that the name given is an employment agency. You will not want to contact an employment agency for an externship position.

Some want ads seem too good to be true. They offer high pay and vague job descriptions. These often turn out to be positions in sales or telemarketing that have high turnover rates.

Because of the use of several abbreviations, want ads can be difficult to read. See Table 2–3 for common abbreviations and their meanings.

TABLE 2–3

COMMON WANT AD ABBREVIATIONS LIST

COMMON ABBREVIATIONS IN WANT ADS	
Ans.	Answer
Appt.	Appointment
Asst.	Assistant
B.A.	Bachelor of Arts Degree
Bldg.	Building
Bus.	Business
Co.	Company
Const.	Construction
Corp.	Corporation
D.O.B.	Date of Birth
Dept.	Department

(Continued)

2

TABLE 2–3 (Continued)

Dir.	Director
Div.	Division
E.O.E	Equal Opportunity Employer
Empl.	Employment
Eqpt.	Equipment
Eves.	Evenings
Exc.	Excellent
Exp. or Exper.	Experience
Ext.	Telephone Extension
Gen.	General
Grad.	Graduate
Htrs.	Headquarters
Incl.	Including
Ins.	Insurance or Insured
Int.	Interview
Maint.	Maintenance
Manuf.	Manufacturing
Mech.	Mechanic or mechanical
Med.	Medical
Metro.	Metropolitan
Mgr.	Manager
Min.	Minimum
Mo.	Month
N/A	Not applicable
Nec.	Necessary
Pref.	Preferred

TABLE 2–3 (Continued)

Prof.	Professional
Req'd	Required
Veh.	Vehicle
A.A.	Associate in Arts (2 yr. degree)
A/P	Accounts Payable
Begnr.	Beginner
Bcgrd.	Background
B.S.	Bachelor of Science Degree
Col.	College
Cdt.	Credit
Hndl.	Handle
Knldg.	Knowledge
Loc.	Location
M.A. or M.S.	Master's Degree
Mag.	Magazine
Neg.	Negotiable
Ofc.	Office
Pers.	Personnel
PR	Public Relations
Prev.	Previous
PT	Part Time

Study the Want Ad

When searching want ads, ask yourself enough questions about the want ad so that you will have a clear picture of the opportunity presented.

- Is this job full or part time?
- In what area is the job located?

- Is there company training?
- What experience is necessary for the position?
- What educational requirements are there for the position?
- What skills are necessary for this position?
- How well do I meet the requirements for this ad?
- What personal traits does this ad require?
- Is there a salary given?

TABLE 2–4

EXAMPLES OF WANT ADS

SAMPLE WANT ADS		
Receptionist	**Administrative Assistant**	**Office Manager**
Busy office requires answering phones, meeting and greeting customers, filing, and computer skills. Must have ability to handle multiple tasks.	Full-time position. Requires associate degree, knowledge of MS Word, Excel, and PowerPoint. Must have good communication skills and the ability to multitask.	Excellent opportunity requires a flexible team player with excellent organizational and communication skills. Supervisory experience required.

THE HIDDEN JOB MARKET

Hidden jobs are the ones that are not advertised to the general public. It takes effort to find these positions, but they generally pay well and there is less competition for them. The majority of the jobs are in the hidden job market, meaning that they are not advertised by traditional means. Oftentimes, they are not advertised at all.

From your perspective as a job seeker, it would be wise to search out hidden jobs. Many of them pay better than those that are advertised to the public. Also, the more job leads you have, the better your chances of finding the right position for you. If you only apply for the visible jobs, it may seem like there are not many available; because the majority of jobs are hidden. How, then, do you find the hidden jobs? A variety of methods follow.

Apply Directly

Mail resumes, or stop in and drop off copies at companies. Applying directly to a company is one of the most effective ways of finding hidden jobs, especially ones that have recently become available. Maybe there is an unfilled opening in the company or perhaps someone just quit, creating an immediate need to fill a position. Perhaps the employer will see something on your resume that leads to a future discussion and creation of a new position or externship just for you.

Dress in business attire when you visit a company to ask for an **application**, which is a form used to request your background information, or to drop off a resume. Sometimes employers are willing to talk to walk-ins even if they do not have an immediate opening. You will want to be prepared for such a possibility. Also, other employees such as the receptionist or secretary may evaluate your appearance.

When you walk in to a company, look confident, smile, and ask to talk to the person in charge of the externship program. If no one is available to speak with you, ask if you may leave a resume for that individual.

Other ways of applying directly to companies include contacting employers by telephone, doing a **job shadow** (defined later in the chapter), arranging an **informational interview**, and answering help-wanted signs displayed in company windows. An informational interview is one where you make contact with someone in the field you would like to pursue and ask that individual questions related to the field. Also, check with your local Chamber of Commerce and/or Small Business Administration for details on companies that are hiring in your area.

SEARCH TELEPHONE BOOKS

Search the phone book yellow pages for business names located in an area in which you would like to work. These pages list companies by the services they provide, so match your skills with companies that are most likely to need them.

For instance, if you are an accounting major searching under the heading *accountant*, broaden your search to include not only businesses, but also hospitals, restaurants, school districts, colleges, utility companies, retail stores, nonprofit organizations, churches, etc. All of these businesses need accounting employees. Think about all the different headings a company might use to advertise positions.

You can find telephone books at your local library, in your school career center, and on the Internet at http://www.bigyellow.com/.

EXERCISE 2-E

Using your local telephone book, Yellow Pages directory, or the Internet, make an extensive list of possible companies to contact and/or which to send resumes. Write your findings in Table 2–5. Opportunities may occur in any company at any time, so broaden your possibilities to as many different companies as possible.

Table 2–5 CREATE A LIST OF POSSIBLE COMPANIES TO CONTACT

MY LIST OF POSSIBLE COMPANIES TO CONTACT			
Company Name	Address	Telephone No.	Job Requirements

USE YOUR NETWORK

Many companies rely on their employees to refer friends and family members to positions they have available. Therefore, let everyone know you are looking for an externship—friends (especially working ones), family members, neighbors, teachers, employees at places where you do business, etc. If you belong to clubs and organizations, spread the word among the members that you are seeking employment.

Networking or making contacts can help you uncover positions as soon as they become available, because the people in your network are in a position to know where these openings are. They also have friends in their networks who may know of additional openings for which you may be qualified.

Networking can give you a decided edge over other students seeking externships. Refer to the networking section that follows to learn how to network your way to success.

NETWORKING

Networking is taking advantage of support from others who encourage and motivate you and offer to help you develop a career. To network is to talk with people from all areas of your life and form connections with them that may benefit both of you. Networking is one of the best ways to search for and locate a job. Tell everyone you know that you are looking for work, which is the ultimate way to network. Friends, family members, neighbors, former teachers, classmates, coworkers, and chat groups are good contacts for job leads. Tell members of clubs to which you belong, former employers, sports contacts, and even the local grocer that you are job hunting. Everyone you meet is a potential contact and job source.

MAKE CONTACT

When it comes to job searches, you never know who might be able to help you or who knows of someone else who can. The more people you talk to, the more opportunities that will open up for you. Even if your contacts do not know people who hire in companies or know the owners personally, they may be able to introduce you to key people who will offer you a job.

GATHER INFORMATION

Networking is a great way to gather information, advice, and referrals. Most of us encounter hundreds of people, many of whom could help us further our careers. When used in job hunting, networking is a skill that dramatically increases your chances of landing a job. It brings you into contact with people who might lead you in the right direction, and then those individuals could lead you to other contacts. Ask your contacts how they learned about and applied for their current jobs.

Networking can increase your self-confidence as you receive information and support from personal and professional relationships. Through networking, you can find a mentor, make contacts, and gain moral support. You may be able to arrange an externship, job shadow, or informational interview. You might locate hidden jobs not advertised to the public.

Remember, the purpose of networking is to gather information, not to get a job. Networking cannot guarantee you a job, especially if you are not qualified. However, your efforts may lead to information about a position for which you are qualified, or to a means by which you can become qualified for an opening.

MEET PROFESSIONALS

The best place to meet people in your field is at professional association meetings and events. Networking with these professionals will not only help you with job leads but also serve you throughout your career. These networks provide referrals and job contacts. They can make information available that will help you advance in your career and provide friendships. In an effort to get support and advice, join an association and become involved. Head a committee to gain the visibility to display your skills and abilities. Give back to the association by becoming and staying active.

Make the best use of networking opportunities by thinking about what you would like your contacts to know about you before you meet with them. For instance, before attending a meeting, you might think about how you can let members know about your particular skills, abilities, and experiences. How can you give them particulars about the type of job you would like to have?

When questioning your contacts about their jobs, refrain from asking personal questions regarding their pay.

NETWORKING QUESTIONS

Some questions you can ask when networking to get information include:

1. What is a typical day like in your position?
2. What qualifications are necessary for a position like yours?
3. Is there an opportunity for advancement?
4. How does an individual qualify for advancement in this position?
5. Do you have any special advice for me?
6. What is the most interesting aspect of your job?
7. Is there anyone else I should speak to within the company?
8. What types of entry-level jobs are there in this field?
9. How can I best prepare myself for a position in this field?
10. What are the specific skills required for this position?
11. Do you have any suggestions about where I can apply for a job?
12. What does your company expect of new hires?
13. What kind of training do new hires receive in your company?

SHARE WITH OTHERS

Networking is a two-way street. Although you will be calling on people to help you, it is important for you to reciprocate and give referrals to others as well. Be generous when sharing your time and advice, and be courteous and professional at all times. Introduce your contacts to people you know who can help them in their careers. Share your expertise as well.

GET STARTED

With whom will you network to find a job? Take into consideration where you would like to work and the kind of work you would like to do when you decide which people to contact. It will be helpful to keep your **job objective**, which is your main career goal, in mind as you write up a list of networking prospects.

To create a network list, write down the names of everybody you already know, including friends, family members, neighbors, classmates, coworkers, supervisors, and teachers. Next, list the individuals who work in your school placement center, people you meet during part-time work experiences, and members of professional groups and organizations to which you belong. These people should form your basic network. Then, expand your network by asking the people you know if they can recommend anyone else for your list.

Reach Out

Do not hesitate to approach people you do not know. It is surprising what you will learn by talking with people. Tell everyone you know that you are looking for work, and do not discount small talk. Never assume you can get along without networking with a particular person or that you have enough people in your network. Keep in mind that the next person you talk with could be THE ONE who helps you get the job. When you put yourself in positions where you can meet other people, it is easy to form a network of helpful friends. Networking is an investment in your career and your future.

EXERCISE 2-F

In Table 2–6 list all the people you can think of who would make good networking contacts.

Table 2–6   NETWORKING CONTACTS LIST FORM

NETWORKING CONTACTS LIST			
Name	Address	Telephone No.	E-mail Address

GET ORGANIZED

After you have completed a list of networking contacts, organize them as to how they might help you. Weigh each contact carefully to determine their value to you.

NETWORKING STRATEGIES

There are several ways to network, including these:

1. Join a **professional organization** or association in your field. Select an organization that will best fit in with your career goals and personality. If there is a specific association for your profession, join it. (Take advantage of student rates.) Other organizations you might wish to join include college and alumni, business and professional, and civic and religious. You will be able to give back to your community and gain professional visibility through organizations. Your library, the telephone book, or the Internet can help you locate information on professional organizations. Introduce yourself to as many members as you can, and commit their names and faces to memory. Read the organization's newsletters and journals to learn of technical changes, industry trends, and membership listings. Become active in the group to get the most benefit. Go to workshops, luncheons, and other events.

2. Volunteer for a nonprofit agency or organization. Doing something for others always has positive benefits for a volunteer, including the opportunity to learn new skills, to gain experience, and to get personal satisfaction.

3. Take a course or workshop, and get to know your classmates.

4. Write articles for newsletters.

5. Stay in touch with former coworkers, employers, classmates, etc.

6. Read newsletters and trade publications in your field.

FOLLOW-UP

Turn your contacts into opportunities by following up on leads they give you. Immediately send your resume and **cover letter** to the companies you have been given. The cover letter is a letter that accompanies the resume, highlighting the important information about your background. Telephone leads if time is a concern.

CAN YOUR NETWORKING CONTACTS

- Provide you with information and advice?
- Link you with other people who can help you?
- Link you to companies that might hire you?
- Review your resume and **portfolio** (defined later in the chapter)?
- Suggest places you might send your resume?
- Tell you of specific job openings?
- Give your name to employers they know who are hiring?
- Introduce you to contacts for job shadows, informational interviews, and/or externships?

2

To keep track of your contacts, any activity taken, and follow-up information, set up a tracking system such as the one in Table 2–7. Your computer will be helpful for this task. Any system that works for you will do.

TABLE 2–7

NETWORKING CONTACTS REFERRAL FORM

NETWORKING CONTACTS REFERRALS		
Name	Organization	Comments

Organize your network contacts, and call or write to them as often as you feel comfortable doing so. You will have a closer relationship with some people more than others. Always send thank-you notes to people who help you, and keep them posted as to your progress. You could also send cards for special occasions and congratulatory messages for promotions and newsworthy items.

Tips & Tricks

Networking Tips

- Make a list of networking contacts.
- Talk to people everywhere you go, especially at workshops, classes, company gatherings, meetings, etc.
- Get out where the people are—go places to meet others.
- Do a follow-up by making calls and appointments, writing e-mails, visiting locations—whatever it takes to get people to remember you.

(Continued)

Tips & Tricks (Continued)

- Follow-up with networking contacts by making calls and arranging appointments with them and by writing e-mails and personally visiting them.
- Join professional organizations.
- Keep in touch with former coworkers, classmates, friends, etc.
- Volunteer.
- Attend workshops and classes.
- Remember that networking is a two-way street and be willing to help others.
- Incorporate networking into your life.
- Be positive when networking.
- Create a file for your contacts and update it often.

PROFESSIONAL ORGANIZATIONS

Professional organizations are available for the majority of professions and industries. While you are in school, you will find that the student rates of many organizations are affordable. This provides a great opportunity to break into the group and join the professional organizations for your field.

Members of professional organizations often know where to find externship positions and other job openings. Names and addresses of professional organizations can be found at libraries. Ask your local librarian to help you find appropriate organizations.

Another good source for locating organizations is the Internet. Do a search to find an appropriate one in your field. A professional organization's **Internet site** provides a lot of information about them. Some sites list names and contact information on a variety of companies in their particular industries, including externship programs, available job openings, requirements, and contact people. Professional organization sites update their members on industry trends and technology, workshops, and job openings.

Many professional organizations have their own Web sites, trade publications, and newsletters that might list details on industry openings, current trends, members, and who to contact to obtain a membership application.

CHECK JOB BOARDS IN LOCAL COLLEGES, HOSPITALS, COMPANIES, ETC.

College campuses often post externship positions and job opportunities on their student bulletin boards or in their career centers. Other companies may use various display boards to post openings and locate prospective employees. In addition, supermarkets and stores sometimes post jobs from local companies on their community bulletin boards.

Resume

When applying for a job found posted in newspaper or Internet want ads, you will be required to send a resume. In addition, use a resume when applying directly to companies.

WRITING AN EFFECTIVE RESUME

A resume is a summary of your work experience, education, skills, and anything else you have to offer an employer. It will show an employer what you have done and what you can do in the future. The resume is essentially a one-page sales pitch of your skills, education, and abilities. Be sure to use proper spelling, punctuation, and grammar. Pay attention to every detail so mistakes do not cost you an interview. Never lie or exaggerate.

There are a number of resume styles, and yours must stand out in order to get an employer's attention. Resumes could have wide margins and lots of white space, or else they may have very little white space. Some resumes have large-font headings, while others would be too many pages long if such sizes were used. Bullets, underlines, bold, and indentions may be used or not. Some resumes concentrate on skills and education listed in chronological order; others concentrate on work experience using a functional style.

When determining how to set up your resume, you will need to consider how much information you have, what you want to emphasize, and what you want to downplay. You also need to decide if the resume will be placed on the Internet or with a company that scans resumes into a database to be accessed later using key terms. There is no one-size-fits-all resume that serves everyone's needs; rather, there are many styles and formats. Check one of the resume books on the market or one of the many on-line resume sites for a style suitable for your purposes. A sample resume is provided in this chapter, as well as a detailed explanation of each section. Choose one that best reflects your personality and background information. Make the format easy to read so employers will be able to spot pertinent information at a glance.

No matter what style you choose, the resume should be arranged in logical order with basic headings, such as personal information, education and training, work experience, and clubs/special achievements.

Target a resume to a specific employer when you know the position for which you are applying. For instance, match your resume to the newspaper want ad by including examples that show you are the person for whom they are looking. If the ad states the company is looking for someone with initiative, give an example of how you took initiative on a previous job or during your education. Other considerations include: Does your job objective relate to the position for which you are applying? Did you compose the resume for a specific job and, therefore, include key terms and skills?

Resumes can be arranged (1) chronologically, by listing education and work history beginning with the most current and working backwards, or (2) functionally, emphasizing skills and responsibilities.

You will also need references—individuals who can vouch for your education, work history, and personal characteristics. References are listed on a separate sheet and will be discussed in more detail later.

PERSONAL INFORMATION

Begin with your name (spelled in full), complete address (spell out all words such as street, road, avenue, boulevard), and telephone number, including area code. Use an alternate telephone number if one is available (i.e., cell phone, work phone, or number to leave a message). You may include a fax number and/or e-mail address if available. Set your name off in some way so it is highly visible by using bold, all caps, centering, etc. Do not include other personal information like health, age, or marital status.

JOB OBJECTIVE

A job objective states the type of work you would like to do. It is optional on the resume, but many employers like to see an objective that indicates your job preference. You can use a general objective or a specific one slanted to an exact position. The objective is a brief statement. For example, *Seeking a position in accounts payable that will lead to advancement.*

EDUCATION AND TRAINING

This section should present all education related to your job objective or to the job you are seeking. Begin with the highest level of education you have attained and the degree held. Then, list others, working backwards. If you have a college degree, you need not put high school information on the resume.

List the names of the educational institutions you attended, addresses, telephone numbers, degrees, and dates you received the degrees. Give major subject areas and add specific skills you have learned that are related to the position you are seeking. If you did not attain a degree but attended college, list the number of credits you obtained, years attended, and any certificates and diplomas you acquired.

After listing educational institutions, add any other training you have had, including on-the-job training and individual courses, workshops, or seminars. You may indicate the name of the programs, dates, and certificates received if applicable. If your training has nothing to do with the job you are pursuing, it is not necessary to mention it.

As a subsection of education and training, detail your major courses, including specialized training, computer software, foreign languages, and machines operated.

Example

TABLE 2–8
EDUCATION AND TRAINING: MAJOR COURSES TAKEN
Medical Courses
Anatomy & Physiology, Medical Coding and Billing, Medical Terminology, Insurance, Medical Office Procedures, Computerized Medical Office Management
Specialized Training
Taking height, weight, pulse; CPR; autoclaving; blood pressure cuff
Machines Operated
Computer, printer, fax, copier, multiline phone, autoclave
Personal Charactertistics
Dependable, Caring, Honest, Responsible

WORK EXPERIENCE

Employers are interested in seeing a successful work history, especially in the field for which you are applying. All work experience will add to your background in some way and can be used to your advantage if presented correctly. What jobs should you list? How far back in your work history should you go? The answers to these questions are (1) list whatever you think will help you get a job, and (2) go back as far as you need to in order to impress employers.

If you are short on full-time work experience, you will need to include part-time jobs. If you have a lot of experience, you can select those work experiences that best represent your background and relate to future positions for which you are applying. For instance, if you have worked as a salesclerk, you need not mention your paper delivery route.

Look at each of your work experiences and decide which would be best to include on the resume. Pay particular attention to your job duties and responsibilities. Think about how your skills might transfer to another job. For instance, if you are like the salesclerk mentioned earlier who waited on customers, you can carry that customer service experience over to any other job, not just another retail position. All companies deal with customers. You can transfer your customer service experience to a position as a customer service representative, receptionist, administrative assistant, manager, health care professional, hospitality worker, and so on. Think about your transferable skills as previously discussed. All companies need people who operate computers, write and keyboard information, handle money (payroll/taxes), train and supervise others, etc. Be sure to analyze every task you have performed and attempt to link it to the next position for which you are applying.

List work experiences in chronological order (by date), starting with the most current job you have held and working backwards. Include complete names, addresses, phone numbers, job titles, responsibilities, and dates. You may also include supervisors' names.

Closely examine and summarize your specific duties, responsibilities, and skills. Emphasize your duties with action verbs and numbers where applicable. For instance, *Supervised three salesclerks* or *am able to keyboard 55 wpm.*

2

EXERCISE 2-G

Ask yourself: What do I have to offer an employer? Then, answer the question in as much detail as possible on the lines provided.

_____

_____

_____

_____

_____

_____

Action Verbs

TABLE 2–9

ACTION VERBS LIST

Motivated	Initiated	Advised	Organized
Assessed	Communicated	Supervised	Trained
Managed	Solved	Controlled	Expedited
Explained	Exhibited	Filed	Coordinated
Inventoried	Investigated	Established	Demonstrated
Installed	Illustrated	Handled	Generated
Wrote	Compiled	Operated	Assembled
Analyzed	Projected	Conducted	Interpreted

CLUBS AND ACHIEVEMENTS

This section of the resume should include professional organizations and clubs to which you belong. Include offices held, duties you performed, and years as a member.

Also, list academic awards, grade point average, special honors, scholarships received, and information on workshops and seminars you have attended. Extracurricular activities such as volunteering and coaching can be added. Achievements and awards can be the result of education, work, or community involvement.

Figure 2–1

SAMPLE RESUME WITH AN OBJECTIVE STATEMENT

CARYN KLINGS

153 Phillipson Drive
Pittsburgh, PA 15222
774–668–8477 (home)
774–998–5465 (cell)
cbklings@mail.com

OBJECTIVE: Seeking a position utilizing my skills and ability to work as a team member to provide quality, dependable patient care.

WORK EXPERIENCE

1992-Present Health Center, Pittsburgh, PA 774–834–5555

- Provided personal in-house care as required for elderly patients, including bedridden care, tube feedings, catheter tending, giving medications, repositioning, and regulating oxygen
- Facilitated physical therapy exercises, including maintaining proper alignment and seeing that exercises were performed correctly
- Managed and maintained files and data regarding billing and medical expenses, including Medicare
- Gave treatments as required
- Wrote out lab records for patients who needed them
- Took doctors' orders
- Helped with patient admissions
- Trained CNAs and aides
- Gave tours of the personal care center to families seeking care
- Interacted with families and doctors
- Ordered supplies for facility
- Maintained oxygen tanks, concentrators, and inhalers
- Directed air mattresses to proper patients

EDUCATION

Westmoreland County Community College, 2000   Microsoft Office Courses
Westmoreland School of Nursing, 1990–1992   Registered Nurse

SPECIAL ABILITIES

- Used preprogrammed laptops to dispense meds and sign off on medications
- Can operate computer, fax, multiline telephone, and navigate the Internet
- Reliable, ethical healthcare provider

2

FIGURE 2–2

BASIC SAMPLE RESUME

CARYN KLINGS

153 Phillipson Drive
Pittsburgh, PA 15222
774–668–8477 (home)
774–998–5465 (cell)
cbklings@mail.com

EDUCATION _____

Westmoreland County Community College, 2000   Microsoft Office Courses
Westmoreland School of Nursing, 1990–1992   Registered Nurse

WORK EXPERIENCE _____

Health Center, Pittsburgh, PA 774–834–5555   1992-Present

- Provided personal in-house care as required for elderly patients, including bedridden care, tube feedings, catheter tending, giving medications, repositioning, and regulating oxygen
- Facilitated physical therapy exercises, including maintaining proper alignment and seeing that exercises were performed correctly
- Managed and maintained files and data regarding billing and medical expenses, including Medicare
- Gave treatments as required
- Wrote out lab records for patients who needed them
- Took doctors' orders
- Helped with patient admissions
- Trained CNAs and aides
- Gave tours of the personal care center to families seeking care
- Interacted with families and doctors
- Ordered supplies for facility
- Maintained oxygen tanks, concentrators, and inhalers
- Directed air mattresses to proper patients

SPECIAL ABILITIES _____

Used preprogrammed laptops to dispense meds and sign off on medications
Can operate computer, fax, multiline telephone, and navigate the Internet
Reliable, ethical healthcare provider

FIGURE 2–3

VARIATION ON A SAMPLE RESUME

CARYN KLINGS

153 Phillipson Drive
Pittsburgh, PA 15222
774–668–8477 (home)
774–998–5465 (cell)
cbklings@mail.com

PROFESSIONAL WORK EXPERIENCE

HEALTH CENTER

Pittsburgh, PA 774–834–5555   1992-Present

- Provided personal in-house care as required for elderly patients, including bedridden care, tube feedings, catheter tending, giving medications, repositioning, and regulating oxygen
- Facilitated physical therapy exercises, including maintaining proper alignment and seeing that exercises were performed correctly
- Managed and maintained files and data regarding billing and medical expenses, including Medicare
- Gave treatments as required
- Wrote out lab records for patients who needed them
- Took doctors' orders
- Helped with patient admissions
- Trained CNAs and aides
- Gave tours of the personal care center to families seeking care
- Interacted with families and doctors
- Ordered supplies for facility
- Maintained oxygen tanks, concentrators, and inhalers
- Directed air mattresses to proper patients

SPECIAL ABILITIES

Used preprogrammed laptops to dispense meds and sign off on medications
Can operate computer, fax, multiline telephone, and navigate the Internet
Reliable, ethical healthcare provider

EDUCATION

Westmoreland County Community College, 2000   Microsoft Office Courses
Westmoreland School of Nursing, 1990–1992   Registered Nurse

2

ELECTRONIC RESUMES

Resumes sent electronically or stored in a company database should be prepared in a simple format. Avoid fancy fonts, bold, underlining, and italics. Do not use tables or tabs as these may not be compatible with a company's software program.

FIGURE 2–4

SAMPLE ELECTRONIC RESUME

ELECTRONIC RESUME

Electronic resumes have no fancy fonts or formatting. This type of resume is e-mailed to potential employers or posted on-line.

CARYN KLINGS

153 Fern Drive
Pittsburgh, PA 15222
774–668–8477 (home)
774–998–5465 (cell)
cbklings@mail.com

OBJECTIVE: Seeking a position utilizing my skills and ability to work as a team member to provide quality, dependable patient care.

WORK EXPERIENCE
1992-Present

Health Center, Pittsburgh, PA, 774–834–5555

Provided personal in-house care as required for elderly patients, including bedridden care, tube feedings, catheter tending, giving medications, repositioning, and regulating oxygen
Facilitated physical therapy exercises, including maintaining proper alignment and seeing that exercises were performed correctly
Managed and maintained files and data regarding billing and medical expenses, including Medicare
Gave treatments as required
Wrote out lab records for patients who needed them
Took doctors' orders
Trained CNAs and aides

(Continued)

FIGURE 2–4 (Continued)

Gave tours of the personal care center to families seeking care

Interacted with families and doctors

Ordered supplies for facility

Maintained oxygen tanks, concentrators, and inhalers

Directed air mattresses to proper patients

EDUCATION

Westmoreland County Community College, 2000, Microsoft Office

Westmoreland School of Nursing, 1990–1992, Registered Nurse

SPECIAL ABILITIES

Used preprogrammed laptops to dispense meds and sign off on medications

Can operate computer, fax, multiline telephone, and navigate the Internet

Reliable, ethical healthcare provider

Tips & Tricks

Resume Tips

- Use a good quality paper with matching envelopes, an easy-to-read font, and a quality printer.
- Keep the resume to one page if possible; eliminate unnecessary words.
- Choose a format that will let your best qualifications stand out at a glance.
- Custom design the resume, rather than using templates or wizards.
- Do not mix too many different fonts.
- Be brief, but specific.
- Make your name stand out by using bold or caps.
- Use action verbs.
- Stress past accomplishments and responsibilities.

(Continued)

Tips & Tricks (Continued)

- Double-check everything and pay particular attention to dates, names, and your contact information.
- Get someone else to proofread your resume.
- Do not exaggerate.
- Do not add unnecessary personal information (age, height, weight, etc.).
- Do not include references on the resume.
- Do not include salary desired.

WRITING AN EFFECTIVE REFERENCE SHEET

A **reference sheet** is a listing of people who will be references for you regarding your job search. References are people who will provide employers with additional information about you, such as verification of work and school. References are not listed on the resume. Instead, a separate sheet should be prepared.

Begin the reference sheet with a heading that includes your name, address, and telephone numbers keyed at the top. Follow the heading with the names, titles, company names, work addresses, and telephone numbers of your references.

Professional references are those who will verify your work habits, skills, and academic history. These individuals may be former teachers and supervisors. Personal references are people who will attest to your personal character. These individuals may be friends, coworkers, and classmates. Avoid using family members.

Choose from three to five references who will say good things about you. Ask permission before giving an individual's name as a reference.

Reference sheets are not sent out with resumes. Instead, take a copy with you on the interview or send one separately when asked to do so by an employer. The employer will check with references to be sure you are the right candidate for the position.

You may use any style and format to type the reference sheet, but make sure it is easy to read and error free. Use the same paper for the reference sheet as you did for the resume.

FIGURE 2–5

SAMPLE REFERENCES PAGE

REFERENCES
OF
CARYN KLINGS

---

153 Phillipson Drive, Pittsburgh, PA 15222
774–668–8477 (home) or 774–998–5465 (message)
cbklings@mail.com

John Smith, M.D.
Health Center
887 Robinson Way
Pittsburgh, PA 15222
774–834–5555

Mary Jones, M.D.
Health Center
887 Robinson Way
Pittsburgh, PA 15222
774–834–5555

Scott Brown
Medical Billing Center
334 Main Street
Pittsburgh, PA 15219
774–856–9987

2

Tips & Tricks

Tips for Choosing References and Writing a Reference Sheet

- Use the same bond paper as your resume.
- Provide a heading with your name, address, and phone numbers.
- Choose three to five references.
- Choose previous employers and teachers, as well as other professionals.
- Provide references that will enhance your chances for a job.
- Provide individual names, titles, company names, addresses (preferably work), and phone numbers of references.
- Contact references and ask permission to use their names.

EXERCISE 2-H

1. Fill out the resume information sheet in Figure 2–6.
2. Design and key your resume in an appropriate format.
3. Create and key a reference sheet.

FIGURE 2–6

RESUME AND JOB APPLICATION INFORMATION SHEET

RESUME INFORMATION SHEET

Name _____

Address _____

Phone Number _____ Alternate Phone Number _____

Job Objective _____

_____

Education and Training _____

_____

_____

_____

_____

(Continued)

FIGURE 2–6 (Continued)

Specialized Courses _____

_____

Diploma/Degree _____

Work Experience _____

_____

_____

_____

_____

Achievements/Awards _____

_____

Clubs _____

WRITING AN EFFECTIVE COVER LETTER

2

A cover letter should accompany every resume you send in the mail or by fax. The cover letter should grab the attention of a perspective employer and hold it.

In the first paragraph, use an attention getter, such as naming a degree you hold, the specialized skills you have, the type of position you are seeking, who recommended you, or where you heard of the opening.

In the middle paragraph, discuss your education and employment history, as well as your skills and qualifications for the particular position for which you are applying. Include transferable skills.

In the last paragraph, request an interview to discuss how your qualifications fit the position. Be sure to give contact information.

Be sure to use action verbs and match yourself to the requirements of the position. Be concise, but specific. Use an appropriate letter format, a return address, and an enclosure notation. Proofread carefully and sign your letter. Do not staple or paperclip your resume to the letter. Instead, fold the resume and letter together.

FIGURE 2–7

RESUME COVER LETTER OR LETTER OF APPLICATION

CARYN KLINGS

153 Phillipson Drive
Pittsburgh, PA 15222

724–668–8477 (home)   724–998–5465 (cell)

cbklings@mail.com

Current Date

Mr. John Doe
ZZZZ Company
99 One Central Way
Freeport, PA 16229

Dear Mr. Doe:

   An associate degree prepares me for the administrative assistant position you advertised in the January 25 edition of *Daily News*. The position seems a perfect fit for my career goals, experience, and education.

   For the past two years, I worked as a salesclerk at Terrific Sales, while taking classes for my degree. These experiences increased my organizational skills and taught me how to manage my time.

   As you can see from my resume, I have taken a variety of computer courses, including MS Office. Independent classes I took gave me experience in making decisions and solving problems. Group projects and presentations provided team-building skills.

   Please review my qualifications to see how they might be an asset to ZZZZ Company. I am available to discuss this position with you at your convenience. Please contact me at the above address and telephone number.

Sincerely yours,

Caryn Klings

Enclosure

Match your resume and cover letter to the job you are applying for as closely as possible, but do not simply repeat the wording in the ad. For example, if the ad requests someone who is dependable and takes the initiative, do not say, "I am dependable and take initiative." Instead, give specific examples of how you are dependable (received attendance awards) and how you take the initiative (have successfully completed an independent study course).

COVER LETTER

A cover letter must accompany every resume sent through the mail. Tailor your letter to a specific person, taking care to spell his or her name correctly and to use a proper title.

If you do not have a specific person's name for addressing your letter, call the company and ask to whom a cover letter should be addressed. If there is no company name given in the ad, use the salutation "Ladies and Gentlemen." Avoid the outdated salutation "To Whom It May Concern."

In addition to checking the want ads, read the business section of the newspaper to learn about companies that are expanding, adding new products and services, merging, or breaking sales records in their industry. These companies may be looking for new employees, even though they have not advertised.

EXERCISE 2-1

Select three want ads from your local newspaper or from the Internet. On the lines, make a list of the skills and personal traits the ad requires.

_____

_____

List any abbreviations in the ad and then write out the meaning by checking Table 2–3. If you come across an abbreviation that is not listed in the table, ask your school placement director or instructor what it means. If your school does not have a placement office, ask your local librarian.

_____

_____

_____

DEVELOPING INTERVIEW SKILLS

Many qualified candidates compete for the same position, so you must be well prepared for an interview. You only make a first impression once; make it a successful one. Do research on the company to which you are applying. Learn about its products and services, locations, types of positions, number of employees, profits/losses, and future plans for growth. Information can be found in libraries, on the Internet, in annual reports, through employees, and by telephoning the company.

If you telephone a company, tell the receptionist you are researching the company for a job interview, and ask him or her to send you appropriate information.

Go alone to the interview and know the location and time. If you are unfamiliar with the exact location of the company, take a ride past it a day or two before the interview. Being late because you did not know where you were going is not an acceptable excuse.

Check the pronunciation and spelling of the interviewer's name. Greet the interviewer with a smile, a firm handshake, and direct eye contact. Speak confidently and clearly.

TYPES OF INTERVIEWS

An interview is a meeting between a job candidate and a perspective employer. It can be formal or informal, depending on the size of the company. For a job candidate, the purpose of the interview is to get a job. For an employer, the purpose is to determine the most qualified candidate.

The interview process is not mysterious, however. Interviews do follow certain patterns. **Screening interviews**, where the interviewer is checking to see if the candidate is qualified, may be conducted by phone or in person. A **structured interview** follows a set question/answer format, where the interviewer determines if the candidate has sufficient skills and experience to do the job and a personality that will fit well with other employees. This is the most common type of interview. **Stress interviews** put the candidate under pressure to see if he or she can handle stressful situations. These interviews are common for upper management positions. **Committee interviews** are conducted with two or more interviewers. **Group interviews** are held with two or more interviewees. In **situational interviews**, you are asked how you would handle specific situations.

It is also common for a job candidate to be scheduled for second and third interviews before being offered a position with the company.

DRESS

Your appearance is an important part of the interview process. Professionally dressed individuals have the highest success rate in landing jobs. You want to leave the interviewer with the impression that you are serious about the position. Therefore, dress professionally for an interview by leaning toward conservative outfits.

Men's Wardrobe

Traditionally, men should wear a business suit in blue, gray, or black. A white shirt with a nice tie presents the best image. Wear basic black or brown wing-tip or oxford shoes that are well kept and polished. Do not wear casual shoes to an interview.

Men should wear a watch and may, if appropriate, wear a wedding ring. Avoid earrings, gold chains, and ornate cufflinks. Do not have body piercings or tattoos showing.

Women's Wardrobe

Women should wear a business suit or basic dress and jacket. Gray, navy, and black are good colors for the interview suit. Add a white or pastel blouse. It is appropriate to wear pale-colored suits in the spring and summer, but stay away from bright colors such as red or hot pink. Avoid fancy styles, fad fashions, and frills; think conservative. Do not wear plunging necklines or skirts with high slits.

Wear neutral-colored pumps with low or medium heels. Hosiery should be of a neutral color. Make sure shoes are in good repair and well polished. Shoe color should match the hemline.

Accessories should be conservative. Avoid flashy, dangling jewelry. A watch, ring, and simple necklace and earrings are good choices. Do not have body piercings or tattoos showing.

Clothing Care

Choose fabrics that are easy to care for and of good quality. Wools, silks, cottons, and linens will provide years of wear. All clothing should be cleaned and pressed after each wearing, and shoes must be kept polished.

2

PROFESSIONAL IMAGE

Use proper hygiene—clean body, hair, teeth, and nails. Bathe or shower daily. Wear a deodorant or antiperspirant.

Men should wear short, conservative hair styles. Women may wear their hair short or long; but if hair is long, it should be pulled back away from the face. Hair should be washed daily.

Do not overdo perfume/cologne, as too heavy a scent is offensive and some interviewers may be sensitive or allergic to fragrances.

Women should use a light touch when applying makeup. Use just enough makeup to enhance your features.

ANSWERING QUESTIONS

Prepare for an interview by thinking about the type of questions that are likely to be asked during the interview and then practicing your answers. (Some typical interview questions are given at the end of this chapter.)

When answering questions, maintain a positive attitude, speak clearly and confidently, and look directly at the interviewer. Answer sincerely, honestly, and with enthusiasm. Be sure to get across your skills and qualifications by telling employers what you can do for them. Communicate achievements in a clear, concise manner, using complete sentences and proper grammar. Give examples as proof of your qualifications, and support your answers with facts, not opinions. Maximize your strengths and minimize your weaknesses. Stick to relevant, job-related information, and do not discuss personal business. Be courteous and respectful; do not criticize former employers. Emphasize your positive personal characteristics and skills.

Do not let your mind wander while the interviewer is speaking or interrupt him or her. Ask appropriate questions about the position or the company when the interviewer finishes speaking. (See sample questions at the end of the chapter.)

Express your interest in the company by discussing the information you have learned about it, and show how your skills will be beneficial to the company. Do not ask about salary unless the interviewer brings it up or you are offered the position. Avoid controversial subjects like politics and religion.

ALLEVIATE NERVOUSNESS

Nervousness is to be expected during the interview. However, you can alleviate some of it by bring prepared. Practice interviewing with a friend. Go over answers to sample interview questions. Take a trial run to find the company you are interviewing with if you are not sure of the location. Arrive a few minutes early. If possible, stop in the restroom to freshen up and dry your hands if they are sweaty.

Take a few deep breaths, and tell yourself you are prepared. Look through your portfolio a few minutes before the interview so your background information is fresh in your mind. Avoid smoking, caffeine, and chewing gum.

Tips & Tricks

Tips to Alleviate Interview Nervousness

- Know exactly where the company is located.
- Practice interviewing with a friend.
- Practice answers to interview questions.
- Look over your portfolio.
- Arrive early.
- Freshen up.
- Avoid caffeine, smoking, and chewing gum.
- Take a couple of deep breaths.
- Mentally recite positive sayings.

EXERCISE 2-J

On the lines provided, list some things you can do to alleviate your nervousness during an interview.

_____

_____

_____

_____

_____

_____

CLOSING THE INTERVIEW

At the close of the interview, thank the interviewer for his or her time. If you were not told when you would hear about the position, ask when you may call to see if a decision has been reached. If you are interested in the position, make sure you get that point across to the interviewer. Ask for the job. The interviewer cannot read your mind.

Send a thank-you letter as soon as possible to show your appreciation for the interviewer's time. Express your eagerness to work for the company. Ask for a business card so you are sure to get the correct spelling of the interviewer's name. In certain cases it may be appropriate to send a card or e-mail in lieu of a letter, depending on the formality of the interview and how you were contacted regarding it.

FIGURE 2–8

SAMPLE THANK-YOU LETTER

> # CARYN KLINGS
> 153 Phillipson Drive
> Pittsburgh, PA 15222
>
> 724–668–8477 (home)   724–998–5465 (cell)
>
> cbklings@mail.com

Current Date
Mr. John Doe
ZZZZ Company
99 One Central Way
Freeport, PA 16229

Dear Mr. Doe:

Thank you for interviewing me yesterday for the administrative assistant position open at ZZZZ Company. I enjoyed meeting you and found your comments very helpful.

I am more convinced than ever that this position fits perfectly with my career goals. I believe my education and experience are suited to the position and that I could make a valuable contribution.

I look forward to hearing from you and to be given the chance to show you how well I could handle the position. Thank you for your time and encouragement.

Sincerely yours,

Caryn Klings

Tips & Tricks

Interview Tips

- Research the company.
- Know the correct pronunciation of the interviewer's name.
- Know the company's location, and be sure to have money for parking.
- Dress and act professionally.
- Know the correct interview time; arrive ten minutes early.
- Take extra copies of your resume and reference sheet.
- Carry a briefcase or portfolio.
- Greet the interviewer with a smile, and introduce yourself.
- Do not sit until invited to do so.
- Use direct eye contact and a firm handshake.
- Be respectful of everyone you meet, including the office staff.
- Sit erect and listen carefully.
- Be sincere and friendly, but professional.
- Watch your body language.
- Do not place materials on the interviewer's desk.
- Show enthusiasm, and be positive.
- Carry a pen and small notebook.
- Do not be overly nervous.
- Do not give simple "yes" or "no" answers.
- Do not smoke or chew gum.
- Send a thank-you letter as soon as possible after the interview.

Prepare three to four questions to ask during the interview. These questions should relate to the company, position, and responsibilities. Avoid questions about salary, benefits, vacations, and the like until after an offer has been made. The following list of questions is suitable for the interviewee to ask.

EXERCISE 2-K

On the lines provided, write a three or four sentence answer to "Tell me about yourself."

_____

_____

_____

_____

QUESTIONS FOR THE INTERVIEWEE TO ASK

- What are the advancement opportunities in the company?
- Do you have a company training program?
- How do you get into the company training program?
- Do you have tuition reimbursement?
- What is the starting date for this position?
- Do you have a dress code?
- What happened to the last person who had this position?
- What kind of training will I get for this position?
- Can you describe a typical day in this position?
- How are the employees evaluated?
- What type of employee are you looking for to fill this position?

QUESTIONS AN INTERVIEWER MIGHT ASK

- What can I do for you?
- Tell me about yourself?
- What would you like to be doing a year from now? Five years?
- What degrees/diplomas do you hold?
- Would your previous employer recommend you for a job?
- How long would you work for the company if hired?
- What kind of benefits are you looking for with this position?
- What do you expect to be paid?
- Are you a good manager?
- Do you manage your time well? Give an example.
- Do you plan to go on to school?
- Are you willing to travel?
- How did you learn about this position?
- What are your strengths?
- What are your weaknesses?
- Why do you want to work for this company?
- What qualifications do you bring to this position?
- What skills do you have that will help you perform the tasks required of you?
- What can you do for this company?
- Why should I hire you?

Laws prohibit interviewers from asking questions that discriminate against applicants. All people must be treated fairly regardless of age, race, gender, sexual orientation, disability, religion, or national origin. Asking questions with regard to these areas is illegal. An applicant who is asked an **illegal question** may choose to answer, inquire as to the relevance of the question, or refuse to answer based on appropriate laws. The applicant may ignore the interviewers' behavior or contact the appropriate agency, such as the Equal Employment Opportunity Commission (EEOC).

EXERCISE 2-L

Discuss with a friend how you would handle an illegal question if it were asked of you during an interview.

EXERCISE 2-M

Ask a friend to do a practice interview with you. Have him or her ask appropriate questions. Ask questions of your own. At the conclusion of the practice interview, print out a copy of Figure 2–9 from the CD and have your friend critique you. Also, critique yourself by filling out Figure 2–9.

FIGURE 2–9

SAMPLE EMPLOYER INTERVIEW RATING SHEET

INTERVIEW RATING SHEET

Applicant's Name   Date

Interviewer   Position

RATING SCALE (CHECK ONE RATING PER FACTOR)				
	Outstanding	High	Average	Low
Personal Grooming				
Clothing				
Overall Personal Appearance				

(Continued)

FIGURE 2–9 (Continued)

RATING SCALE (CHECK ONE RATING PER FACTOR)

	Outstanding	High	Average	Low
Self-Confidence				
Poise				
Maturity				
Career Goals				
Character				
Motivation/ enthusiasm				
Warm/friendly				
Interactive skills				
Initiative				
High energy				
Interpersonal skills				
Fluency				
Quick thinking				
Good listener				
Relationship between job and background				
Work experience				
Related life experience				
Degrees/diplomas				
Self-improvement				
Related skills				

(Continued)

ILLEGAL QUESTIONS

- How old are you?
- Are you married? Divorced?
- Do you have young children?
- Are you pregnant now?
- Do you have any heart disease?
- What are your religious beliefs?

2

FIGURE 2–9 (Continued)

RATING SCALE (CHECK ONE RATING PER FACTOR)				
	Outstanding	High	Average	Low
Overall recommendation				
Comments				
Final recommenda-tion (Circle one)	Hire	Do not hire	Hold	
Signed			Date	

LEARNING TO SELL YOUR SKILLS

During an externship interview, you are essentially a salesperson. You must sell your unique skills and abilities to the interviewer. Jobs are available, but you must do your part to obtain one. Employers want to hire people who can add value to their companies, so it makes sense that they would want the same thing from an extern. If you can prove that you can add value during your externship, you might be offered a job after completing it. The more time you spend preparing yourself for the externship, the better your presentation will be.

The interviewer will attempt to determine throughout the interview process if you have the skills necessary to perform the tasks required of the job and if you are a **team player**, who is someone who gets along with and works well with others. Therefore, you need to convey the message that your skills match the company's needs and that you will fit in with the other employees. On the other hand, the interview is also your opportunity to see if the company is a good match for you.

Typical areas an employer is concerned about include (1) competence, (2) attitude, (3) communication skills, (4) personal traits, and (5) problem solving.

In Chapter 1 you assessed your skills and character traits. Now, how do you get these accomplishments across to the interviewer? You must somehow show the company will benefit if you are hired.

First, create a polished professional image through your dress, behavior, and words. This will encourage the employer to take you seriously. Pay attention to your nonverbal body language and voice tone.

Second, have confident answers ready to basic questions. Use action verbs to state how you have benefited other companies where you have worked. Communicate your accomplishments in a clear, concise manner. By concentrating on your experience, education, and skills, you will be focused on your strengths. Give examples of how you can solve problems through critical thinking, and mention that you are ready for a challenge. Highlight personal traits on which you want to focus, such as organization, communication skills, dependability, etc. Remain professional, though, and keep your personal life to yourself. Always show courtesy and respect.

EXERCISE 2-N

Answer the interview questions below on the lines provided.

1. What are your strengths? Weaknesses?

_____

_____

2. What can you do for this company?

_____

_____

3. What unique skills and abilities do you have?

_____

_____

4. Give an example of how you are a team player.

_____

_____

5. Give an example of a problem you have encountered and how you solved it.

_____

_____

2

MORE WAYS TO SELL YOUR SKILLS

Let the interviewer know you are a well-rounded person who has positive work habits and personal qualities. This should be done through providing examples of your dependability, responsibility and **work ethic**, which is the moral code by which you operate in the workplace, such as attendance record, honesty, maintaining confidences, and the like. You also need a clear sense of where you are going and should be able to state goals and communicate effectively.

The first few minutes of contact with the interviewer are crucial, so you need to build rapport quickly. Rapport is the ability to make a common connection, which puts both of you at ease. Listen carefully and pause before giving thoughtful, sincere answers to the interviewer's questions. Employers want confident, prepared employees. Do your part to meet the interviewer's expectations. Remember, you are selling your skills, so you must show the employer that you are valuable. Make yourself stand out from other candidates.

APPLICATION

Another way to sell your skills is through the proper completion of an application. Most businesses require job applicants to complete an application before the interview process begins. Job candidates are frequently eliminated by the way they fill out the application. It is important to write neatly and to fill out the answers to all questions completely and accurately. Read and follow directions carefully. Check and double-check your spelling, grammar, dates, and numbers.

PERSONAL DATA

In the personal data section of the application, spell out your full name (no nicknames), your address, telephone number(s), social security number, and the current date. You may be asked to write your name in several places on the application. You will need to fill in your current address and years of living at that location. Some applications ask for previous addresses and the number of years at each of those places. Spell out words in the address such as road, boulevard, and street. List a phone number where you can be reached during the day and an alternate number if you have one. There may be a reference to age, asking if you are over the age of 18.

When filling in the answer for "position for which you are applying," do not say "any job." Write the name of a position. If you read of the job opening in a want ad, word the name of the position exactly as stated in the ad. You can add the words "or similar position" afterwards if you wish (i.e., administrative assistant or similar position).

Most applications will ask about your citizenship or eligibility to work in the United States and whether or not you have a criminal record.

When filling in the date you are available to start working, remember that it is a professional courtesy to give current employers a two-week notice. Figure that time period into the starting date for a new job. If you are not employed and are able to start immediately, say so.

General Information

The general information section of the application includes work experience, education, extracurricular activities, and references. Sign and date the application when you have completed it.

Work Experience

For work history list the company names, addresses, telephone numbers, dates worked, whether the work was full or part time, job titles, previous salaries, supervisors' names, and reasons for leaving. In addition, detail your duties/accomplishments, including any skills used and machines operated. There may be a separate skills section, where you can list additional ones. The work section may include military and volunteer experience.

It is helpful to create a master list of your work experience to carry with you. This will enable you to fill out applications quickly and accurately.

Education

For the education section, list the school names, addresses, telephone numbers, dates attended, diploma/degrees/certificates you received, and major areas of study. The education section generally includes high school, technical and trade schools, and colleges.

Achievements

There may be a section on the application where you can list your awards, certificates, special achievements, and interests. If so, fill it in with applicable accomplishments.

References

Give three or four names, titles, addresses, and telephone numbers in the reference section. Be sure to select people who will give you a good reference.

EXERCISE 2-O

Fill out the application in Figure 2–10.

Figure 2–10

APPLICATION FOR EMPLOYMENT

(Please print)

PERSONAL INFORMATION

Name _____   Date _____

Present Address _____

Telephone No. _____   Social Security No._____

Were you previously employed by us?_____ If yes, state when_____

EMPLOYMENT DESIRED

Position(s) applied for _____   Expected pay _____

Are you legally eligible for work   Are you over 18 and
in the US? _____   under 70? _____

When are you available to   Are you willing to
start work? _____   travel? _____

Available to work full time _____   part time _____

Special skills _____

(Continued)

FIGURE 2–10 (Continued)

FORMER EMPLOYERS

List below all present and past employment, beginning with the most recent.

Employer Name	Address	Phone No.	Dates Employed	Start Salary	End Salary
Job Title	Supervisor's Name	Describe duties			Reason for leaving

Employer Name	Address	Phone No.	Dates Employed	Start Salary	End Salary
Job Title	Supervisor's Name	Describe duties			Reason for leaving

Employer Name	Address	Phone No.	Dates Employed	Start Salary	End Salary
Job Title	Supervisor's Name	Describe duties			Reason for leaving

(Continued)

2

FIGURE 2–10 (Continued)

EDUCATION

School	Name/ Location	Course of Study	Yrs. Completed	Graduated (Yes/No)	Degree Received
High School					
College					
Business/ Trade/ Other					

PERSONAL REFERENCES (Not a relative)

Name/Occupation	Address	Phone Number

MIILITARY SERVICE RECORD

Were you in the US Armed Forces? _____   If yes, what branch?_____

Dates of duty _____   Rank at Discharge _____

List duties and special training _____

_____

Tips & Tricks

Tips for Filling Out Applications

- Keep a copy of your resume handy to refer to company names and addresses.
- Be prepared by having your background information with you.
- Print or write neatly, staying within the space provided.
- Use a black pen.
- Answer every question. Use NA if a question does not pertain to you.
- Give complete information on names, addresses, and telephone numbers.

Tips & Tricks (Continued)

- Check your spelling.
- If you make a huge mistake, ask for another application. Never turn in a sloppy application.

PORTFOLIO

One terrific tool for selling your skills is the portfolio, which is a compilation of samples of your work, skills, and achievements. Choose a professional looking portfolio with plastic insert sheets to hold your documentation. Include resumes; reference sheets; recommendation letters from employers, teachers, and your externship supervisor; grade transcripts; educational awards (attendance, dean's list, keyboarding, computer software, machines, etc.); class projects; and community service and/or volunteer awards. Anything that documents your accomplishments should be included in the portfolio.

Separate the portfolio into sections by using dividers that identify documents within that section. For instance, a section marked "awards" should contain dean's list letters, attendance and academic awards, employee of the month and safety awards, and so forth. Have one example showing (i.e. resume and reference sheet) and put the other copies behind it.

In the projects section, include sample documents of all the software you can operate. For example, include a sample Peachtree report and Word and Excel documents. Choose work examples with care. The best ones will show skill development, creativity, proficiency, and logical thinking.

When you put something concrete in front of an interviewer, he or she can readily see what you have done and will perhaps mentally link your skills to the tasks required for the available job opening.

Show It

Carry your portfolio to every interview. Women should not carry both a purse and a portfolio. Never place the portfolio (or anything else) on the interviewer's desk. Keep it in your lap until the interviewer asks to see it. Remain alert during the interview to determine the right time to ask if the interviewer would like to see samples of your work. A good example is if you are asked about software that you know how to operate, say, "Yes, I am proficient in Word and have a sample project in my portfolio if you would like to see it."

At the beginning of the interview, if the interviewer looks as if he or she is searching for your resume, offer one of your extra copies from the portfolio.

Tips & Tricks

Portfolio Contents

- Resume
- Reference sheet
- Documentation for degrees, certificates, licenses
- Recommendation letters from former employers
- Recommendation letters from externship supervisor(s)
- Educational awards (attendance, dean's list, certifications, honors, etc.)
- Documentation for organizations (honor society, student services, etc.)
- Class projects (computer programs, writing samples, presentations you have given, PowerPoint presentations, etc.)
- Workshop participation certificates

EXERCISE 2-P

What documents do you have that you can use to build a portfolio? List them on the lines provided.

_____

_____

_____

_____

_____

_____

_____

_____

_____

_____

_____

GETTING HIRED WITHOUT WORK EXPERIENCE

Employers look for job experience whenever they screen job candidates. So, what can you do if you have no actual job experience? Think creatively. Externships, as discussed earlier, are invaluable to students. Although externships are a learning experience for students, they are also an opportunity to impress employers. Do your best work and act in a professional manner.

Externships are a way for employers to try out a person to see if he or she has the required skills and the personal traits necessary for the position. Students have the opportunity to try out the employer, sharpen their skills, and gain experience. Many people are hired permanently because of externships they completed.

VOLUNTEER

Volunteering is another good way to show an employer what you can do, which often leads to a permanent job. Join a professional organization in your field, and become an active member by volunteering for

2

EXERCISE 2-Q

Where can you volunteer your services? Consider locations and types of positions that will give you experience in your field. On the lines provided, list the names of companies and organizations where you might volunteer.

_____

_____

_____

_____

_____

_____

_____

_____

_____

_____

an office or else organizing a program. In addition, nonprofit agencies are always looking for volunteers. Check with hospitals, schools, Girl/Boy Scouts, churches, youth groups, sports teams, animal shelters, and other special agencies. Another volunteer situation for students is helping instructors with projects.

Volunteering shows you are an involved member of society, and you will gain valuable contacts and real work experience.

JOB SHADOW

You could arrange to "shadow" or observe an individual in the workplace. Job shadows are helpful for gaining insight into a particular position or career. During the job shadow, you can offer to perform routine tasks, ask questions about the profession, and have your resume and portfolio reviewed by the individual you are job shadowing. A job shadow is a chance to see the internal workings of a company.

Call friends, relatives, or companies and ask if you may shadow an employee for a few hours or more.

EXERCISE 2-R

Where can you job shadow someone? Consider locations and shadowing someone working in the field you intend to enter. On the lines provided, list the names of companies and organizations where you might job shadow.

_____

_____

_____

_____

_____

_____

_____

_____

WHAT EMPLOYERS WANT

What do employers look for when they want to fill job openings? The answer to that question should be of concern to everyone who hopes for career placement or success. Job seekers should be concerned with what employers want from their workers so they can address those concerns during the interview.

According to many employers, job seekers must possess a good work ethic, be educated and skilled, and get along with others. Employees must have the ability to communicate effectively—both orally and in writing—with customers, coworkers, and supervisors. They must be able to locate information in a timely manner, use higher-level thinking skills to complete tasks, solve problems, listen, follow directions, and develop good judgment. They must also be willing to accept responsibility, supervision, and constructive criticism.

The list sounds like a tall order, but employers want well-rounded employees who will be an asset to their companies. Therefore, you must do everything you can to prepare yourself to meet employers' needs and wants. This preparation is discussed in detail in this and the following chapters.

EMPLOYERS WANT EMPLOYEES WHO ARE

- active listeners
- loyal
- at work every day
- willing to accept supervision
- willing to accept responsibility
- able to work in a group
- able to speak and write clearly
- independent workers
- positive/cheerful
- able to maintain confidences
- professionally dressed
- professionally behaved
- dependable
- goal oriented
- organized
- eager to learn
- skilled
- able to use good judgment

◗ punctual
◗ flexible
◗ ethical/honest
◗ able to follow directions
◗ willing to learn from constructive criticism
◗ accurate/efficient

EXERCISE 2-S

In the space provided, give an example of a time that you:

1. Accepted extra responsibility at work or at school.

_____

_____

2. Showed dependability.

_____

_____

3. Worked independently at school or work.

_____

_____

4. Were loyal to someone.

_____

_____

5. Kept a confidence.

_____

_____

6. Behaved professionally.

_____

_____

7. Faced an ethical situation.

_____

_____

8. Worked in a group.

_____

_____

DEVELOP A GOOD WORK ETHIC

Employees who have a good work ethic are highly valued. Conversely, poor work habits and attitudes are the main reasons why people are fired. A good work ethic is comprised of a number of personal characteristics.

Attendance

Employers expect employees to report to work when they are scheduled. Do not take off unless absolutely necessary. Make every effort to get to work every day and on time. Employees who do not report to work when scheduled are a detriment to their employers. Their absence creates a hardship for coworkers who must fill in for them. Sometimes other people are too busy to do the absent person's work in addition to their own, which means some work goes unfinished. Also, productivity drops when all employees are not present to do their jobs.

If you do need to take time off, be sure to call your employer to explain that you will not be at work. Never abuse sick days by taking them for reasons other than illness. Keep in mind that many companies have a set number of sick days that employees can miss in a year without penalty.

Punctuality

Be **punctual** by arriving at work on time every day. Being five or six minutes late on a daily basis may not seem like a big deal, but that amounts to a half hour or so of missed time per week. And that half hour quickly adds up over the months and years.

Sometimes employees who come in late work through their lunch periods to make up lost time and to justify their lateness. However, working through lunch does not always satisfy employers when it is used to cover for consistent tardiness. Most employers feel every employee should follow the rules (i.e., working during scheduled hours) to be team players and to prevent discord among other employees. When people consistently come in late, their coworkers may waste time by complaining, or they may resort to coming in late, too.

Employers need employees who are willing to work the hours the business is open. Otherwise, the business may suffer reduced income and a tarnished service image.

2

When you do arrive at work, be prepared to begin working. Do not linger over coffee or chat with coworkers. Take breaks when they are scheduled and get back to work on time. When you need to make copies or send faxes, do not stand around talking with coworkers. Work your required number of hours until quitting time.

Meetings can be a waste of time if attendees wait for missing people, sit around talking, or linger over lunch and snacks. Be prompt, avoid chatting, and stick to the agenda.

Integrity

Maintain **integrity** by being honest. Never lie, cheat, or steal. Many companies suffer losses due to employee theft of money, equipment, and office supplies. Do not take anything that belongs to the company or other employees, no matter how little it may be worth.

Do the right thing at all times, and respect yourself and others. Take proper care and precautions with equipment, furniture, and tools. Keep confidential information to yourself.

Telephones and the Internet

Business phones are meant for business use, and so is your time when the business pays you. Make personal calls in emergency situations only. This includes using company phones and personal cell phones. Many employers have banned personal cell phones in the office due to excessive personal calls. Spending an excessive amount of time on personal calls is the same as stealing time from the employer. Employees are paid to do company work while they are on the job.

Companies are increasingly having difficulties with Internet abuse, and many have strict policies against personal Internet use. Internet abuse, an unwelcome problem, includes sending jokes and e-mails to friends, searching for personal information, and accessing questionable sites. All of this abuse wastes company time and ties up company equipment. Internet abuse in the work environment will not be tolerated for long.

Maintain Accuracy and Efficiency

Quality work is extremely important to a company's success. How well you perform your job says a lot about you. Aim for positive results. When confused, go over tasks with the employer so you will understand how to do them properly. Work quickly to complete tasks in a timely manner, but maintain a high degree of accuracy. Errors negate the work you do.

You will be expected to complete a certain amount of work in a specific timeframe. Give to your employer the time he or she is entitled to by doing an honest day's work each and every day.

Be Flexible

Today's employees must be willing and able to adapt to the changing workplace. Technology, skills, job titles, and information are constantly changing. Flexibility is the key to meeting these challenges.

Use Good Judgment

Think about each task you do and figure things out for yourself, rather than run to the boss with every problem. Do be sure, though, you are doing tasks correctly.

While developing personal judgment, ask yourself these questions: Do I complete tasks properly? Do I double-check for accuracy? Do I work efficiently?

BE A TEAM PLAYER

Employees must get along with supervisors and coworkers and be able to work with them in teams to accomplish company goals. On the job you may have to work closely with someone you do not like. You will have to put your personal feelings aside and do your part to get the job finished.

Show that you are ready to help the team. Do whatever needs to be done as best as you can. Share your ideas and propose solutions, but do not dominate others. Encourage everyone to share ideas and participate in discussions.

Companies today rely on the combined expertise and efforts of employees to reach productivity, quality, and service goals. Teams often brainstorm ideas, conduct research, and work on projects.

Besides working together, teamwork applies to respecting the property and space of others. Follow the company rules and regulations to show you are a team player, and do not think you are better than others. All employees should be able to work effectively in a group as well as independently.

EXERCISE 2-T

In the previous summary list, look over the traits that employers want. From the list, write down the character traits you are lacking. Work on improving these traits in order to meet the employers' wants.

_____

_____

_____

_____

If you were to develop a plan of action to begin your self-improvement, what steps would you take? Write your answer on the lines provided.

_____

_____

_____

_____

● BENEFITING FROM AN EXTERNSHIP

Externship is one of the names given to paid or unpaid positions, usually entry level, where you can gain first-hand experience by using your skills and abilities in a company setting. (This type of experience may also be called work-study or internship). Other programs are available, such as the federal school-to-work, co-ops, or cooperative learning.

Externships provide a transition from classes to work, providing students with an opportunity to apply what they learned in the classroom. Working in a "real world" setting makes classroom training more meaningful by helping students make the connection between what they learn in a classroom and what they do at work. Externships promote skill development and problem-solving ability.

Since employers want to hire people with job experience, an externship provides an invaluable opportunity for both employers and job seekers. The extern can establish a work experience record, and his or her future employer gets an experienced employee.

Through externship programs, employers can try out individuals to see how well they meet their company's needs with regard to having the ability to do the job. They can evaluate interpersonal skills to see if they fit in with other employees and can determine their work ethic.

Externs, who will be seeking future jobs, have an opportunity through their externships to decide if the companies they extern for, and the type of industry in general, are what they really desire for a career. Externs can gain knowledge and develop employable skills through on-the-job training. They have the opportunity to establish contacts with professionals and add to their network contact lists. Hopefully, externs will develop desirable work habits, such as dependability, initiative, team building, and punctuality. If the extern and the employer are compatible and there is an opening, the extern may be offered a permanent position with a company.

USE SCHOOL PLACEMENT SERVICES

Keep in touch with your school or college throughout your job search. Many schools and colleges have placement departments that will to assist you in finding a job. If your school has a placement department, sign up and take advantage of the services it provides. Oftentimes businesses will contact professors, counselors, and placement directors for employee leads. In addition, you may get referrals from these individuals and/or the placement department, directing you to companies that are hiring.

If your school has an alumni association, consider joining it. These organizations keep up-to-date information on industry trends and employment opportunities. They are also a great way to network.

LEARNING FROM AN EXTERNSHIP

You will have the opportunity to learn many different things from an externship. It will be up to you to take full advantage of the experience. Although you may have been a disciplined student, you may find that even more discipline is necessary whenever you work. Employer expectations are high when it comes to quantity and quality of work, skills, character traits, and attendance. What may have been enough to "get by" in school will not be acceptable to most employers.

TAKE FULL ADVANTAGE OF YOUR EXTERNSHIP EXPERIENCE, FOR IT CAN PROVIDE AN OPPORTUNITY TO

- gain real-world work experience
- develop skills that make you more employable
- interact with coworkers
- establish contact with professionals
- add to a network contact list
- increase judgment skills
- expand problem-solving ability
- sharpen interpersonal skills
- learn to get along with others in a team
- develop good work ethics
- decide what type of career you would like
- determine if you would enjoy working for the company on a full-time basis
- be offered a full-time job
- get a reference for a future job
- get job leads

SUCCEEDING AT AN EXTERNSHIP

Employers appreciate externs who can work independently, listen carefully, and follow directions. They also look for a willingness to learn, a positive attitude, and a high degree of accuracy.

When you obtain an externship position, dress and act the part of a professional. Follow the company's dress code, and always present a neat, clean appearance. Conservative dress is best for most offices.

Employers expect all workers, including externs, to have good work ethics. This includes coming to work every day and being on time. Take breaks when they are scheduled, and get back from them on time. You will be expected to work until quitting time, which means no slacking off 10 or 15 minutes early. Show up when you are scheduled to work.

Communication skills are a necessity in a work environment. Communicate effectively through clear, concise language. Listen carefully when you are given directions and information. Instead of relying on memory, write everything down in a notebook. When you are confused about directions, ask appropriate questions, but refrain from asking the same questions again and again. In addition to remembering directions, make an effort to remember names and faces of coworkers and supervisors.

Do not make or receive personal calls at work, including those on cell phones, except for emergencies. The Internet should be used for business purposes only. Be respectful of the property of others, and clean up any messes you make.

ACCEPTING CRITICISM

Since the externship is a learning situation, there may be times when your employer criticizes your work. Hopefully, this will be done in a constructive manner. Separate your personal feelings from the criticism, which is of your work, not of you personally. Do not get defensive or offer an array of excuses. Listen carefully, learn as much as you can about what you did wrong, and figure out how you can correct the error. Take the initiative to do the job correctly in the future. Whenever you are confused about how to do a job, ask for specific directions.

EXERCISE 2-U

Complete the self-evaluation in Table 2–10.

Table 2–10 SELF-EVALUATION FOR EXTERNSHIP CHECKLIST

Self-Evaluation for My Externship

Check the following items by finishing this statement:

On my externship I will:

Work at developing my skills.	_____
Seek out professionals that can help my career.	_____
Practice good human relations skills when interacting with coworkers.	_____
Add names to my network list.	_____
Work on developing good judgment.	_____
Work at team-building skills.	_____
Get to work and back from breaks on time.	_____
Work until my scheduled quitting time.	_____

(Continued)

Table 2–10 (Continued)

Keep confidences.   _____

Be dependable.   _____

Work on problem-solving skills.   _____

Decide if this is the right career for me.   _____

Learn from criticism.   _____

EXERCISE 2-V

Interview a student who has completed an externship, and then answer the following questions on the lines provided.

• Did he/she gain new skills?

_____

_____

• Did he/she develop his/her current skills?

_____

_____

• Did he/she have to work independently doing tasks?

_____

_____

• Did he/she have to work with others on a team?

_____

_____

• Did he/she gain some network connections?

_____

_____

• Did he/she learn more about the industry?

_____

_____

(Continued)

EXERCISE 2-V (Continued)

• Did he/she need additional skills for the externship? If so, what were they?

_____

_____

• Was he/she exposed to a variety of duties?

_____

_____

• Was he/she offered a job through the externship?

_____

_____

• How many hours a week did he/she work at the externship?

_____

_____

2

END OF CHAPTER WORK

CASE STUDIES

● ETHICS CASE STUDY

Bob works in a small company, where he does the accounts payable. One day he received an invoice for a two-week late bill that he should have paid. He checked his records and found that he had forgotten to mail the payment for the original invoice, and now the company must pay a late charge. Bob is hesitant to tell his employer. He does not want to get fired for incompetence.

Questions to Ask Yourself

1. Should Bob pay the bill with the late charge and keep quiet about being late?

_____

_____

2. Do you think telling the employer about his mistake would jeopardize Bob's job?

_____

_____

Things to Consider

Employers value honesty and integrity. Chances are that Bob's employer would be far more upset to learn that he tried to cover up a mistake rather than admit the error, even if it meant a reprimand. Bob should explain the situation to his employer. It is unlikely he would be terminated after admitting an error. However, he would be expected to learn from his mistake and not repeat it. Double-checking work will eliminate many errors.

TEAM PLAYER CASE STUDY

Zoey was working on an important project with Justin. After several days of intense discussion on how to do a particular summary for the project, Justin went to the supervisor (without telling Zoey) and got her to agree with his idea for the summary. Zoey was furious. For spite, she called in sick the next two days so Justin would have to complete the project himself.

Questions to Ask Yourself

1. Did Zoey have a right to be upset with Justin?

_____

_____

2. How should Zoey have handled the situation?

_____

_____

Things to Consider

Justin was not being a team player by going behind Zoey's back to get the supervisor on his side. He should have guessed Zoey would be upset with his actions, and he lost integrity with her.

However, Zoey did not handle the situation in a professional manner. Although it is understandable she would be upset, Zoey should have sat down and discussed the matter with Justin. She also could have expressed her ideas or concerns to the supervisor.

Afterwards, if the supervisor still prefers Justin's method, Zoey should acquiesce and help complete the project.

Sometimes things do not go your way when you are working in teams. However, you are still obligated to the team, the company, and yourself to complete projects and tasks assigned to you.

NETWORKING CASE STUDY

Casey's teacher Ms. Smith invited her to a professional organization meeting. Casey went to the meeting but stayed near Ms. Smith all evening. When Ms. Smith introduced her to people, Casey smiled and answered their questions. She did not volunteer extra information or ask questions of her own. By the end of the evening, Casey had collected one business card from someone who knew her mother and asked her to pass along the card with her phone number.

Questions to Ask Yourself

1. How could Casey have taken advantage of the opportunity to learn about the professional organization and its members?

   _____

   _____

2. How could Casey have increased her chances to build a network list?

   _____

   _____

Things to Consider

Casey lost out on a great opportunity to build a network list because she did not leave her teacher's side and seek out other professionals. She also missed opportunities when she limited her answers and did not express an interest in the people who questioned her. Casey should have taken business cards of her own to distribute, and she should have actively sought cards from members.

Casey should have prepared a list of questions to ask about the professionals before the meeting. She should have attempted to arrange an informational interview or job shadow with a member. She also could have asked about job opportunities and requirements.

● **EXTERNSHIP CASE STUDY ONE**

Tina accepted an unpaid externship at a large company, where she performed administrative assistant duties. After a week of working, her supervisor reprimanded her for using the phones during work hours for personal business. It seems Tina made and received several calls a day, many of which lasted a half hour or so. Tina agreed she would not use the company phone for her personal calls.

The supervisor then reprimanded Tina for being away from her desk for long periods of time. One day he found Tina standing in the parking lot talking on her cell phone. He immediately terminated her externship.

Tina expressed her surprise to a friend. "I don't know why I was fired. After all, I quit using the company phones. Besides, I'm working for free on the externship, so I think it takes a lot of nerve for him to fire me."

Questions to Ask Yourself

1. Did the supervisor act appropriately in terminating Tina's externship?

   _____

   _____

2. Should Tina have been surprised at being fired?

   _____

   _____

3. What should Tina have done after the supervisor warned her about personal calls?

   _____

   _____

Things to Consider

An externship provides work experience, whether it is paid or unpaid. All externship participants must treat the experience as a "real" job, because it is. The gains in most cases will outweigh the extern's efforts.

When given a warning, Tina should have ceased making personal calls on company time. She also should have stayed at her desk working.

● EXTERNSHIP CASE STUDY TWO

Jason liked his externship because the company had Internet access, and he often "surfed the 'Net" when he did not have a lot of work to do. His supervisor told him the Internet was for company use only. Jason avoided the Internet a few days, but soon was back "surfing." He received another warning and stayed off the Internet until his supervisor went out of town on business. Jason had a great time on the Internet for the three days his supervisor was gone.

When the supervisor returned, he did not reprimand Jason. Relived, Jason thought he had gotten away with abusing Internet privileges. What Jason did not know was the company had checks in place that allowed supervisors to determine when and where a person surfed on the Internet. They knew Jason had spent considerable hours doing personal business on the Internet. Although there was a job opening in the company, Jason's supervisor did not offer it to him when he finished his externship.

Questions to Ask Yourself

1. What did Jason lose by ignoring his supervisor's warnings?

   _____

   _____

2. Do you think Jason's supervisor would give him a good job reference?

   _____

   _____

Things to Consider

Not only did Jason lose out on a job opportunity, he also lost integrity, honesty, and a good work ethic in his supervisor's eyes. He should have heeded the supervisor's warning. In addition, Jason's supervisor probably would not give him a good verbal recommendation or a recommendation letter. Think about the far-reaching effects a person's actions have.

● EXTERNSHIP CASE STUDY THREE

Ryan has a chance to do an externship at a large, successful company. His duties will include skills he learned at school.

The company has the latest computer software and equipment. It seems like it will be an excellent experience.

His friend Tom, who works at a smaller company, wants Ryan to work with him. Tom believes they would have fun working together. Ryan realizes he will not gain as much experience at the smaller company, but he likes the idea of working with a friend.

Questions to Ask Yourself

1. What do you think should Ryan do?

   _____

   _____

2. What do you think you would do in a similar situation?

   _____

   _____

Things to Consider

Working at an externship is an important career step and should be treated as such. Ryan should disregard the fact that he would be working with a friend. Instead, he should consider the position; duties; and skills, equipment, and software used at each company. Other considerations are company reputation and location, and the chance for future employment. Treat the externship as the vital work experience it is, not as a place to have fun with friends.

● RESUME CASE STUDY

Billie saw an advertisement for what she considered to be an ideal job. A tinge of disappointment hit her when she saw the requirement for a software program with which she had no experience. Billie decided to list the program on her resume anyway and "fake" her way into the job. A week later, Billie was hired for the position.

Questions to Ask Yourself

1. How do you think Billie's employer will react when he learns she cannot operate the required software?

   _____

   _____

2. Do you think Billie was smart to obtain a job through deceit?

_____

_____

Things to Consider

When you list skills on your resume, a perspective employer will expect you to be able to use those skills. Employers know that new hires will need training for a new position, but they do not expect to have to teach skills. When a job applicant lists a skill on a resume, an employer will assume he or she is proficient in that skill. Lying about your skills and background is grounds for being fired.

Billie did not do herself a favor by taking a job she is not qualified to do. She will likely be stressed and on edge most days. She may even be dismissed from the job for her incompetence.

● **REFERENCE CASE STUDY**

While preparing his resume, Davlin debated about whom to list as his final reference. The choice was between his best friend and a former employer. Davlin knew his friend would give him a terrific reference, although he knew nothing about his actual work habits. On the other hand, he had worked at his last job for two years, and Davlin's supervisor knew his work well. However, he left on not-so-good terms with his supervisor and did not know if he would give a good reference.

Questions to Ask Yourself

1. Whom would you choose as a reference if you were Davlin?

_____

_____

2. Why would you choose this person?

_____

_____

Things to Consider

Employers are interested in your work experience and habits. If possible, list a work reference rather than a personal one. If you feel your former employer may give you a bad reference, you might want to call and discuss the matter with him or her. Many employers will give other employers very little information about former employees. They do so to avoid time-consuming, costly lawsuits from disgruntled employees who are denied jobs because of what the former employer said about them. If you worked at a particular job for a considerable length of time, it may be beneficial to list it and the duties you performed, even if you left under less than desirable circumstances.

You could tell an interviewer that there was a personal conflict, but you did your job to the best of your ability. Never bad-mouth a former employer. Doing so will reflect poorly on you.

END OF CHAPTER QUESTIONS

1. List five traits that employers want in employees.
2. Name three things you should consider when studying a want ad.
3. Name three things that a good work ethic encompasses.
4. Name two things you can do to show you are a team player.
5. List five things you should determine when researching a company.
6. Why should you prepare for an externship interview as if it were an actual job interview?
7. What is an informational interview?
8. What are three questions you can ask on an informational interview?
9. Why would you want to do a job shadow?
10. Name three ways you can find hidden jobs.
11. How can you find a company's Web site?
12. Do you have to include a cover letter if a want ad asks for a resume but does not mention sending a cover letter?
13. What are three benefits of networking?
14. Why should you join a professional organization?
15. What are two advantages of working for a temporary employment agency?
16. What is the main purpose of networking?

17. What are three things you should consider before taking an externship position?

18. On an application, what should you write if a question does not pertain to you?

19. Define integrity.

20. Name three ways you can find information on a company.

21. What extracurricular activities can you list on your resume? If you have none, is there an activity in which you can participate?

22. What information should you include in a cover letter?

23. Can you think of at least two professional references you can list on your reference sheet?

24. Define a screening interview and a structured interview.

25. What can you do to follow-up after an interview?

26. Can an employer legally ask your age during an interview?

27. What can you do to alleviate nervousness before an interview?

28. Is it proper to list references on a resume?

2

CHAPTER 3

Communicating on the Job

3

LEARNING OBJECTIVES

After completing this chapter, you should be able to:

1. Develop oral communication skills.
2. Give an effective speech.
3. Improve listening skills.
4. Practice good telephone techniques.
5. Communicate properly via e-mail.
6. Observe nonverbal communication.
7. Demonstrate effective nonverbal communication.
8. Ask questions effectively.
9. Use feedback to your advantage.
10. Explain directions clearly.

Chapter 3 provides an overview of effective communication by presenting information on how to improve speaking and listening skills, as well as being aware of nonverbal communication. Details are provided on proper telephone techniques, e-mail communication, giving and receiving directions, and using feedback advantageously.

KEY TERMS

articulation	inflection	oral communication
concrete words	jargon	paraphrase
empathy	listening barriers	tone
etiquette	monotone	visual aids
feedback	nonverbal communication	voice mail

INTRODUCTION

Read through several job want ads from the classified section of a newspaper or from the Internet. You will see "excellent communication skills" listed as a requirement in many of these ads. Employers are always looking for people who can communicate well through writing, speaking, and listening.

Because we speak and listen to others on a daily basis, it is easy to assume we are doing both properly. Although we may communicate fine in personal situations, speaking and listening for business encompasses far more than speaking and listening for entertainment and fun. For one thing, the level of concentration must be high in the business world. For another, business professionals must always be at their best through positive, friendly, and helpful attitudes. In order to succeed, they must develop highly effective communication skills for dealing with customers, coworkers, and supervisors in a number of situations.

Business professionals must be able to

- give clear, explicit directions
- follow the directions others give them
- gather and disseminate information quickly and accurately
- demonstrate products
- remain calm and professional in the midst of difficult situations
- maintain goodwill for the company

In this chapter you will find helpful information on developing and improving oral, nonverbal, and listening skills.

DEVELOPING ORAL COMMUNICATION SKILLS

Oral communication is the use of spoken words to exchange or convey information. In the business world, employees must be able to orally communicate in a clear, distinct manner in a variety of situations. They will speak to supervisors, coworkers, and customers on a regular basis. They will give directions, explain about products and services, give presentations and speeches, and ask questions in face-to-face situations and on the telephone.

Employees will communicate on an informal basis, as well as in formal settings and with one person or a large number of people. To be effective, employees must orally communicate in a manner that will be understood by their listeners. No communication will take place if the listener does not understand the message conveyed.

When communicating orally, think about what you want to accomplish. *Why* are you speaking? About *what* are you speaking?

ORAL COMMUNICATION TIPS

Your communication approach will differ in various situations, but some general tips apply to all oral communication situations.

LANGUAGE

In every situation, use clear, easy-to-understand language so your message will be understood. Words are crucial to the listener's understanding, so choose ones that are familiar to most people. Use concise words that have precise meanings and eliminate wordiness. Filling a message with complicated, academic words does not make a speaker look more intelligent, but rather may confuse the listener, resulting in miscommunication. Make sure your sentences are complete and grammatically correct.

Avoid **jargon**, which is the language spoken in a specific industry. For example, it is the use of medical terms in a medical office, legal terms in a legal office, or computer terms in a computer office. Many industries have specialized terminology that is usually understood by people in those industries. The general population, however, may not be familiar with the words. If you must use terms that are unfamiliar to your listener, define them.

Refrain from using slang or cultural comments, which could be confusing or even rude. Always be sensitive to people from other cultures.

DO YOU WANT TO

- give directions?
- improve yourself or others?
- ask about directions you have been given?
- convey goodwill?
- persuade someone?
- advise someone of a problem?
- investigate a problem?
- solve a problem?
- give information?
- ask for information?
- sell a product?
- offer a service?

3

EXERCISE 3-A

On the lines provided, rewrite the following wordy expressions to make them more concise.

1. The sound of the ringing phone

_____

2. Due to the fact that

_____

3. Return back to you

_____

4. Repeat that again back to me

_____

5. This e-mail is being sent as your confirmation

_____

6. Endeavor to attend the meeting

_____

7. At this point in time

_____

8. Please call at your earliest convenience

_____

9. Let me have your comments

_____

CONSIDER THE LISTENER

What do you know about your listener? The more you know about your listener, the more you can slant your words to him or her and create a better understanding. Consider the listener's age, experience, education, interests, cultural background, and knowledge level when selecting your words and presenting information.

Before speaking, try to determine how much your listeners already know about your subject. This information will allow you to determine what material you should cover in specific detail and what to leave out so as not to bore the listener. Learning what listeners know gives you the insight needed to prepare a message that is relevant to them.

BE SPECIFIC

Words can have multiple meanings. Make messages clear to your listener by choosing **concrete words**, which are specific, over abstract ones, which are vague. Specific words will increase your chances of achieving the results you want.

Instead of saying "this afternoon," say "at 3 p.m." Instead of saying "next week," say "Monday, December 2." Times, dates, numbers, locations, distances, colors, sizes, and the like provide concrete details and reduce misunderstandings. Give enough specifics to paint a clear picture in the listener's mind.

Notice how the use of the *specific* words in Table 3–1 express a clearer meaning than the *vague* ones.

BE CLEAR

Along with using specific words, arrange ideas in logical order starting with the most important. Emphasize main points by repeating them often, and give sufficient supporting details so listeners understand.

Avoid speaking with a condescending attitude; be courteous, positive, and tactful. Provide appropriate information and cut unnecessary words. Clarify difficult information by breaking it down into manageable steps.

Find common ground with listeners; having something in common will make for a smoother communication transfer.

PROJECT A QUALITY VOICE

The sound of your voice can be pleasing to listeners, or it can grate on their nerves. Your sound, **inflection** (raising and lowering your

3

TABLE 3–1

LIST OF VAGUE AND SPECIFIC WORDS

Vague	Specific
This morning	10 a.m. today
Early next week	Thursday, May 1
This year's figures were close to last year's	$105,000 in 2005 vs. $105,391 in 2006
A few feet	3 feet
A dark color	#395 navy blue
A few thousand dollars	$3,000
A tall man	A 6'1" man
In the future	Thursday, May 1
A number of people	65 people
Several respondents	65 respondents (or people)
Slow delivery	Three-day delivery
For the entire amount	$566
Soon	July 2
Later	July 2
In time	Two weeks from today (or July 2)
At a future date	Monday, July 2
This week	The week of July 2
A good response rate	56 percent response

voice), volume, **articulation** or pronunciation, and speaking rate all send messages to listeners. Work on sending the right message by practicing positive speaking techniques.

Volume

Speak loud enough to be heard, but do not shout. Speaking too softly frustrates listeners, causing them to miss words or to misunderstand the message. Listen for clues such as, "What did you say?" and "Could you speak up?" These comments indicate you need to raise your voice.

Speaking too loudly may annoy listeners and/or give the impression the speaker is angry or upset. Take into consideration the room's

EXERCISE 3-B

Choose specific, concrete words for each of the following expressions, and write them on the lines provided.

1. Soon

_____

2. Often

_____

3. A close distance

_____

4. A few minutes

_____

5. Inexpensive

_____

6. Short

_____

7. After a while

_____

8. Small

_____

9. In due time

_____

10. Cold

_____

acoustics, which affect how your voice sounds. The acoustics of the room can absorb or project sound, so you will need to adjust your speaking volume accordingly.

EXERCISE 3-C

Think of a time when you gave someone directions for doing a job, but he or she did not do the job correctly. What do you think went wrong? Write your answer in the space provided.

_____

_____

_____

Fill out Table 3–2 to determine where the communication breakdown occurred.

Table 3–2 EVALUATING GIVING DIRECTIONS

EVALUATION FOR GIVING DIRECTIONS		
	Yes	No
Directions were not clear enough		
Directions were clear, but listener misunderstood		
Information was missing from the directions		
Listener did not understand the language/words used		
Listener understood the directions, but was not capable of doing the job correctly		
Directions were clear, but the listener did not pay attention when they were given		

In face-to-face conversations, seek nonverbal **feedback** or reactions and responses by watching listeners' facial expressions and gestures.

Inflection

Inflection is raising or lowering your voice, emphasizing key points. Adding proper inflection creates enthusiasm, friendliness, and sincerity in your voice, which in turn creates more interesting messages. A flat voice, or **monotone**, may bore the listener, who will tune out the message by mentally shutting down or by letting his or her mind wander. Inflection affects the meaning of what you have to say.

Tone

Tone is closely tied to inflection, for *how* you say something leaves a positive or negative impression on the listener. Your tone should fit the mood of the situation. For example, you might use a lighthearted tone when entertaining, a serious one for a solemn occasion, a stern one to reprimand, and a sincere one to help.

For instance, you might say, "May I help you?" in a warm and sincere way, or in a way that implies you are busy and do not want to be bothered.

Speaking Rate

Speaking either too slowly or too quickly can distract listeners. If you speak faster than the listener can comprehend, your message obviously will miss its mark. Once you have lost the listener, he or she will most likely tune out the remainder of the message. A slow speech pattern may suggest that you are not enthusiastic about what you are saying or are droning on and on about insignificant details. Vary your speaking rate, slowing for emphasis and pausing for effect, but picking up the pace when appropriate.

Articulation

Articulation is enunciating or pronouncing words correctly. Do not mumble or mispronounce words; articulate clearly. Consult a dictionary whenever you do not know how to pronounce a word. If it is a person's name that you cannot pronounce, find a way to get the correct pronunciation, such as calling his or her company to ask.

If you mispronounce words, listeners may not recognize the word you are using at all or else may confuse the word you meant to use with one that has a different meaning. If the listener pauses to figure out the meaning of your words, he or she may miss other important details or give up listening all together. Distorting words frustrates listeners who may not be clear about your message. Be particularly articulate when addressing people who do not speak English well. Match your style to your audience.

Positive Words

Use positive words, eliminating as many negatives as possible. State what you *can* do for the caller. The positive words in Table 3–3 are

TABLE 3–3

USE OF POSITIVE AND NEGATIVE LANGUAGE

Positive	Negative
I will call by 3 p.m.	I don't know when I can call.
We can repair your watch for a nominal fee.	We cannot replace your watch.
Your new computer was shipped today.	We are sorry your computer is late.
Thank you for your letter.	We received your complaint letter.
Thank you for your order. As soon as we receive the following information, we will ship your products.	Your order was incomplete. We cannot ship your products until we get the following information necessary to process it.
T116, which replaces T115, is now available.	T115 is no longer available.
No. 425 is available in blue and green.	No. 425 does not come in the color you ordered.
Please resend your order as we have not received it.	We never received your order.
No. 265 will be available December 1, and we will ship it immediately.	We are sorry to disappoint you, but No. 265 is currently out of stock.
We have corrected your order and apologize for the error.	We're immensely sorry for the mistake we made.

more likely to satisfy a customer than the negative ones, which are an instant turnoff.

WORD CHOICE

Be cautious of words that are similar in meaning and/or spelling, taking care to choose correct words that express the meaning you intended to convey. Consult a dictionary when you are unsure of a word's meaning or else choose a different one.

GIVING SPEECHES

Employees may be called upon to give speeches or presentations to customers and/or coworkers. If they refuse, their jobs could be in

EXERCISE 3-D

Using a dictionary, define the words in Table 3–4 on a separate sheet of paper. Be able to use them in a sentence.

Table 3–4 **CHOOSING THE CORRECT WORD**

WORD CHOICES	
CAN YOU USE THESE WORDS PROPERLY?	
Affect/effect	Than/then
Personnel/personal	Accept/except
Beside/besides	Farther/further
Formally/formerly	Later/latter
Adapt/adept	Good/well
Leave/let	Who/whom
Proceed/precede	Passed/past
Among/between	Adapt/adept
Fewer/less	Imply/infer
Access/excess	Lie/lay
In/into	Can/may

jeopardy or they risk losing out on advancement opportunities. Therefore, it is in their best interest to learn how to deliver professional speeches and presentations. All of the previously discussed oral communication tips apply to giving speeches. A few additional guidelines will prepare employees to make presentations.

Effective speakers think before they give presentations and, therefore, plan their messages. They know why they are speaking and what material they should cover. They highlight and reinforce major points, give supporting points and details, and summarize. They do not fill their speeches with unnecessary words and descriptions. Rather, they make their points in easy-to-understand language and arrange the material in logical order.

Unlike informal situations, when people listen to a speech, they do not always have the opportunity to interrupt the speaker to ask questions and/or make comments when they do not understand something. Therefore, steps should be taken to minimize any confusion by reinforcing main points and presenting enough supporting points to be clear.

EXERCISE 3-E

Think of a time you had to give a speech, and answer the following questions on the lines provided.

1. How did you feel getting up in front of people to speak?

_____

_____

_____

2. Is there something that you did to keep yourself calm?

_____

_____

_____

3. Is there something you could have done to make your presentation better?

_____

_____

_____

CHOOSE A TOPIC

ASK YOURSELF THESE QUESTIONS:

- Do you want to inform?
- Do you want to persuade?
- Do you want to entertain?
- Do you want to demonstrate or describe something?

Is your topic interesting? If you have control over the topic, select something of interest to your audience. However, sometimes you have no choice in the matter. If this is the case, is there some way that you can make the material interesting for the listeners? Also, consider how much time you will need for the speech. Will you be able to hold the audience's attention for that length of time? Can you finish within the allotted time? The answers to the last two questions will determine how long your speech should be to remain effective.

CHOOSE A PURPOSE

Decide the purpose of your speech. Your purpose will determine how you should proceed with writing and presenting your speech.

CHOOSE AN APPEAL

You can make an appeal in several ways. Logical appeal incorporates facts, examples, statistics, and expert testimony. Emotional appeal calls upon a personal story or sincere anecdote. Anecdotes (or stories) should be short and have relevance to the main speech. Problem-solving appeal takes the audience through a problem/fact-gathering/solution sequence. No matter what appeal is used, the speaker's attitude should be focused on the audience and getting the message across.

RESEARCH

Plan what you want to say whenever you must give a speech or presentation so you will be able to state your message as effectively and intelligently as possible. Your audience will expect you to know your subject, so prepare yourself by researching it thoroughly. Gather enough material to provide main points and supporting details with ease.

Always check your speech content to be sure it is current and accurate, or you risk losing credibility. Your audience will be able to tell if you are not prepared, and you will lose their attention. Double-check dates, times, numbers, names, and specific details. Content must be accurate, timely, ethical, and well researched. Back it up with statistics, comparisons, charts and graphs, tables, slides, models, handouts, and the like.

Organize the content of your speech into parts—introduction, body, and conclusion. The introduction should preview your speech and let the audience know what you are going to tell them. Start by giving your topic (example, "Today I am speaking about..."). Then tell the listeners why you are speaking to them about the topic. Get their attention right away and go over the main ideas. State your main ideas, using key words and phrases, and reinforce them throughout the speech.

The body is the main part of your speech, where you tell the audience what they need to know. Elaborate on ideas by presenting supporting details in logical sequence. Use adjectives and adverbs to add interest and make ideas connect with the audience, but avoid flowery language or giving too much information, which could overwhelm listeners. Use supporting material to get the message across.

The conclusion should summarize what you have said. Emphasize critical points and make requests and recommendations. Give handouts at the end of the presentation so listeners are not distracted from what you are saying by reading the handouts during your speech.

3

VISUAL AIDS

If possible, provide **visual aids** to keep the audience's attention and give concrete examples to reduce or eliminate confusion. Visual aids may include handouts, products, samples, equipment, slides, DVDs, wall charts, blackboards, and the like. Visual aids are important for the listeners' retention and understanding, and they help the speaker clarify points. Visual aids keep the speaker on track throughout the talk. Visuals should be simple.

NONVERBAL

On the day of the presentation, wear comfortable but professional clothing and shoes. Do not wear distracting accessories such as ties and scarves in bold colors and prints, dangling jewelry, or faddish styles. Have a confident stance, a pleasant tone, and natural gestures and facial expressions. Look at the audience and speak clearly and with enthusiasm.

PACE YOUR SPEECH

A common trait of nervous speakers is talking too fast. Take two or three deep breaths before you begin, and remind yourself to speak slowly. Preview and then cover all main points thoroughly, reinforcing them when necessary. Present your main ideas, give supporting information, reinforce, and summarize. Stay within the allotted time by keeping the topic and ideas narrow. Writing each idea on an index card is helpful.

KNOW YOUR AUDIENCE

Knowing something about your audience will be helpful in selecting the right content and language for your speech. If possible beforehand, determine gender, age, educational level, cultural background, interest and needs, and the audience knowledge of the subject matter.

Some of this information will be obvious because of where you are speaking and the nature of the presentation. For instance, if you are speaking to coworkers, you will already know a lot about them. Some information you will gather as you look over your audience, such as age and gender. Asking key questions of your audience before you begin can provide broader background information.

BE PREPARED

If you are preparing to give a formal speech or presentation, be sure you have everything you need for a successful outcome. Check the microphone, overhead projector, computer, and other equipment you will use. Prepare handouts, visuals, and note cards. Practice your speech and time it. Ask a friend to listen to and critique it.

MISCELLANEOUS CONCERNS

You will want to determine if your speech will be informal or formal, the size of your audience, and if you or members of the audience have any special requirements. Respect your audience by showing courtesy and proficiency. Greet them before you begin, and thank them when you are finished. Maintain eye contact. Avoid a condescending manner, tactless humor, and biased language. Anticipate listeners' expectations, and look for ways to meet them. Be confident in the knowledge that you have researched the subject matter and know it well.

Have your notes, water, and a watch or clock handy.

OVERCOMING LISTENING BARRIERS

Consider what **listening barriers** or obstacles might sabotage your speech and then eliminate as many of them as possible for your audience. These barriers include the audience talking, late arrivals who bang doors, loud music playing, too hot or cold temperatures, the listeners' preoccupation with other thoughts, the speaker's message being delivered in a monotone voice, and uninteresting content.

Many of these barriers are within your control to eliminate. Doing your part as a speaker to overcome or minimize these barriers can enhance your listeners' experiences.

BE INCLUSIVE

Use language that is inclusive to all people. For example, say "he or she" instead of "he" when referring to a hypothetical person. Say "spouse" or "partner" instead of "husband" or "wife," and use "police officer" instead of "policeman." You cannot assume a certain occupation is for all men or all women. Not all doctors are men and not all nurses are women.

3

Look over the list of barriers to listening to learn the kinds of things listeners face. Which of these items could you, as a speaker, eliminate?

BARRIERS TO LISTENING TO A SPEAKER

▶ Background noises.

▶ Bias against the speaker's message or opinion.

▶ Preconceived notions about the speaker's dress/mannerisms.

▶ Listener is preoccupied with other thoughts.

▶ Listener is disinterested in the subject matter.

▶ Listener is prejudiced against speaker.

▶ Temperature in the room is too hot or cold.

▶ Listener is tired or in pain.

▶ Visuals are not visible to everyone.

▶ Listener cannot identify main points of the speech.

▶ Late arrivals who bang doors.

▶ People shuffling papers.

▶ Members of the audience who talk/whisper.

▶ Listener cannot understand speaker's words or misinterpret them.

▶ Speaker has an unpleasant voice.

▶ Speaker talks too fast.

▶ Speaker has annoying nonverbal habits.

▶ Listener is thinking of something he forgot to do.

▶ Listener is thinking of lunch.

▶ Speech's content is boring.

Tips & Tricks

Speaking Tips

- Decide the purpose of your speech.
- Plan what to say.
- Give main points and reinforce them.
- Speak loud enough to be heard.
- Use easy-to-understand language.
- Vary your pitch and speaking rate.
- Be positive, courteous, and tactful.
- Speak clearly.
- Pronounce words correctly.
- Use proper grammar.
- Avoid jargon, slang, and technical language that is unfamiliar to the listener.
- Be specific.
- Use visual aids.
- Arrange ideas in logical order.
- Research information.
- Know something about the audience.
- Eliminate distracting noise.
- Be inclusive in your language.
- Clarify information.
- Dress appropriately.
- Check equipment.

EXERCISE 3-F

Get together with a friend and evaluate each other's everyday speaking qualities. Take into consideration volume, rate, tone, grammar, and articulation.

Each of you write down your comments on a separate sheet of paper and then exchange them with one another. Look over your friend's comments about your speech and decide how you can improve your speaking.

EXERCISE 3-G

Select a topic of your choice. On a separate sheet of paper, prepare an outline for a speech on the topic. Include in your outline the introduction, body (with main points and secondary points), and the conclusion.

EXERCISE 3-H

The next time you go to a lecture or other situation where there is a speaker, analyze his or her effectiveness by checking the items in Table 3–5.

Table 3–5   EVALUATING A SPEAKER'S PRESENTATION

Evaluate a speaker. Did the speaker:	Yes	No
Hold your interest?		
Speak clearly?		
Use easy-to-understand language?		
Seem prepared?		
Know the subject matter?		
Use nonverbal gestures in a positive way?		
Use proper grammar?		
Reinforce main points of the lecture/speech?		
Use visual aids?		
Provide handouts?		

What would you change about the speaker's presentation?

_____

_____

_____

_____

_____

_____

IMPROVING LISTENING SKILLS

Hearing is the physical ability to hear sounds. Listening, an important form of communication, is concentrating on the words you hear. Sometimes we hear, but we are not listening.

Everyone in business will be called on to give and receive instructions and share ideas in some way. People may need to listen to directions, explanations, complaints, and demonstrations. They do so to gain knowledge or to develop goodwill. Listening may be on a one-on-one basis or in large audiences at conferences and workshops.

Listening is a skill that can be improved with practice and is well worth the effort. Improving your listening skills will make you a better communicator and a valued employee.

CONCENTRATE ON THE SPEAKER

Have you ever tried talking to someone who was not listening? Even if the person pretends to be listening, you can usually tell that he or she isn't. As you know, it can be very annoying. Remember that feeling whenever you need to listen to someone else, and give the speaker your full attention.

You cannot gain information or gather all the facts without listening carefully to what is said and then concentrating. Refrain from thinking about what you want to say or do next, as this may cause you to miss important facts.

Do you usually remember what a speaker says to you? Sometimes we hear words coming out of a speaker's mouth but do not attach meaning to them. Concentration is the key to gaining meaning and understanding. When someone is speaking to you, whether in an informal or formal situation, concentrate on the message, and get involved in the communication process. Is there anything you already know that you can relate to the talk? If so, it could help you stay with the speaker. Interpret the speaker's message by putting it in your own words. Commit key information and instructions to memory, or write them down.

Do not finish the speaker's words in your mind or jump to conclusions before he or she is finished. Doing so may cause you to misinterpret something important. Do not work on other activities or let your attention drift to other thoughts.

Skillful listening goes beyond hearing words. It includes taking into account the speaker's tone of voice and nonverbal cues. Oftentimes, *how* something is said is more important than *what* is said. Tone of voice lets you know if someone is happy or unhappy, stressed, excited, disgusted, and any number of other emotions. Listen beyond the words by listening for feelings.

3

USE EMPATHY

Show **empathy**, which is understanding and compassion. It is putting yourself in the other person's place. Empathy allows you to relate better to another person's needs and wants because you attempt to understand how he or she feels. It allows you to imagine how you would feel in a similar situation. You can also surmise how you would like a particular situation handled, which is helpful when determining how to resolve problems and/or provide customer service. Try to be understanding.

ANALYZE WHAT IS SAID

While listening, analyze what is being said. Think about the main points and examples given. Sift through the information, retaining important facts. Be objective whenever you sort through the facts so your biases and prejudices do not flaw your interpretation of the message. Listen without passing judgment on the speaker or the message. Relate anything you know about the subject.

If you do not understand what the speaker is saying, formulate questions in your mind that you can ask once he or she has finished speaking. You can also ask for needed clarification at that time.

PARAPHRASE

It is a good idea to **paraphrase** what has been said to be sure you have internalized the correct message. Paraphrase means to restate or summarize something in your own words. Sometimes we attach a meaning to what is said, but it is not the one the speaker had in mind. For example, if your supervisor says "I need this right away," does that mean to drop everything and do it? Or does it mean to finish the job you are doing (which will take five minutes) and then do the new one? The only way to be certain what the supervisor meant is to ask for clarification. (Say, "Do you want me to stop what I am doing right now or take five minutes to finish this task?")

STATUS AND PREJUDICES

Some people have a problem dealing with status, and they tune out others they think are not in a position of power. With status, the opposite can also be true. People may not listen because the speaker is a supervisor who makes them nervous.

Do not let prejudices keep you from listening. Ignore things about the speaker that bother you or prejudice you, such as dress, behavior, or physical traits. This includes a speaker's gaudy outfit and jewelry, annoying mannerisms, and wild hairdo.

Make an effort to stay focused on the message, not the speaker's appearance. Judging people by their looks and mannerisms may cause you to miss an important part of the message. In addition, keep an open mind; do not get defensive if you disagree with the speaker. Ignore preconceived notions you may have. In order to learn something new, listen before you make up your mind.

FOLLOWING DIRECTIONS

You will need to follow directions on the job. Employees spend time listening to directions from supervisors, coworkers, and customers. Sometimes they will be given directions and information from several people in a single situation, such as during a meeting. They need to listen actively, paying attention to the facts. Passive listening is hearing the words, but not concentrating enough on them to get the meaning of what is said and retain it.

ANALYZE DIRECTIONS

Employees will need to interpret directions by analyzing what they hear and determining how to use the information. They will need to remember directions given to them in order to use the information properly.

When listening, pay particular attention to names, dates, terms, figures, and other pertinent details so you will remember them. Maintain eye contact with the speaker, and do not allow your mind to wander while you pretend to listen. Some people are masters at looking as if they are fully engaged with the speaker. Then they are asked a question and cannot answer because they were not actually paying attention.

WRITE IT DOWN

Write down everything important that you will need to remember, especially names, dates, technical information, figures, and complicated data. It is not necessary to write down every word, and it is

3

helpful to abbreviate. Keep a pen and paper handy so you do not have to search for them when someone is speaking to you.

You must learn to interpret complicated instructions. One of the best ways to do this is to break the instructions down into steps and then arrange the steps in a logical order. Ask questions to clarify anything you do not understand or of which you are unsure. Never assume; missing information causes problems. Paraphrase directions, and pay attention to small details. When necessary, ask, "What did you mean by that statement?"

EXERCISE 3-1

Think about the last time you went to a lecture, class, or other activity that involved a speaker. Using the form in Table 3–6, evaluate listening to a speaker.

Table 3–6 SPEAKER EVALUATION

Evaluate a speaker by checking the appropriate boxes.

	Yes	No
Did the speaker hold your interest?		
Was the content of the speech of interest to you?		
Did you take notes?		
Did you put yourself in the speaker's place?		
Did you analyze what was said?		
Did you relate what you already knew to the subject?		

Write down key points that you remember from the lecture/speech.

OVERCOME BARRIERS TO LISTENING

It is easy to miss information when you put up physical and mental barriers. Physical barriers include people talking, noisy machinery and papers, traffic, temperatures that are too hot or cold, dirty surroundings, frequent interruptions, and so forth.

Imagine sitting at a dinner table listening to a keynote speaker as the waitstaff clears the dishes. It would be difficult to hear the speaker and even more difficult to concentrate. The noise from the clinking of dishes, and watching the waitstaff move around, will interfere with concentration.

Mental barriers include preoccupation with other thoughts, worry, fatigue, hunger, and headaches. If you are tired mentally, it will be difficult to focus on the message.

Overcome barriers by looking at the speaker, sitting close to the speaker, sitting where distractions are minimal, dressing for comfort, taking notes, concentrating on the message and the visual aids, keeping an open mind, and participating mentally. In addition, refrain from whispering to others, doodling, and thinking about what you will say next. Stay involved while listening so you will build knowledge, gain information, and/or be able to follow directions. Review the barriers to listening in the summary list given earlier in the chapter.

Tips & Tricks

Listening Hints

- Concentrate on the speaker's words.
- Relate anything you know to the talk.
- Listen for the emotions behind the words.
- Avoid jumping to conclusions.
- Do not interrupt the speaker.
- Show empathy.
- Paraphrase the speaker's words.
- Analyze what is being said.
- Ask for clarification.
- Take notes.
- Sit where distractions will be minimal.
- Avoid daydreaming.
- Avoid preconceived notions.

3

LISTENING AND SPEAKING SITUATIONS

- ▶ Giving/receiving directions and information.
- ▶ Listening to and talking with customers, clients, supervisors, and coworkers.
- ▶ Listening to presentations, speakers, class instructors, and workshop facilitators.
- ▶ Delivering presentations and speeches.
- ▶ Running classes and workshops.

▶ Listening or speaking for entertainment purposes.

▶ Evaluating others or interpreting others' evaluations of you.

▶ Participating in discussions and meetings.

▶ Brainstorming with team members.

EXERCISE 3-J

Evaluate your listening habits by filling out Table 3–7.

Table 3–7　EVALUATING A LISTENING EXPERIENCE

Think of a situation when you had a difficult time listening to someone. What were the major problems? Answer Y (yes) or N (no) in the boxes provided.

	Yes	No
Monotone voice		
Boring content		
Speaker used poor grammar		
Outside noise		
Could not understand the speaker		
Speaker did not know the subject matter		
Speaker had distracting mannerisms		
Speaker talked too fast		

Other (explain)

EXERCISE 3-K

Think of a time when you were given directions for performing a task, but it turned out that you did the job incorrectly. What do you think went wrong? Write your answer in the space provided.

Is there anything you could have done to increase your chances of doing the job correctly?

EXERCISE 3-L

Complete the self-evaluation in Table 3–8 by checking the appropriate column to determine how well you follow directions.

Table 3–8 **EVALUATING YOUR LISTENING SKILLS**

Complete this self-evaluation by checking the appropriate column to determine how well you follow directions.

	Always	Sometimes	Rarely
1. Do you ask people to repeat information?			
2. Do you miss key information from speakers?			
3. Do people frequently ask, "Are you listening?"			
4. Do you daydream while others speak?			
5. Do you miss nonverbal clues people give?			
6. Do ringing phones, machines, and general noise bother you when someone is speaking to you?			
7. Do you become distracted when coworkers are talking or whispering while you are listening to a speaker?			
8. Do you frequently miss crucial steps when someone gives you directions?			
9. Do you lack focus when someone speaks to you?			

TELEPHONE TECHNIQUES

One of the primary forms of communication for companies is the telephone. Business is conducted by phone within and outside the company. Employees take and place calls for customers, clients, supervisors, and coworkers. During calls, employees provide customer service, take and place orders, provide information, sell products and services, generate goodwill, and handle complaints. It requires skill and preparation to handle calls in an efficient, professional manner.

Your handling of workplace telephone calls says a lot about you and your company. You could be conveying an efficient, helpful attitude or an incompetent, negative one. Often customers and clients form their impressions of companies based solely on a telephone conversation with an employee. Therefore, employees must be effective on the telephone by using professional language and positive statements. Some employees imply through their tone of voice or language that phone callers are a bother. Others leave callers cold because they have an indifferent attitude.

To be successful on a business telephone call, you must train yourself to appreciate every caller and then convey the appreciation to him or her. The message you should send is "I'm ready to help you." First impressions are lasting; make yours a good one.

LANGUAGE

Use correct grammar and simple language. Failure to use the right language could cause miscommunication, and the caller may not comprehend your message. Avoid slang and jargon as they distort your message. Incorporate common business language to show competence (use business words such as correspondence, satisfaction, applications, solutions, quality, and the like). If technical terms will not be understood by your caller, do not use them, or else explain the terms. Develop a smooth flow to your sentences by using transitional words to move from one to another.

ENUNCIATE

Learn correct word usage and pronunciation. Make a conscious effort to speak properly. Keep a list of words you typically abuse, such as "like" or "um," and try to rid them from your speech. Do not cut word endings short by saying "callin'" instead of "calling." Enunciate all word endings such as -d, -t, -ing, and so on. Pronounce all the syllables in a word.

SPEAKING VOICE

Vary your speaking rate so your voice does not sound monotone or flat. Establish a moderate pace, but pause for effect when you want to make a point. Raise and lower the inflection in your voice to add interest. Speak clearly and distinctly in a volume loud enough to be heard, but avoid yelling in the phone. Speak directly into the mouthpiece, using your natural voice. Do not mumble or turn away from the phone while speaking. Do not eat, drink, or chew gum while speaking on the phone. Also, avoid talking with other people in the office while you have a caller on the phone unless you put him or her on hold first.

WATCH YOUR TONE

How you say something can be more important than *what* you say, especially when talking on the phone. Do not sound impatient or distracted. Stand up when speaking to sound more enthusiastic and upbeat. Smile. A smile makes you sound like an agreeable, helpful, and friendly person. Give your voice personality.

Ask friends how you sound on the phone or else leave yourself a message on your answering machine.

ANSWERING

Answer on the second or third ring in a positive, sincere voice. Remember to smile before picking up the telephone, which makes your voice sound pleasant. Give a friendly greeting, identify yourself and your company, and offer to help. ("Good morning. This is Mikaila. May I help you?") Your name adds a personal touch and provides the caller with the information for his or her reference.

When the caller gives his or her name, use it during the conversation. If the caller does not give a name, ask "May I ask who is calling please?" or "May I have your name?" Never say something abrupt, such as "Who is this?" or "Who are you?"

Ask, "How may I help you?" Listen carefully to the caller, concentrate, and be patient. Put other work aside and avoid distractions. Make callers feel important. Give the impression you care about the customer and his or her business.

Paraphrase what the caller says to be sure you understand him or her. After the caller states his or her business, if you do not understand something, ask questions to clarify.

Take notes; do not make the caller repeat the information. Show that you are competent and sincere. Relate what the caller says to what you know about his or her past experience as well as yours.

Some callers may be difficult to understand. Listen for ideas and also for tone and any other hidden meanings. Since you do not have the gestures and nonverbal cues that you do in a face-to-face conversation, you have to rely more on words and tone.

Do not jump to conclusions or finish the caller's sentences. Do not argue mentally. Do not type, comb hair, file nails, or write while the caller is speaking.

Conclude the call on a positive note, thank the caller, and follow-up if necessary. Make sure the caller is listening to you and understands what you have said. Ask him or her to repeat information you gave or to summarize it.

EXERCISE 3-M

On the lines provided, make a list of things you can do to help ensure that you sound helpful and friendly while speaking on the telephone.

_____

_____

_____

_____

_____

_____

DIFFICULT CALLERS

Remain calm and speak slowly when you have an upset or angry customer on the phone. If you must interrupt a ranting caller, use his or her name as an attention getter. Do not minimize the caller's problems in your own mind; instead, put yourself in his or her place. Let the caller speak without interruption unless he or she gets out of control. You do not have to put up with abusive language or behavior. In such cases, turn the caller over to a supervisor or follow company policy regarding such calls.

Sometimes customers just want to express their concerns and know someone is listening to them. Other times they may want you to solve a particular problem. They may have a solution in mind or want you to propose one.

When you are ready to reply to a customer's request, think before you speak and use positive language. Consider possible options that you can offer. What would make the customer happy and retain his or her business?

Show empathy and offer solutions if possible, but be honest. Avoid making promises you cannot keep.

When you end the call, promote goodwill with the caller. Thank him or her for bringing the problem to your attention. Repeat the caller's name when closing the call.

LIMIT HOLD TIME

People do not want to wait on the phone. Limit hold time, as waiting on hold can seem longer to the caller than it actually is. Therefore, keep all messages short, but complete. If you need time to search for files or documents, suggest to the caller that you will call back with the information.

PLACING OUTGOING CALLS

When making outgoing calls, plan before dialing, so you will know what information you need to have available and can gather it. Dial numbers carefully, and keep a directory of frequently called numbers. If you cannot get through to someone you need to speak with, be patient yet persistent as you keep trying.

Planning what to say in advance will save time during the call and will ensure that you complete your business in its entirety. Write down the number to call, the name of the person to be called, the reason for the call, and an outline of the message. Have all available files and data on hand.

When the other party answers, identify yourself, the company, and your purpose. Get to the point; keep your message short and focused. When you need a substantial amount of someone's time on the phone, make an appointment to talk with him or her. Call at the appointed time. If someone you called has not returned your call, be patient. Allow the person you called enough time to return your call.

3

ELIMINATE DISTRACTIONS

Both you and your caller face many distractions during phone conversations. Eliminate as many as possible from your end. Do not eat, chew gum, or drink while on the phone. Avoid thinking about others, reading, or writing personal notes while you are participating in the call. Minimize background noise such as loud machines, talking, music playing, paper shuffling, and so forth.

TRANSFER CALLS

Be sure that you understand how to transfer a call on your company's phone system. Callers become frustrated when they are transferred from one person to another again and again or else are disconnected during the transfer. Ask permission before putting a caller on hold and/or transferring him or her. It is a good idea to give the caller the extension number to which you are transferring before you make the transfer. (Say, "I'll transfer you to Extension 2561, Mr. Smith. Should you accidentally get disconnected, you can dial that number directly.")

VOICE MAIL

Although **voice mail**, or recorded telephone messages, is widely used, callers will become frustrated if their calls are not returned in a timely manner. Therefore, check voice mail boxes frequently and retrieve your messages. Return customers' calls as soon as possible. Doing so maintains goodwill for your company and shows you are efficient.

If you leave a message on someone's voice mail, give complete information, including your name, company, telephone number, and a brief message. Try to make it easy for someone to return the call by stating the specific times that you will be available.

Also, if you can save the caller from returning your call, do so by leaving an appropriate message. For example, say, "This is Jim Smith at Extension 235. I'll be at Tuesday's meeting. You don't need to return this call."

EXERCISE 3-N

On the lines provided, make a list of things you can do to project a positive image to customers while speaking on the telephone.

_____

_____

_____

_____

_____

_____

TAKE ACCURATE MESSAGES

When taking telephone messages, record complete information. Using a telephone message form will help guard against forgetting pertinent details. A telephone message form provides a space for the name of the person who was called; the date and time; the writer's initials; and the caller's name, company, and phone number. In addition, check boxes are often included with options such as *telephoned, returned your call, please call, came to see you,* and the like.

Ask the caller to spell his or her name, and then repeat the phone number to the caller to be sure you have recorded it correctly. Write a complete, but concise, message. Incomplete numbers and inaccurate messages cause delays, confusion, and irritation. Date the message and record the time and your name or initials.

Deliver messages promptly. Do not let them pile up on your desk, where they can be misplaced or forgotten.

EXERCISE 3-O

Angelo Haas of XYZ Company called for Anita Duncan. He would like her to return his call. His number is 777–330–0303. Fill out the telephone message form in Table 3–9 using the current date and time.

Table 3–9 SAMPLE PHONE MESSAGE FORM

Phone Message		
For	Date	Time
From		
Of		
Phone Number	FAX	
Message	☐ telephoned	
	☐ returned your call	
	☐ please call	
	☐ stopped to see you	

THINK BEFORE SPEAKING ON THE PHONE

When you must answer the phone, think before speaking. Be helpful to the caller, but do not give out confidential information or say anything that reflects poorly on you or anyone else in the company.

WHAT NOT TO SAY

▶ She never came back from lunch.

▶ He's golfing today.

▶ He's in a meeting with XXY Company.

> He left early today.
> What?
> Speak up. I can't hear you.
> Bye-bye.

WHAT TO SAY

> Hello and goodbye.
> I'm sorry, he is unavailable. May I help you or take a message?
> I'm sorry, he is at lunch. May I help you or take a message?
> He is not in today. May I help you or take a message?
> He is not in today. Mr. Smith is taking his calls if you would like to speak with him.
> He is out of the office. May I help you or take a message?
> I will give him your message when he returns.
> Excuse me. Could you repeat that? I'm having difficulty hearing you.

Tips & Tricks

Telephone Tips

- Smile when you pick up the phone.
- Use conversational words and correct grammar.
- Answer on the second or third ring.
- Personalize the call—use the caller's name.
- Take complete messages.
- Say please and thank you.
- Be sincere, polite, and friendly.
- Listen actively.
- Greet the caller; identify the company and yourself.
- Say goodbye, not bye-bye

Tips & Tricks

- Use your natural voice; speak clearly.
- Use a positive tone.
- Avoid slang, jargon, and technical terms.
- Take notes.
- Show empathy.
- Vary speaking rate and pitch.
- Speak directly into the mouthpiece.
- Limit hold time.
- Plan outgoing calls.
- Minimize or eliminate distractions.

EXERCISE 3-P

Telephone Self-Assessment

Fill in the telephone assessment in Table 3–10. To have a good telephone presence, you should be able to answer yes to all of the questions.

Table 3–10   **SELF-EVALUATION: TELEPHONE VOICE AND ETIQUETTE**

Answer yes or no to the following by checking the appropriate boxes.

	Yes	No
I have a pleasant speaking voice.		
I smile before picking up the phone.		
I speak at a normal rate.		
I speak clearly and naturally.		
I use proper grammar.		
I use inflection in my voice.		
I speak directly into the phone.		
I use positive language.		
I speak at a normal volume.		
I identify myself.		
I take complete, correct messages.		
I deliver message promptly.		
I give my company's name.		
I offer assistance.		

3

E-MAIL COMMUNICATIONS

E-mail is a rapid form of communication used to send and receive messages. Many companies have policies that state their e-mail is to be used for business purposes only. Employees must abide by the policy and refrain from sending jokes and personal e-mails during company time on company computers.

Messages should be short, to the point, and complete. Use proper grammar, punctuation, and sentence structure. Common abbreviations may be used, such as ASAP (as soon as possible) and FYI (for your information). Fill in the subject line with a concise title that describes the e-mail contents. Proofread carefully.

The ability to create a mailing distribution list is an important e-mail feature that allows you to send the message to multiple recipients at once. However, send the e-mail only to people who should receive the information. Never send confidential information via e-mail.

Files can be attached to e-mails, so documents and projects can be sent easily and quickly to several people at various locations. Most e-mail applications have an address book, where you can store the e-mail addresses of individuals.

NONVERBAL COMMUNICATION

Nonverbal communication includes body language (gestures, nodding, eye contact, smiling, etc.), appearance (dress and grooming), and more. Being aware of your nonverbal cues can increase your effectiveness in dealing with supervisors, coworkers, and customers. Your nonverbal cues send messages about your attitude and personality, and people will form perceptions (or their interpretations) based on these cues. These perceptions, based on beliefs and past experiences, may not be accurate and may cause miscommunication. Backgrounds, cultures, and other things influence people's interpretations. Therefore, think about the nonverbal messages you send.

BODY LANGUAGE

Direct eye contact is important when speaking and listening in face-to-face conversations. Avoiding eye contact could be construed as having a lack of interest or being intimidated or nervous. People also tend to avoid eye contact when they are lying or have something to hide.

As a sign of friendliness and helpfulness, smiling promotes goodwill, whereas a frown shows displeasure. Nodding signals agreement or disagreement. Gestures provide clarity and enthusiasm. They can signal openness (relaxed arms) or restraint (crossed arms) or insecurity (covered mouth). An erect posture with a slight forward lean can signal you are interested, as can nodding affirmatively. If you shake hands, use a firm, but not bone-crushing, grip. Limp handshakes are a turnoff, as are damp or clammy hands.

Keep a proper distance from others. Invading someone's personal space may cause him or her to become uncomfortable or offended.

APPEARANCE

Appearance conveys an image of you and the company. Good personal hygiene comprises clean hair, body, nails, and clothes. Use deodorant and mouthwash. Avoid heavy perfumes and colognes, as they may be offensive, especially to people who have allergies. Makeup should be minimal and natural. Hair styles should be simple.

Clothing must be cleaned and pressed. Polish shoes, as this shows you pay attention to details. Follow your company's guidelines for proper business dress.

PROPER ETIQUETTE

Etiquette is showing customers proper respect and courtesy. Remember to use "please" and "thank you." Do not talk with food in your mouth, interrupt, burp, scratch, tug at clothing, fidget with jewelry, and the like in front of your customer. Do not talk about personal problems.

TABLE 3–11

LIST OF NONVERBAL COMMUNICATION CUES

Positive	Negative
Smiling, laughing	Frowning, wrinkling brow
Maintaining eye contact, but not staring	Staring
Keeping arms at side or using them to gesture positively	Playing with hair, a pen, jewelry, etc.
Nodding affirmatively	Crossing arms
Listening	Fidgeting, tapping fingers
Naturally gesturing with hands	Frequently looking at watch
Dressing professionally	Wearing dirty, torn, or sloppy clothes
Using pleasant facial expressions	Yawning
Relaxed posture	Ignoring the speaker
Walking briskly; posture erect	Sighing, groaning
Pleasant speaking tone	Slouching

EXERCISE 3-Q

For an entire day, pay attention to the typical nonverbal clues you may be sending to others. On a separate sheet of paper, make a list of good and bad nonverbal behavior. Think about the list and determine what you can do to eliminate negative behaviors and/or add positive ones.

EXERCISE 3-R

In the space provided, write down your perception of each of these examples:

• Customer has arms crossed.

_____

_____

• Customer avoids eye contact when explaining a problem.

_____

_____

(Continued)

EXERCISE 3-R (Continued)

• Customer is smiling and nodding positively.

_____

_____

• Customer shows no expression.

_____

_____

• Customer frowns as you discuss a solution.

_____

_____

EXERCISE 3-S

Think of a time when you interpreted someone's nonverbal communication, but you discovered that you were wrong in your interpretation. Then, in the space provided, answer the questions.

1. Why did you interpret the nonverbal communication the way you did?

_____

_____

2. Why do you suppose you were wrong?

_____

_____

3

COMMUNICATE CLEARLY

ASKING QUESTIONS

Some people question everything, while others are afraid to ask a single question, even when they should. Business professionals do not have time to continually answer frivolous questions, nor do they want to be bothered with questions when the person asking should know the answer. On the other hand, they would prefer that someone ask for clarification rather than do a job incorrectly.

Ask questions when you are not clear about directions and other information. However, do not ask so many questions that you become a nuisance. Also, avoid asking questions that are not relevant to your work or that are bothersome. Think before asking.

If a simple yes or no answer will suffice when you ask a question, word your question with that intention in mind. If you require more than a yes-or-no answer, ask an open-ended question that elicits a longer response. For instance, word a question similar to this one: "What were the sales figures for the years 2004, 2005, and 2006?"

ASK YOURSELF THESE QUESTIONS

- Are you asking something the speaker already covered?
- Is your question intended to clarify something the speaker said?
- Is your question meant to learn something new or obtain a missing fact?
- Is your question meant to examine the speaker's facts?
- Is the question valid?
- Does the question have one point or objective?
- If the question has multiple parts, is each part clear?
- Does your question bring up another question?
- Does your question require research?
- Can your question be answered in a brief period of time?

USING FEEDBACK

Employees have the opportunity to receive feedback from customers, coworkers, and supervisors. This feedback might come from written instructions and questionnaires, by telephone calls to customer service, or in face-to-face conversations.

Consider feedback with a positive attitude, learning as much as you can from it. For instance, if your supervisor gives you feedback on your job or attitude, look at it as constructive criticism that will help you improve in those areas. If it is positive feedback, state your appreciation. If it is negative, ask what you can do to improve in that area.

When customers provide feedback on products and services, learn what you can from the evaluations and comments in order to improve. If feedback was positive, state your appreciation for taking time to let you know. If feedback was negative, make sure the proper personnel are notified in order to have the problem resolved.

When coworkers give you feedback, analyze their comments to determine if there is something you should act upon. Keep in mind that people have different work habits, which could influence their criticisms. For example, you may be a thoughtful, thorough employee who takes his or her time working on tasks. Your coworkers, however, may work quickly and not pay much attention to detail. Your different work habits may be a problem whenever you work together. In such cases, think about what you can do to be more compatible without sacrificing efficiency.

If the feedback provided to you is incomplete or of little value, try to elicit additional information by asking open-ended questions that require more than a yes-or-no answer. Use feedback to learn about problems and concerns and to correct them.

EXERCISE 3-T

Your supervisor may criticize your work or your work habits. In such cases, ask yourself what you can learn from the criticism.

- How can you improve your attitude or work?

_____

_____

- How can you incorporate the supervisor's suggestions into your daily work?

_____

_____

- Is there something you learned that you were doing incorrectly?

_____

_____

- Can you correct what you were doing incorrectly?

_____

_____

3

EXPLAINING CLEARLY

Be thorough when giving directions, presentations, and speeches, or when demonstrating products or procedures. Understandably, people become frustrated whenever the information they need is incomplete. This breakdown in communication causes errors, delays, and loss of credibility.

Write down what it is that you need to get across to your listeners. List main points, secondary points, and supporting information. Write the steps to take in a logical sequence and double check them. Review directions and demonstration procedures before you relay them to others. Be sure there is no missing information.

If you are demonstrating a product or service, inform your audience or participants of everything you are doing or going to do to operate the equipment or product. Make eye contact with participants and pay attention to their nonverbal cues. If it seems your audience is confused, pause and ask if there are any questions. At the conclusion of the demonstration, provide an opportunity for listeners to ask questions, and welcome any questions they may have.

Break down information into manageable parts or steps. Use easy-to-understand language and concrete or specific words. Define unfamiliar terms in detail. Provide handouts if they will increase learning.

EXERCISE 3-U

Working with a partner, explain to him or her how to ride a bike. When you are finished, ask him or her to fill out the evaluation in Table 3–12 to determine if your directions succeeded.

Table 3–12   **EVALUATION FOR GIVING DIRECTIONS**

	Yes	No
Directions were not clear enough		
Directions were clear, but listener misunderstood		
Information was missing from the directions		
Listener did not understand the language/words used		
Listener understood the directions, but was not capable of doing the job correctly		
Directions were clear, but the listener did not pay attention when they were given		

END OF CHAPTER WORK

CASE STUDIES

● NONVERBAL LANGUAGE CASE STUDY

Holly and Barry were discussing a sales report. As Barry liberally gestured with his hands, Holly sat back in her chair with her arms crossed, staring at her desk. When Barry asked if she understood, Holly said, "Yeah, I got it."

Questions to Ask Yourself

1. What can you surmise from this scene?

   _____

   _____

2. Do you think Holly is listening?

   _____

   _____

3. Do you think Holly understands what Barry said?

   _____

   _____

Things to Consider

Holly's crossing of her arms, staring at the desk, and distancing herself by leaning back would seem to indicate she is not receptive to what Barry is saying. Barry's liberal use of gestures could indicate frustration, anger, or simply that he is explaining his point. Overall, it does not appear that communication is taking place. Holly's response is a further indication of her unwillingness to listen to Barry. It is hard to tell if she actually does understand what he said.

   No matter what seems to be occurring between Holly and Barry, keep in mind that our perception does not always give a true account of what is actually taking place.

● FOLLOWING DIRECTIONS CASE STUDY

Mr. Jenners gave Cassidy directions for a graph he wanted her to create. When Cassidy finished and gave Mr. Jenners the graph, he said, "What is this? This graph is not arranged the way I asked you to do it."

   "I followed your directions," Cassidy said.

   "I don't know what directions you followed," Mr. Jenners said, "but this is not what I described to you."

Questions to Ask Yourself

1. Who was at fault in this situation?

   _____

   _____

2. What could Cassidy have done to be sure the graph was correct?

_____

_____

Things to Consider

Obviously, there was a communication failure between Mr. Jenners and Cassidy. It is hard to say who was at fault. Perhaps the directions were unclear, or they were misunderstood.

Cassidy should have paraphrased (or restated) the directions and should have taken notes. Perhaps Cassidy did not have the skill to complete the project. When she started the task, she could have checked with Mr. Jenners to make sure it was correct.

For his part Mr. Jenners should have been clear, giving Cassidy step-by-step directions. He also could have had Cassidy repeat the directions and/or asked to see a draft of the project.

● GIVING A SPEECH CASE STUDY

After Dara attended a presentation on how to use new software her company intended to purchase, the supervisor asked her to demonstrate it to her coworkers. Dara felt confident that she could operate the software, but she was terrified to get up in front of her coworkers and speak. The mere thought of doing the presentation made Dara ill.

Questions to Ask Yourself

1. What can Dara do to ease her fear of speaking?

_____

_____

2. What are your suggestions for Dara on how to give the presentation?

_____

_____

Things to Consider

Dara should remind herself that she knows her subject matter—the software. That should build her confidence. Perhaps instead of standing in front of the group, Dara could sit at a computer and demonstrate the software or else use an overhead and have participants focus on the slides. She could develop a handout, distribute it, and refer to it during her talk. In that way, participants could look at the handout and not stare at Dara.

Before the presentation, Dara should take some deep breaths and focus on a positive outcome. She may want to practice what she intends to say or demonstrate.

TELEPHONE TECHNIQUE CASE STUDY

Leanne was working on a difficult project. The phone kept ringing and interrupting her. At one point, she snatched up the ringing phone and brusquely said, "Hello. Sales Department."

When the caller started explaining his problem, Leanne interrupted, telling him to please get to the point as she was busy.

Question to Ask Yourself

1. Should Leanne have rushed the caller in order to get the project finished?

   _____

   _____

2. What could Leanne do to alleviate some of her stress?

   _____

   _____

Things to Consider

If possible, Leanne could ask a coworker to answer her phone for a while. If that is not possible, Leanne would have to use restraint and answer the phone properly with a helpful attitude. In this particular case, she could have taken the customer's number and told him she would return the call as soon as possible.

Never give callers the impression they are a bother. They are bringing the company business. Office workers must be flexible and be able to multitask.

FOLLOWING DIRECTIONS CASE STUDY

As the manager in a retail store, you continuously give directions to your salesclerks. Jim, one of the salesclerks, does not pay attention when you give the directions and later asks you several questions about things you covered. If he would have listened, you would not have to repeat yourself.

Questions to Ask Yourself

1. How can you get Jim to listen?

   _____

   _____

2. What suggestions do you have to help Jim remember directions?

   _____

   _____

Things to Consider

The manager could mention to Jim that all details were given during the directions and suggest that he concentrate on what is being said and take notes of important information. When finished giving directions, the manager could ask Jim to summarize in his own words what was said. The manager could also keep Jim's attention by periodically saying, "Are you with me, Jim?" or "Do you understand what I mean, Jim?" By using Jim's name and making eye contact with him, the manager is letting Jim know that he or she expects him to pay attention.

END OF CHAPTER QUESTIONS

1. Name three things that you can do to improve the quality of your speaking voice.
2. What two things can you do to make a speech interesting when you are the one giving the speech?
3. Give an example of the proper way to answer a business telephone.
4. What is jargon?
5. What are two things you can do to ensure that you get complete information when someone gives you directions?
6. List five ways to overcome listening barriers for the audience when you are the one giving a speech.

7. List five ways to overcome listening barriers when you are listening to a speech.

8. Give an example of using empathy toward a customer who calls.

9. List four ways you can improve your telephone speaking voice.

10. What additional information can you obtain from observing a person's nonverbal communication?

11. What are three things you should include on a telephone message form?

12. Name three situations where employees communicate orally.

13. How can you use evaluations from customers to your advantage?

14. Why are excellent communication skills in such demand by employers?

15. List five positive examples of nonverbal communication.

3

CHAPTER 4

Providing Customer Service

LEARNING OBJECTIVES

After completing this chapter, you should be able to:

1. Better serve customers by identifying their needs.
2. Display professional customer service traits.
3. Treat customers professionally and courteously.
4. Learn to deliver positive face-to-face and telephone service.
5. Improve listening skills.
6. Resolve customer complaints.
7. Obtain feedback.
8. Observe nonverbal clues.
9. Retain customers.

Chapter 4 discusses how to provide the best possible customer service by being courteous and professional at all times. Tips are given for dealing with problem customers and their complaints, obtaining customer feedback, and learning to provide positive customer service. A section on problem solving will guide you in meeting the needs of your customers.

KEY TERMS

biases	cultural differences	customer loyalty
customer service attitude	empathy	goodwill
open-ended questions	perception	professionalism
product knowledge	rapport	

4

INTRODUCTION

Why do companies believe customers are so valuable when there are plenty of them? There may be a lot of customers, but there are also a lot of companies to which they can turn for products and services, which creates strong competition. This competition keeps companies vying for each customer, whether it is for a first-time sale or repeat business. If companies do not attract enough customers, they will go out of business.

PROVIDING EXCELLENT CUSTOMER SERVICE

Since selling products or services to customers is a major moneymaking activity for every company, it makes sense to attract as many sales as possible. Without customers who bring in the money, companies would not stay in business for long. Therefore, every customer must be considered an opportunity to generate business.

Customer service deals with the way you treat customers when they request information, buy products or services, or interact with your company in any way. Everyone likes to feel appreciated and important. It is your job to serve customers in an efficient, effective way so their dealings with your company will leave them with a positive feeling.

You do not have to like every person you serve, but you must treat each one fairly and respectfully. Make customers feel they are special and that you are acting in their best interests when you answer their questions, and guide them toward the purchase of products that are right for them. You also make customers feel special when you provide exemplary service.

Businesses rely on top-quality customer service providers to keep their customers satisfied and loyal. Knowing what to say and how to say it leaves people with a positive impression. Training customer service providers to anticipate customer needs and to be alert to potential problems is, therefore, a top priority for most companies. If customer service providers can spot a minor problem, they can deal with it before it escalates into a major headache and lost business that might never be recovered.

It is important for each individual in a company to do his or her part to gain and keep customers. The best way to do that is to deliver quality products and effective customer service. As a service provider, treat every customer you deal with as if he or she keeps your company in business, which in turn keeps you employed.

Customer service providers must have excellent communication and listening skills if they are to receive and give information in an efficient manner, as well as process it. If they do not provide high-level service, they will lose customers. When customers feel good, they will likely return to do business with companies, and they will be good word-of-mouth advertisers for them.

EXERCISE 4-A

In the space provided, answer the following questions:
Do you think customer service providers as a whole have become better or worse at their jobs over the last five years? Explain your answer.

_____

_____

_____

What is one step a customer service provider can take to provide a positive experience for customers?

_____

_____

If you were a customer service provider, what would you do to improve the quality of your company's service?

_____

_____

_____

4

KNOW YOUR CUSTOMERS

To better serve customers, get to know them. Take the time to find out as much as possible about their backgrounds, experiences, and needs. The more you know about customers, the better you will be able to relate to them and, therefore, to serve them. Attempt to learn age, gender, educational level, cultural background, and economic level if necessary.

Some details about your customers you will determine as soon as you see them, such as age and gender. You may even be able to determine cultural background. If you require other information to better serve customers, such as educational or economic levels, ask them.

Sometimes you will need to learn a lot of information pertinent to sales or services. In other cases, depending on the products or services you offer, you do not need any background information at all.

Engage in a casual conversation with the customer to gain valuable facts, and also to build a connection that will make him or her feel special.

ASKING THESE REFLECTION QUESTIONS WILL PROVIDE SUBSTANTIAL BACKGROUND INFORMATION ON CUSTOMERS.

- Who are my customers?
- Why did these customers come to my company?
- How can I obtain information on my customers?
- What do my customers need and/or want?
- Can I provide what my customers need and/or want?
- If customers are not sure what they need, can I help them decide?
- What do my customers expect with regard to my products and services?
- Do my products and services meet or exceed customer expectations?
- How can I keep my customers satisfied?
- How can I understand my customers better?
- Do my customers have a problem with my company's products or services?
- How can I show concern for my customers when they encounter a problem?
- Can I do anything to become more sensitive to my customers' needs?
- How can I help my customers solve problems?
- Do I know what will satisfy my customers?

EXERCISE 4-B

On a separate sheet of paper, develop a short questionnaire that you will be able to fill out whenever you want to learn more about your customers. Consider the previous reflection questions when preparing your questionnaire.

IDENTIFY CUSTOMER NEEDS/WANTS

Most customers want the same things you do—excellent products and service. Discuss the customers' needs and wants with them, and pay attention to what they have to say by concentrating fully, maintaining eye contact, and using positive gestures (i.e., smiling and nodding). Make customers feel appreciated by showing a sincere desire to help them.

Customers may not accurately convey what they need or want, making it necessary for you to rephrase what they have said. For instance, "Let me see if I understand you, Ms. Sockes. You said you are interested in Model 750, which is electrically propelled? Is that correct?"

At times, you might need to clarify what the customer has said. If so, ask pertinent questions such as the ones in these scenarios:

Customer: I have a problem with this shovel.

Customer Service Provider: I will be glad to help you. May I get a little more information? What exactly is the problem with the shovel?

Another example of clarifying is this:

Customer: This printer doesn't work right.

Customer Service Provider: I'll be glad to help you. What seems to be the problem with the printer?

Customer: It smudges my paper.

Customer Service Provider: Would you like to have a seat so I can get a few more details?

When you are trying to make a sale, it is helpful to know not only what products and services customers want, but also what they expect from those products and services. Ask yourself and the customers some questions regarding both. Be specific in your request to get the best answers. Consider the customers' education and background when you speak to them so your message will be understood.

To get all the facts from a customer, listen to his or her complete request or explanation without interrupting. Look for facts; do not assume anything about the situation. When the customer has finished, ask clarifying questions if you are not certain what the customer wants, or if you need additional details. Ask **open-ended questions**, which are ones that require an explanation. Closed questions can be answered with a simple "yes" or "no."

By asking open-ended questions, you can more closely match the product or service with the customers' wants. Consider this scenario:

Customer: I'm looking for a washing machine.

Customer Service Provider: What type of washing machine are you looking for, gas or electric?

Customer: Electric.

Customer Service Provider: Do you want front load or top load?

Customer: Top load.

Customer Service Provider: Do you have any particular color in mind?

Customer: White.

Customer Service Provider: (While walking to the washing machine area) I can show you what we have over here. About how many loads per week do you wash?

Customer: Six to ten.

Customer Service Provider: And are the clothes heavily soiled?

Customer: No.

Customer Service Provider: I think one of these models would be a good choice.

This conversation required more than yes-or-no answers. Although the customer did not give long explanations, the customer service provider was able to learn which washing machine to show the customer.

Sometimes you are not sure what the customer wants, and you may need to verify the information you have been given. Check this scenario for an example of verifying information:

Customer Service Provider: I believe you said you have operated this model washing machine before. Is that correct, Mrs. Garcia?

Keep asking questions until you get enough information to make a sale, i.e., "Do you have other concerns about what this washing machine can handle or which detergents are best to use in it?"

Tune in to the customer's body language to pick up additional signals and clues to his or her true feelings.

Once you have an idea of what customers want, explain how your company's products or services can help them. Knowing your products well will help you determine the right selections to match the products or service to their needs. Take steps to get customers to purchase from you by doing your best to provide complete information in a friendly, competent manner. If customers are wavering, find out what further details they need to finalize their decisions, but do not pressure them. When giving details, solicit feedback from the customer so you will know if your message was received the way you intended.

PROVIDING EFFECTIVE SERVICE

Effective service is giving customers what they want and doing it in an efficient, timely manner. Always provide the best customer service no matter what the circumstances, as it will affect future business.

Superior service brings satisfied customers back, whereas substandard service drives dissatisfied customers away.

One negative incident may permanently turn off a customer who has done business with your company for years, costing the company a valuable source of consistent income that was maintained through repeat business. Unfortunately, a customer will remember the one bad experience, or the one employee who was nasty, even if he or she was treated well many other times by other employees. One negative experience may also be the determining factor of whether or not a person will become a customer in the first place. Therefore, provide your best service to each customer with whom you interact.

If you are busy when a customer approaches you, acknowledge him or her with a smile or nod and say, "I will be with you in a moment."

If you know you will be a while, ask the customer if he or she prefers to wait or would like to see someone else. Most people do not mind waiting a few moments, but they do expect prompt service. Customers should not be made to wait while you fix equipment breakdowns or technology problems. Apologize for such incidents and offer a perk such as a discount coupon. Providing excellent customer service promotes **goodwill** for your company. Goodwill is the feeling created by displaying a helpful, friendly, concerned attitude.

EXERCISE 4-C

Turn back to Chapter 1 and look at the interpersonal skills you listed. On the lines provided below, write down the interpersonal skills you feel will make you a successful customer service provider.

_____

_____

_____

_____

_____

_____

4

PROVIDING SERVICE TO TELEPHONE CALLERS

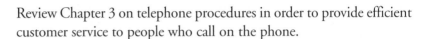

Review Chapter 3 on telephone procedures in order to provide efficient customer service to people who call on the phone.

TELEPHONE TIPS

▶ Smile, greet the caller, and identify the company.

▶ Use the caller's name when he or she gives it.

▶ Listen actively.

▶ Take complete messages.

▶ Maintain a positive tone and natural voice.

▶ Use conversational words, correct grammar, and clear language.

▶ Be friendly and sincere.

▶ Avoid slang, jargon, and technical terms the caller may not understand.

▶ Vary your voice inflection.

▶ Show empathy.

▶ Speak directly into the mouthpiece.

▶ Ask before putting the caller on hold.

▶ Eliminate distractions.

▶ Conclude calls professionally by using the caller's name, maintaining goodwill, and summarizing what you have discussed.

GO THE EXTRA MILE

It is your job to provide excellent service to every customer on a consistent basis, even when you are busy with other duties. Go the extra mile with your customers by taking time to learn exactly what they want, being efficient, and/or offering additional services or products. Advertising strategies keep customers well informed about products and services. These days customers are generally better educated and more knowledgeable than ever before about price, quality, availability, and service. They expect excellent service and products.

Customers will shop around and compare, thus creating a competitive market. They will also rely on word of mouth from friends and relatives. For the most part, customers expect top-notch service and quality products, and if they do not get them from one company, they will go to another.

If you provide customers with what they want and need, you will be able to retain them. If you do not give customers what they want, they will go to a competing company. Lost customers equal lost revenue.

EXERCISE 4-D

Find out what the return policies are for two stores in your area and write a summary of each on the lines provided by answering these questions:

Do you feel the policies are fair?

Why or why not?

Would you change either of the policies?

Why or why not?

4

DISPLAY A CUSTOMER
SERVICE ATTITUDE

Providing customer service involves more than what you do for some-one. It encompasses your attitude, knowledge, and appearance, which is your **customer service attitude**.

Company policies sometimes do not encourage positive customer service, so you will need to be creative in order to satisfy the people with whom you deal. For instance, if the company does not permit returns, customers may get angry upon hearing about that policy. In such a case, the customer cannot be given what he or she wants (the return). Is there something else you can do to let the customer know you appreciate his or her business even if you cannot take a merchandise return? For instance, can you offer a discount coupon or give early notice of a special upcoming sale?

BE COURTEOUS

Treat customers with respect and courtesy. Smile and maintain direct eye contact to express a genuine interest. Make your tone of voice friendly and sincere. It is important to let customers know you care about them and their business. They will be able to tell if you do not truly want to help them or if you do not care about them.

BE RESPECTFUL

Show respect for everyone you speak with by displaying proper etiquette. Say "please" and "thank you" and "you're welcome" in an upbeat tone to come across as a helpful, polite individual. Do not assume it is all right to use someone's first name or nickname unless they give you permission to do so.

Good manners play an important part in leaving customers with a favorable impression. Talking with food in your mouth, cracking gum, pointing a finger in someone's face, and interrupting others who are speaking show bad manners and a lack of respect.

Do not let distractions such as writing, reading, daydreaming, and letting your mind wander keep you from providing efficient service. These actions are rude; concentrate on helping the caller. No matter how busy or rushed you are, never show disrespect or take out your frustrations on customers.

EXERCISE 4-E

Evaluate your customer service attitude by asking yourself these questions and writing your answer in the space provided.

Am I helpful and friendly to each and every customer?

_____

Do I provide the best service I can to every customer?

_____

Do I obtain necessary information to assist my customers?

_____

Do I have the ability to make all decisions regarding what my customers want?

_____

If I do not have the ability to make decisions, can I refer the customer to someone who can?

_____

Am I learning how to provide better service?

_____

What am I personally doing to promote excellent customer service?

_____

Do the policies of my company promote good customer service?

_____

Is there anything I feel should be changed about my company's policies in order to provide better service to customers?

_____

Do I retain my customers' goodwill through my attitude?

_____

(Continued)

4

EXERCISE 4-E (Continued)

Do I pay attention to nonverbal cues from my customers?

Do I pay attention to my own nonverbal cues?

Am I respectful to every customer?

BE HELPFUL AND FRIENDLY

Greet customers with a friendly, helpful manner. Because you may be the initial contact a customer has with the company, you will want to make a favorable impression. Conversely, you may be one of a long list of customer service providers a person has dealt with that keeps him or her returning for your company's products and services. Let your helpful attitude show through your smile and in your eyes, giving you an open and friendly nonverbal appearance.

Customers often treat customer service providers as they are treated, so remember to treat everyone as you would like to be treated.

LISTEN

You will not learn what the customer needs without concentrating on what he or she tells you. Customers will know when you are not paying attention, just as you are aware when people do not pay attention to you.

Listen carefully to the customer's entire message, not just one or two points. Do this without interrupting, unless you need to stop customers to clarify, obtain additional information, or correct facts. Adapt your conversation style to the customers' styles by mirroring their speaking rate, volume, and language level.

Sometimes customers may request information about products or services, or even want to purchase them, but they cannot adequately express their wants. If necessary, ask questions that allow the customer to further identify needs or wants; find out exactly what it is that he or she expects you to provide. Your questions and the feedback from the customer will help you gather the necessary details.

Pay particular attention to the customer's tone of voice and emotional state to get a clearer understanding of the overall message. Does the tone conflict with the words being spoken? Could there be any hidden meaning in the message?

When dealing with a customer face-to-face, be aware of what his or her body language is communicating. Oftentimes, nonverbal expressions say a lot more than words do. This includes gestures, speech patterns, emotions, and dress. If body language suggests the customer is unhappy or frustrated, try to reassure him or her that you intend to provide efficient service.

EXERCISE 4-F

Look for ways to provide excellent customer service by answering these questions in the space provided:

What can you do to improve your customer service skills?

_____

_____

_____

What journals or magazines in your field can you read to keep up to date?

_____

_____

_____

Can you improve your skills by enrolling in workshops offered at your local community college on the subjects of customer service and/or building a positive attitude?

_____

_____

_____

Do you know of an excellent customer service representative you can emulate as a role model?

_____

_____

_____

(Continued)

4

EXERCISE 4-F (Continued)

Have you received evaluations from customers that you can study in an effort to improve yourself?

_____

_____

_____

SHOW EMPATHY

Empathy is imagining what other people feel emotionally and physically by putting yourself in their place. When a customer comes to you with a concern, ask yourself how you would feel if your roles were reversed.

As a customer service provider, you will want to show empathy for others. The best way to have empathy is to refer to your own experiences as a customer. Were you treated negatively by a customer service provider? Were you treated positively by one? Did you feel misunderstood or frustrated? Did you receive satisfaction?

When you deal with customers, try to recall the positive customer service experiences you have had. Analyze what made those experiences positive. Can you emulate the techniques of the person(s) who provided the service?

A good customer service provider will relate to customers' needs and concerns, listen patiently, and make them feel he or she cares. All customers need compassion and understanding. It is your job to find out what they specifically need from you and your company.

EXERCISE 4-G

Show empathy by thinking of a time when you felt sad for a friend or relative who was going through a difficult time and you tried to make him or her feel better. In the space provided, answer the following questions regarding the situation:

What was your friend's or relative's problem?

_____

_____

(Continued)

EXERCISE 4-G (Continued)

Why do you think you felt sad for the friend or relative?

_____

_____

What made you want to help him or her feel better?

_____

_____

How did you express your feelings to him or her?

_____

_____

What steps did you take to help your friend?

_____

_____

Were your efforts successful? Why or why not?

_____

_____

If your efforts were not successful, did you try something else?

_____

_____

4

BUILD RAPPORT

Rapport is the positive feeling you get when you "connect" with someone. It is finding something in common, displaying an interest in another person, and being genuinely likeable. Connecting with customers will make you and them more receptive to conversations.

To build rapport, smile and engage in small talk to get to know the customer. Be helpful and efficient. Call the customer by name, listen carefully, and then work on a solution in a timely manner.

EXERCISE 4-H

Observe the next customer service provider that you come into contact with, and in the space provided, answer these questions about the experience:

Did the customer service provider listen effectively to you?

_____

_____

Did the customer service provider help you with a friendly, sincere attitude?

_____

_____

What could the customer service provider have done to provide better service to you?

_____

_____

BE PERCEPTIVE

Perception is our view or opinion, which is based on our individual background, experiences, education, and life situations. As individuals, we look at situations and facts in different ways, according to what we believe about each situation. This is our perception or "take" on the happening. We arrive at our perception from our beliefs, values, ideas, past experiences, knowledge, and everything else that makes us who we are. Each of us views a situation from our own perception, which is not always a good thing. For example, if you see a customer's problem one way and he or she views it another way, a misunderstanding or serious problem can easily occur and go unresolved. Therefore, try to view the customer's situation from his or her perspective so you can empathize. When you look at things from the other person's side, there is a higher probability of resolving the situation.

Be objective in your dealings. It is important to avoid personal opinions, stereotyping, and judgments, which all form **biases**. If you already have preconceived ideas or opinions, you could make incorrect conclusions and mishandle the situation. In addition, biases may cause you to alienate the customer or not want to deal with a particular individual or issue.

EXERCISE 4-1

Read the bulleted items and write down your perception of each in the space provided.

A customer has his or her arms crossed while listening to you.

_____

_____

When returning a product, a customer avoids eye contact while explaining how the product was damaged.

_____

_____

A customer is smiling and nodding positively while you are speaking to him or her.

_____

_____

A customer frowns while you are speaking to him or her.

_____

_____

A customer blankly stares at you during an explanation.

_____

_____

Now look at your answers and ask yourself, "Could my perception of any of these situations be incorrect?" Give an example of how your perception could be inaccurate by stating another way one or more of the situations can be interpreted.

_____

_____

_____

4

BE POSITIVE

Be aware of the affect your attitude has on people. A positive, helpful attitude makes for effective human relations in the form of satisfied customers. Most people are more agreeable when dealing with a positive person. Therefore, project a positive attitude at all times.

When trying to resolve a complaint or a problem, do not dwell on what you cannot do for a customer but on what you can do. The language you use has a lot to do with how your customers perceive what you tell them. For instance, telling a customer that you *cannot* deliver products on their requested date will leave a negative impression. The customer may even go somewhere else for the products. However, stating the date you *can* deliver the order is a more positive approach that lets the customer know you are trying to meet his or her needs. Perhaps the alternate date will be fine with the customer.

NEGATIVE CUSTOMER SERVICE WORDS AND PHRASES

- can't
- won't
- you don't seem to understand
- our policy is...
- I never told you...
- we cannot deliver the supplies by...
- we do not carry the color red
- that's impossible
- you have got to be kidding
- that's unreasonable
- you cannot...
- we cannot...
- unfortunately
- regretfully
- no...
- we never...

REPLACE NEGATIVE WORDS

Oftentimes, replacing a negative word with a positive one will make a significant difference in satisfaction level. Customers are less likely to tune you out or dispute your options. Speak positive words and phrases such as the ones given.

POSITIVE CUSTOMER SERVICE WORDS AND PHRASES

- I understand how you must feel, Ms. Gonsales.
- Let me get the facts so I can help you.
- I can help you, Ms. Sanchez.
- I will be glad to help you.
- Let's see if we can agree on an alternative solution.
- Let's look at possible options, Mr. Shuster.
- How can I help you?
- What can we do to keep your business, Mrs. Winstinski?
- Here's what I can do for you, Dr. Soferez.
- I understand that you expect quality products.
- You have a right to quality products and service.
- I'm listening.
- You can be sure that we will make every attempt to resolve this matter.
- How do you suggest that we resolve this matter?
- Here are the available options, Ms. Rodriquez.
- Do you feel this is a fair solution?
- Will this option be satisfactory to you?
- I can have your products delivered by January 3, Mr. Wang.

4

▶ If January 3 is acceptable for delivery, I can guarantee that for you now, Ms. Bronsis.

▶ Shall we resolve this problem?

▶ Would you like me to implement that solution?

Tips & Tricks

Characteristics of a Positive Customer Service Attitude

- Respectful
- Knowledge of products and services
- Courteous
- Friendly
- Upbeat tone
- Positive attitude
- Empathetic
- Perceptive
- Positive nonverbal behavior
- Concerned
- Professional
- Open communicator
- Fair
- Consistent

EXERCISE 4-J

Consider a time when you experienced positive customer service and another time when you experienced negative customer service. For each of the situations, answer the following in the space provided:

Describe the situation.

_____

_____

(Continued)

EXERCISE 4-J (Continued)

How did the customer service provider treat you?

What was your reaction to the treatment?

What nonverbal gestures did the customer service provider use?

How did the whole experience make you feel?

Would you use the company's products or services again?

(Continued)

EXERCISE 4-J (Continued)

Did you report the poor service from the representative or send a letter of appreciation to the helpful one?

_____

_____

_____

_____

● DIFFICULT CALLERS

Customers are not always pleasant when they do not get what they want or expect. Their negative attitudes can frustrate a customer service provider, but he or she still must treat the customer with respect and make an effort to maintain goodwill. Do not internalize a customer's unpleasant behavior. He or she is angry with the company or product, not necessarily with you. In difficult situations, make it a habit to set your feelings aside and do your job as effectively as possible. Concentrate on solving the problem with an "I care" attitude.

Acknowledge the customer's anger, and reassure him or her by being sympathetic to his or her problems. Attempt to determine the cause of the customer's anger. Remain objective, and do not be critical or rude. Do not do anything to further upset the customer; rather say what you can do for him or her. If the customer does not calm down, tell him or her you cannot help until he or she does so. If the customer is demanding, remain firm, but do not retaliate because of the behavior. Tell him or her what you can do, and stick to your decision. Contact your supervisor if you need help.

Take a look at how this customer service provider calmed an angry, demanding customer.

Customer: I demand a refund on this lousy product!

Customer Service Provider: I see you are upset, sir, and I would like to help if you could tell me what happened.

Customer: This thing never worked right. I want my money back.

Customer Service Provider: Do you have a receipt?

Customer: No. I threw it away.

Customer Service Provider: I must have a receipt to refund your money. What I can do is exchange the product for another.

Customer: I don't want another one. I want my money.

Customer Service Provider: As I said, I cannot refund your money without a sales receipt. I can give you store credit for the product if you would like.

Customer: OK. Give me the credit.

Customer Service Representative: I will just need some information from you. Would you please fill out this form?

RESOLVING COMPLAINTS

Things sometimes go wrong with products and services, no matter how much you and the company try to prevent that from happening. As a result, you will probably have to resolve complaints some time during a customer service career. If so, do your best to listen, empathize, and help the customer.

Do not think of a complaining customer as the enemy. Instead work on solving his or her problem by determining what the customer wants and then searching for a reasonable solution. Apologize for the problem. When you do whatever you can to resolve complaints fairly, you retain goodwill.

Make a note of key issues like names, dates, amounts of money, questions, and possible solutions. This gives you a permanent record, shows the customer that you are indeed concerned with working with him or her, and prevents your forgetting what was discussed.

You are responsible for ensuring that enough communication occurs so that an understanding takes place between you and the customer. To aid in understanding, ask open-ended questions.

Customers are not interested in company policy; they want satisfaction, and they want it now. Stress what you can do for the customer and de-emphasize what you cannot do. Say, "Here is what I can do for you, Mr. Avanche."

Offer an alternative, which gives the customer some control over the situation, as he or she can agree to it or not. Introducing a customer to an alternative product may be a way of producing a sale where there would not have been one. And getting customers to try new products may result in future sales increases.

If you cannot do what the customer wants, try to negotiate a workable solution by stating what you can and cannot do to resolve the

4

ASK YOURSELF THESE QUESTIONS:

- When did the problem start and what has been done so far to resolve it?
- What exactly is the problem you are experiencing with this product?
- Can you be more specific about what happened when you used the product?
- What is your primary use for the product?
- Do you have other concerns you have not mentioned yet?
- Do you have suggestions about how you would like this problem resolved?
- Is this solution satisfactory?
- Do you need anything else?
- How can I work this out so you will be satisfied with the results?
- You have been a loyal customer for many years, so how can we continue with this relationship?
- Is this option acceptable, or should I look for another one?

issue. If you do not have the authority or the ability to solve the problem, find someone who does. An ideal situation for customer service providers is to empower them to do whatever they can to solve a problem and satisfy the customer.

MAKING CUSTOMER SERVICE DECISIONS

Before making customer service decisions, learn what the customer wants you to do. Are clues presented in addition to the words? If you need additional information that the customer has not provided, try to elicit it before presenting the options or making your final decision.

Your decisions as a customer service provider will be based on your company's policies and guidelines. If you do not have the authority to give the customer what he or she wants, call a supervisor to intervene.

Do not rush a customer who is trying to make a decision. Some people make snap decisions and others labor at length to arrive at one. Be patient and supportive.

EXERCISE 4-K

Recall a situation when you complained to a customer service provider about a product or service you received. In the space provided, answer these questions:

What was the situation?

_____

_____

How did you present the facts?

_____

_____

How did the customer service provider treat you?

_____

_____

(Continued)

EXERCISE 4-K (Continued)

Did the customer service provider understand the situation?

_____

_____

How did the way you were treated make you feel about the customer service provider?

_____

_____

How did the way you were treated make you feel about the company and its products?

_____

_____

Was your problem resolved in the way you wanted?

_____

_____

If your problem was resolved, how was it resolved?

_____

_____

If your problem was not resolved in the way you wanted, why not?

_____

_____

If your problem was not resolved in the way you wanted, were you offered an option?

_____

_____

If you were offered an option, were you happy with it?

_____

_____

(Continued)

EXERCISE 4-K (Continued)

Do you continue to do business with the company?

_____

_____

GET THE FACTS

Do not make assumptions if you are not clear about everything the customer has said while explaining the problem. Missing information causes minor problems to escalate into major headaches.

Ask questions to clarify what you do not understand; and paraphrase, which is restating what the person has told you. (For example, say, "As I understand it, you want your tool replaced. Is that correct, Mr. Smith?")

However, do not try to manipulate customers by telling them what they think or how they feel or by asking questions that are actually opinions. (i.e., "You don't think a replacement for the tool is the best option, do you?" or "You think repairing the tool is the only thing that makes sense, right?")

DETERMINE OPTIONS

Once you have gathered information from the customer's conversation, make a list of possible options for a viable solution. Then look at each option and decide which one would be most equitable to the customer as well as the company. Ask the customer for his or her opinion.

Provide the customer with the facts with sincerity and knowledge. Be fair, respectful, and consistent in dealing with all customers. If the customer is indecisive, be patient, ask more questions, and suggest additional options.

BE HONEST

If you do not know the answer to customers' questions, do not give inaccurate information or try to fake it. Customers do not like being given the runaround by someone who is trying to cover up the fact that he or she does not know what to do. Ineptitude shows. Advise customers that you will find answers to their questions, and then get back to them as soon as possible, or else direct them to someone who does know the answers. Customers resent being lied to or being apprised of a solution that you have no intention implementing. Keep your word; competent people are trustworthy.

WORK ON A SOLUTION

All customers have needs and wants, and if they come to your company, they believe you have what they need and/or want. Most of these customers have something specific in mind whenever they approach you, and they are looking for your help. Many of them do so calmly and rationally, while others may be difficult with which to work.

Unhappy, difficult customers may have been disappointed with the products they received or may have been treated poorly by another customer service provider. Even though you may not have been at fault, the customer might take out pent-up frustrations on you because you are the contact at the moment. Although that seems unfair, you still must do whatever you can to satisfy the customer and to retain goodwill.

▶ Keep a positive attitude.

▶ Listen.

▶ Ask questions to clarify.

▶ Paraphrase what the customer said.

▶ Ask the customer to suggest options.

▶ Suggest options.

▶ Take action.

SATISFY COMPLAINERS

Unhappy customers have a problem and do not want to hear what you cannot do to fix it. They generally do not care if you are busy or overworked or not at fault. They want a resolution, and they want it as soon as possible. On occasion, customers want nothing more than to vent their dissatisfaction to someone who will listen.

If a complainer gets out of hand, ask him or her to stop the behavior or else refer the incident to a supervisor. Do not defensively attack; simply state your unwillingness to put up with any kind of verbal abuse. If you feel you cannot handle a particular situation, get a supervisor involved.

Some customers will be quick to anger; others will be more reasonable. No matter which type of customers you have, you must work on a possible solution and do it with a pleasant attitude. Reacting in anger will only escalate the problem, and you will probably still have to resolve it. Why make the situation worse for yourself? A complaint from an unhappy customer to a supervisor about your negative behavior may jeopardize your job.

IMPLEMENT THE SOLUTION

Study your company's policies and procedures before problems arise so you know what you can and cannot do to handle them. Make only those promises you can keep. Suggest available options, using positive words. Decide what you want to do to solve the problem, and implement the most effective solution that will satisfy the customer. Be specific when providing information, especially names, dates, amounts of money, and other important facts. Follow up in a few days with a phone call or a letter in order to retain the customer's goodwill.

EVALUATE THE SOLUTION

Evaluate the solution you implemented to see if it has successfully satisfied the customer and is working out for all parties concerned. If the solution is unsuccessful, go back to your list of options and try another one. Follow up on that one as well, striving to reach an amicable agreement.

MAINTAIN YOUR PROFESSIONALISM

Although you will be expected to behave in a professional manner, unfortunately, not all customers will do so. Angry customers may want immediate satisfaction or resolutions that you cannot give them. They may shout, blame you, or otherwise cause problems. Accept the faults of others, and ignore their negative behavior. Realize you cannot change someone; you can only control your own feelings. Be patient; do not argue.

It is important to get along with the customers with whom you come into contact, which means you must be in emotional control at all times. This shows maturity on your part and **professionalism**, which includes level-headedness and competence. Words spoken in anger can have a disastrous affect on your career.

Keep your emotions under control while you attempt to learn as much as possible about the customer's problem. Ask enough questions to help you understand what went wrong and what it will take to satisfy the customer, but avoid unnecessary questions and discussions that deviate from the subject. Give the customer your full attention, and listen without interruption. Concentrate on the facts if the customer's behavior is unsatisfactory, so you can sort out the facts from personal opinion and anger.

CONTROL NONVERBAL BEHAVIOR

As discussed in Chapter 3, your nonverbal behavior says a lot about you. For instance, it may be easy to see if you are happy or angry from your facial expressions. If you do feel angry toward a customer, do not let it show. Be polite and courteous through your individual words and actions; display a cooperative attitude. In a controlled manner, let the customer know that you understand his or her problem and want to resolve the matter.

TABLE 4–1

USING POSITIVE NONVERBAL COMMUNICATION

DISPLAY POSITIVE NONVERBAL BEHAVIOR	
Face	Smile; use direct eye contact
Voice	Use a friendly tone and positive language
Gestures	Nod in agreement; display enthusiasm through proper hand gestures
Posture	Stand or sit erect; lean forward slightly; maintain adequate spatial distance

4

EXERCISE 4-L

Observe a friend, classmate, or coworker for the day. In the space provided, make a list of his or her negative nonverbal behavior and positive nonverbal behavior.

_____

_____

_____

What can you learn from the observation that will help you improve your own nonverbal behavior?

_____

_____

_____

Tips & Tricks

Handling Customer Complaints

- Listen carefully.
- Offer advice.
- Assess the gravity of the situation.
- Avoid blaming others.
- Tell the customer you are willing to work with him or her.
- Remain objective.
- Ask questions.
- Thank the customer.

EXERCISE 4-M

Assume that Felicia bought a DVD player from your store. She brought it in for repair after owning it for three weeks. The DVD has a 90-day warranty. The service department discovered the DVD was dropped; therefore, the warranty does not cover repairs. Answer the questions in the space provided.

(Continued)

EXERCISE 4-M (Continued)

As a customer service provider, what would you tell Felicia?

_____

_____

_____

Suppose Felicia becomes angry about your explanation and threatens never to buy anything from your store again. How can you keep her as a customer and also maintain goodwill for your company?

_____

_____

_____

Tips & Tricks

Solving Complaints

- Sincerely apologize.
- Put yourself in the customer's place.
- Build rapport.
- Listen to the customer.
- Be respectful.
- Know your products.
- Use positive words and phrases.
- Remain calm.
- Observe nonverbal behavior.
- Identify the problem.
- Restate the problem.
- Suggest options.
- Choose the best option.
- Implement the solution.
- Evaluate the solution.
- Implement an alternative solution if necessary.
- Maintain goodwill.
- Learn from the problem/complaint.
- Solicit feedback.

MESSAGES TO SEND TO EVERY CUSTOMER

- ▶ I care.
- ▶ I am honest and sincere.
- ▶ I am listening.
- ▶ I am competent.
- ▶ I want to help you.
- ▶ I am able to help you.
- ▶ I will keep my promises.
- ▶ I will find answers.
- ▶ I will provide options.
- ▶ I want to keep you as a customer.
- ▶ I want you to be satisfied.

EXPAND YOUR KNOWLEDGE

People can tell when someone does not know what he or she is talking about or does not have enough knowledge to help with a problem. To be an effective customer service representative, you must continually work toward knowing as much as possible about your company, job, products, services, and policies. Become an expert on them. The more knowledgeable you are, the more competent you will look to your customers.

Both employers and customers appreciate skilled, enthusiastic customer service people who expertly handle a variety of questions and complaints and know what to do and say.

Make it your business to learn everything you can about your company and its products and procedures. Be able to identify and discuss them in detail, including their special features, uses, styles, operation, prices, availability, etc. Try the products yourself to get a personal in-depth look and feel for them. Do it as much for your customers as for yourself.

Some of the things customers will want to know about products and services are cost, options, warranties, operating instructions, uses, colors, sizes, features, benefits, rebates, tests performed on the product, technical information, and so forth. Be able to give short, factual answers. Stress the benefits of using your products and services.

In addition to knowing your products well, know who your competition is and what they have to offer. Also, update your technological knowledge and increase your skills so you are prepared to do your job in the best way possible.

WHAT YOU SHOULD KNOW TO PROVIDE QUALITY CUSTOMER SERVICE

▶ Your company's complete product line and the services it offers

▶ Your company's policies and procedures

▶ What each department within your company does

▶ Key personnel—department heads, supervisors, CEO, etc.

▶ Your company's future product line

▶ What you can and cannot offer the customer as a service provider

▶ Industry trends

COMMUNICATING WITH CUSTOMERS

Remember, communication is a two-part process—sending information and receiving it. Listen carefully to determine what your customer wants. Then, offer to provide him or her with those products or services by communicating in a positive, helpful tone.

Appropriate voice inflection will make your message more interesting. Speak slowly and in a normal volume, giving concise, but complete, information. If it appears that the customer is having trouble hearing you, speak up. Enunciate words clearly and pronounce them correctly. Try to avoid using annoying sounds such as "um" and "ah," which detract from your message.

Greet customers in a friendly, but professional, manner. Repeat a customer's name as soon as he or she gives it, and continue saying it throughout the conversation. Put the emphasis on the customer by avoiding the words "I" and "we." Keep the emphasis on a "you" attitude.

4

Make customers feel special so they are left with a favorable impression of your company. Focus on the customers' needs and wants, letting them know you intend to act in their best interest.

BE CLEAR

Be prepared for questions. Communicate your answers clearly, using straightforward, simple language. Complex words can be confusing and may not be understood by certain cultures, education levels, or ages. Interspersing big, complicated words into your language will not make you appear to be smarter and may cause miscommunication. Do not eat, drink, or chew gum while speaking.

Avoid giving the runaround or the impression that you are stalling for some reason. Have the customer repeat what you have said in his or her own words. Keeping the customer's needs in mind, figure out what to do. Close all conversations by reiterating the solution and thanking the customer in a way that will bring him or her back for future business.

MAINTAINING CUSTOMER LOYALTY

Customer loyalty is when customers faithfully use your products and services by coming back again and again. Repeat business increases a company's success by providing a consistent customer base. It costs the company less to retain customers than to recruit new ones. To gain customers' loyalty, stay focused on their needs. Strive for quality products and service, and stress the benefits of using your company's products and services. Take the time to answer questions, communicating information effectively and with a positive attitude. Treat each customer as a special individual that you want to help. Make him or her feel important by sincerely offering your service, even if you have to go out of your way to do so.

Commit to cultivating positive relationships by meeting or exceeding customer expectations. Get to know repeat customers by name and remember what they usually purchase. Make a note of what you do for customers, as they will expect the same treatment in the future.

Handle complaints by providing solutions that will be fair to the customer and to the company. Do not raise customer expectations if you are not sure you can give them what they want. If you do not have the ability to give the customer what he or she wants, solicit help from someone who does have the authority.

If customers believe they have received fair treatment, they will likely return. Follow up on service provided, which is an excellent way to promote customer loyalty.

EXERCISE 4-N

Choose a product you are loyal to (i.e., you buy it frequently, or it is the only brand you use). On the lines provided, write a paragraph about why you are loyal to the product. Include what makes you keep buying and using it and what it would take to make you switch from it.

_____

_____

_____

_____

_____

_____

_____

_____

_____

_____

_____

RETAINING GOODWILL

To keep customers coming back, customer service providers must make them feel welcome and important. Offer to assist them and/or to solve their problems. Invite the customer to use your products and services in the future. Close the conversation professionally by thanking him or her for using your products and services.

Do what you can to continue an ongoing positive relationship with the customer, keeping him or her coming back again and again. Provide additional information or suggestions, call periodically, provide discounts, advertise sales for preferred customers, and send occasional cards or letters.

Satisfied customers will tell others about your company's products and services. Those people may then become customers. On the other hand, disgruntled customers will tell others about their negative experiences, causing the loss of not only their business, but also the future business of the people to which they complain. It is smart to retain the customers you have rather than constantly look for and acquire new ones only to lose them as well.

If you do not provide exceptional customer service, someone else at another company will. You will lose your customers and possibly your job. That should be enough incentive for you to want to do a superior job.

How do you provide service that will keep customers returning time after time? First, find out what they want. Next, determine what you can do to give them what they want. Third, provide them with quality products and service. Fourth, follow up to make sure they are satisfied. If they are unsatisfied, determine why. Finally, focus on developing a positive relationship with customers, because people do not forget how they are treated.

EXERCISE 4-O

Assume you are a customer service provider, and an unhappy customer comes to you with a complaint. On the lines provided, list the steps you would take to satisfy this customer.

_____

_____

_____

_____

_____

_____

● PROVIDE STELLAR SERVICE

It seems simple enough to provide service that will keep customers happy; however, many are unhappy because of dealings with inefficient, insensitive, and rude customer service personnel.

Let your customers know you are willing to help them get what they want and that you are sincerely prepared to meet their needs. Be sure to follow through with promises you make as quickly as possible. If you cannot address the customer's problem, let him or her know.

Tips & Tricks

Tips for Providing Excellent Customer Service

- Treat every customer as someone special.
- Express a genuine interest in helping the customer.
- Remember that customers bring in business.
- Identify customer needs and wants.
- Empathize with the customer.
- Use the customer's name.
- Listen for feeling.
- Gather information; take notes.
- Ask questions.
- Identify problems.
- Analyze problems.
- Offer solutions.
- Establish goodwill.
- Follow up on the handling of complaints.
- Learn from complaints.
- Know your products and services.
- Be respectful.
- Be positive, friendly, and sincere.
- Solicit feedback.

4

CULTURAL DIFFERENCES

In today's global economy, **cultural differences** are prevalent, as you will probably work with, or come into contact with, people from various cultures. These individuals demonstrate the differences in the beliefs and values people from different countries hold. In dealing with individuals from cultures other than your own, it is important to recognize that not everyone thinks and feels as you do. Cultural values and beliefs dictate acceptable or unacceptable behavior for each culture. What is valued in one culture may not be valued in another; what people do in one culture may not be tolerated in another.

Cultural beliefs and values are instilled at a young age and can have a direct bearing on how customers think, feel, act, and react. For instance, in some cultures it is disrespectful to make direct eye contact or to use certain gestures. In the United States, direct eye contact is a positive nonverbal behavior.

Cultural differences can affect your perceptions. If you believe strongly that people should behave a certain way, you could perceive they are wrong if they do not comply with your way of thinking. However, in their minds, you are the one who is wrong. In truth, neither of you are wrong or right; you just see things from a different viewpoint.

Cultures have different nonverbal language, as gestures are not universal in meaning. A gesture that means something positive in one culture could be an insult in another culture. Therefore, using the wrong gesture could unintentionally offend your customer, but you would have no idea why.

Cultural differences can also affect a customer's needs and wants, as well as how he or she perceives the customer service provider. Some cultures are very family-oriented; in some cultures men do not have any business dealings with women.

To understand customers better, be aware of cultural differences. Read current literature that describes and defines these differences. When dealing with individuals from other cultures, be patient, look for nonverbal cues, and ask someone else to assist if you cannot determine what the customer wants.

EXERCISE 4-P

Choose a country (other than your own) and research the culture. Write a one-page paper on what you learn.

 ## IMPROVE CUSTOMER SERVICE SKILLS

There is room for improvement in most areas of life, and this includes providing customer service. To help achieve and maintain the right customer service attitude, employees should attend customer service seminars and read current magazine articles on the topic of customer service, positive attitudes, and motivation. In addition, seek out other top-notch customer service providers and observe them as they work.

Keep your **product knowledge** and level of commitment high. Learn all you can about your company's current products; strive to learn about new ones that are being developed.

By using creativity in managing customer needs, looking for self-improvement opportunities, and assessing your attitude, you will be an asset to your company. Your goal should be to form a solid, professional relationship with customers, and to provide them with total customer satisfaction.

If you are currently providing excellent service, discipline yourself to maintain that level every day. Providing customer service can be draining and frustrating; therefore, work at maintaining a positive attitude. Find an appropriate release from stress such as exercise, sports, and hobbies. Get enough sleep and eat proper foods. Talk over customer problems with a superior and ask for guidance.

Tips & Tricks

Stress Relievers

- Remain calm.
- Listen to relaxing music.
- Take breaks from your work—even if they are just mental breaks.
- Stretch.
- Use positive self-talk.
- Eat healthy.
- Exercise.
- Be flexible.
- Prioritize.
- Organize.
- Manage your time.
- Get enough sleep.

ACCEPTING DIVERSITY

Besides cultural differences, customer service providers must accept diversity in the workplace, which includes beliefs, religion, dress and mannerisms, educational level, appearance, age, sex, marital status, political affiliation, and the like.

Your awareness of diversity can make a difference in dealing with customers. Consider how you would deal with adults versus children, women versus men, and a wealthy person versus a poor one. One individual may think of an elderly person as slow and out of touch, while another might revere him or her as wise. You may have customers who speak a language that you do not, or who are undereducated and cannot understand what you are telling them.

When dealing with a language barrier, listen patiently, use proper English (no slang, contractions, or Americanized words), pause frequently, and use a normal volume and tone. Smile frequently and use appropriate gestures to aid understanding. Never talk down to someone or demean him or her in any way. Some customers may have disabilities, such as a hearing impairment, that creates a barrier to understanding. All of these customers want to be treated like everyone else, so be sensitive and respectful. Never use demeaning mannerisms or terms.

Tips & Tricks

Overcoming Language Barriers

- Listen carefully and patiently.
- Use proper English—avoid slang and technical terms.
- Pause frequently while speaking.
- Use a normal tone and volume.
- Watch for nonverbal cues.
- Smile.
- Do not talk down to the customer.
- Avoid touching the customer.
- Avoid using first names or nicknames.
- Avoid stereotyping and biases.
- Avoid demeaning terms.
- Get someone else who can help you.

● FOLLOW-UP ON SERVICE

Turn customer complaints to your company's advantage by using them to gain feedback on your products and services. If one customer is dissatisfied, others may be as well. Aim to ensure that all of your customers are satisfied by listening to what they think of your products and by being attuned to their complaints.

To determine if your customers are satisfied, take advantage of follow-up opportunities by soliciting feedback. Send customer satisfaction surveys with postpaid return envelopes. Surveys should be user-friendly, easy-to-check forms with minimal questions. Include a place on the form for comments. In lieu of written surveys, you can call and ask if customers are satisfied. Build additional goodwill by sending holiday and birthday cards and notes if possible.

EVALUATE PRODUCTS

Evaluations from customers provide valuable feedback to companies about their products and services. Think of an evaluation as a chance to determine if customers are satisfied. If they are not, a survey might pinpoint where the problem lies. Evaluations might identify a faulty product or indicate a major or minor problem with the company's products or services.

When customers are given an opportunity to evaluate products, they know the company is concerned with their satisfaction and with quality.

EVALUATE SERVICE

Customer evaluations of customer service personnel let supervisors know if their employees are handling problems and complaints well, giving correct information about products, taking orders properly, answering the phone correctly, and so on. If the majority of customers are dissatisfied, it is an indication that the service provided is poor, and improvements must be made if the company hopes to stay in business for long. If the service lives up to expectations, customers will be satisfied.

Customer service providers who receive positive evaluations feel good about themselves, increasing their self-esteem.

4

EXERCISE 4-Q

Fill out the evaluation form in Table 4–2.

Table 4–2 EVALUATING YOUR OWN EXPERIENCE AS A CONSUMER

EVALUATE A RECENT PRODUCT YOU BOUGHT OR A SERVICE YOU RECEIVED BY CHECKING "YES" OR "NO" IN THE APPROPRIATE BOX.	Yes	No
Did the product/service meet your needs?		
Did the product/service exceed your expectations?		
Was there something wrong with the product/service?		
If there was something wrong with the product or service, what was it?		
Would you buy this product or use this service again?		
Why or why not?		
Is there any way the product/service could be improved?		
If you answered yes to the previous question, how do you think the product/service could be improved?		

PERSONAL APPEARANCE

Your personal appearance says a lot to customers. It can say, "I care," "I am a professional," and "I am neat and organized." On the other hand, your appearance could say, "I am sloppy and disorganized," I don't care about myself or you," and "I am not a professional."

What does your appearance say about you? Project a professional image by dressing appropriately and following good hygiene basics like showering, washing your hair, and brushing your teeth. Pay particular attention to fingernails, which can be a big turn off if they are dirty.

Clothing must be appropriate, neat, clean, and pressed; polish shoes and keep them in good repair.

Go easy on makeup and fragrances. Hairstyles should be neat and flattering. Simple jewelry and accessories that complement outfits are best. Follow your company's guidelines for acceptable dress.

ENVIRONMENT

Your environment leaves an impression on customers. If you have a messy desk and stacks of boxes or things lying around the office, it could indicate to customers that you are disorganized and inefficient. A clean, neat environment will leave customers with a positive impression.

BE PROACTIVE

Companies are becoming proactive with regard to their customers. That means they are not waiting for problems to turn up, but rather are constantly looking for ways to avoid them. They are also searching for new ways to (1) gain customers, (2) serve customers better, and (3) keep customers coming back.

❯ END OF CHAPTER WORK

CASE STUDIES

● CUSTOMER SERVICE CASE STUDY

Ben, a customer service representative for a large company, answered a call from an irate woman customer. The woman opened the conversation by saying, "Your products stink! I want my money back immediately."

Ben remained pleasant and asked questions to learn what he could about the problem. Instead of giving helpful answers, the customer continued to berate him, the product, and the company. Nothing Ben said satisfied the customer, who eventually used abusive language.

Questions to Ask Yourself

1. What should Ben have done differently, if anything, to satisfy the customer?

    _____

    _____

4

2. Should Ben have hung up when the customer used abusive
    language? Explain your answer.

_____

_____

Things to Consider

Customer service providers often deal with irate customers. Ben
did the right thing by remaining pleasant and asking questions.
When he knew there was nothing he could do to satisfy the customer, Ben could have asked a supervisor to intervene.

Customer service providers do not have to subject themselves
to verbal abuse. When the customer started using abusive language, Ben could have interrupted to explain that he would not
tolerate such language, and/or he could have hung up the phone.

● CUSTOMER SERVICE CASE STUDY

Jenna often shopped at ZZ Company. She had been satisfied with
their products and services over the years. One day Jenna made a
return, and the salesclerk gave her a difficult time. She rolled her eyes
and snatched the article from Jenna, treating her as if she were doing
something wrong. She even huffed while refunding the money.

Jenna left the store with a negative impression of ZZ
Company and doubted that she would return in the future.

Questions to Ask Yourself

1. How should the salesclerk have handled the return?

_____

_____

2. What can be done to repair Jenna's goodwill toward the
    company?

_____

_____

Things to Consider

There is no excuse for being rude to customers. A salesclerk may
have to inspect merchandise to be sure it was not worn or damaged, but he or she should do so without making the customer feel
uneasy. If there is a problem with the merchandise, the salesclerk
should state the facts in a professional manner. If there is no

problem, he or she should cheerfully assist the customer with the return or exchange. It is the salesclerk's job to take returns as well as make sales in a professional manner.

● CUSTOMER SERVICE CASE STUDY

A customer approached Malaya with several questions about her company's products. She knew the answer to only one of the questions. The customer asked if someone else could help him, but Malaya was the only customer service representative on duty. The customer said, "Thanks for nothing," and walked away.

Malaya was indigent and muttered, "How rude."

Questions to Ask Yourself

1. What could Malaya have done to satisfy the customer?

   _____

   _____

2. What can Malaya do in the future to prevent such an occurrence?

   _____

   _____

Things to Consider

If Malaya is a customer service provider, she should know enough about her company's products to answer questions satisfactorily. If she cannot answer questions, she needs to learn more about the products, or else learn where she can find the information.

Malaya could have taken the customer's name and phone number to have someone call him with the answers, or she could have given him a name and phone number to contact for the answers.

It is apparent from the scenario that Malaya felt she was wronged and did nothing to invoke the customer's irritation. However, Malaya needs to become more knowledgeable about her company's products and services if it is her job to provide information. In that respect, she is doing a poor job.

● CULTURAL CASE STUDY

Shawn waited on a customer who was returning merchandise. The customer spoke broken English, and Shawn had a difficult time

4

figuring out what he wanted. As Shawn attempted to communicate, he could tell the customer was getting irritated at his lack of understanding. Shawn threw up his hands and shrugged his shoulders, indicating he did not understand.

Questions to Ask Yourself

1. What more could Shawn have done to communicate with the customer?

   _____

   _____

2. What do you think the customer thought of Shawn?

   _____

   _____

Things to Consider

Shawn should remain pleasant while trying to figure out what the customer wants. He should rely on nonverbal gestures from the customer and also use some positive gestures of his own during the explanation. However, so that he does not inadvertently insult the customer, Shawn needs to be aware that gestures are not universal in nature. He could have tried writing his answers, or could have asked the customer to write his message.

If possible, Shawn should ask someone to assist him. Shawn should not have thrown up his hands in apparent defeat. This would probably have left the customer feeling even more frustrated and dissatisfied.

END OF CHAPTER QUESTIONS

1. How can you maintain customer loyalty?
2. What are the two parts of the communication process?
3. What are four questions you should ask about your customers to get to know them better?
4. What does it mean to empathize with a customer?
5. List four things you can do to solve customer complaints.
6. List five ways you can display a good customer service attitude.

7. In what ways can you become more knowledgeable about your products and services?

8. What messages should you send every customer? Name two.

9. Why is it important to consider cultural differences when dealing with customers?

10. How can you improve your customer service skills?

11. Name two ways you can maintain your professionalism when dealing with a difficult customer.

12. In what ways should you follow-up on the service you provided to a company?

13. Name three ways you can positively communicate with customers.

14. Why should you be concerned about your appearance when dealing with customers?

15. What can you do to help yourself whenever you become frustrated providing customer service?

4

CHAPTER 5

Doing the Right Thing

LEARNING OBJECTIVES

After completing this chapter, you should be able to:

1. Define business ethics.
2. Maintain employer/company loyalty.
3. Identify the need for safety in the workplace.
4. Understand the laws for discrimination and harassment.
5. Define corporate culture.
6. Handle mistakes in the workplace.
7. Define ergonomics.
8. Determine the need for ergonomically designed workstations.

Chapter 5 prepares you for dealing with others in the workplace. Information is presented on ethics, loyalty, and corporate culture to help you become the best professional you can be. A section on ergonomics informs you of workplace safety issues and proper workstation design. A brief overview of workplace laws aids you in learning of your rights and those of others with whom you will work.

KEY TERMS

business ethics	chain of command	corporate culture
discrimination	EEOC	ergonomics
harassment	norms	OSH Act
OSHA	repetitive stress injuries	safety

INTRODUCTION

All businesses have set rules and regulations. These rules, many of which are written in policies-and-procedures manuals, define what is expected of employees. You and everyone you work with will be required to follow all company rules and guidelines.

People who disregard company policies create a negative impression on supervisors and coworkers. For example, if you are consistently late for work, frequently make personal calls, are always in a negative mood, or ignore policies, you will be labeled a rulebreaker. Coworkers may avoid you or have a low opinion of you. Supervisors may consider you unworthy of promotion or of no value to the company.

CORPORATE CULTURE

In addition to written policies, there is an underlying set of **norms**, defined as informal, unwritten rules. These norms cover acceptable conduct for employees. They convey various values, traditions, cultures, and rules of behavior for companies, and comprise what is known as **corporate culture**.

It is difficult to define corporate culture because it is unique to each company. This culture pertains to employee dress, attitudes, performance, interaction with customers, and overall knowledge. It deals with communication between coworkers and supervisors, defines which employees do what tasks, and establishes who assigns the tasks. Corporate culture also covers the companies' facilities, furnishings, and equipment.

Every company has informal norms or rules that dictate how employees should act if they hope to fit in successfully with the other workers. Because the norms that comprise corporate culture are unwritten, some employees, especially new hires, have a difficult time figuring out what is required of them. They may inadvertently do something to cause coworkers to ostracize them. They could also sabotage their careers and not even realize they did so until it is too late.

For example, do you know that some companies have a rule against employee dating, although it may not be written in the policies manual? The same can be said of discussing salaries, which is taboo in the majority of companies. One organization might have standard break times; another may not have a particular policy, but everyone takes one or two 15-minute breaks daily. If someone takes a 25-minute break, the grumbling will start.

Along with informal rules, corporate culture deals with how people act and interact in the workplace. To familiarize yourself with how things are run within the company, get to know who does what task, who holds the power, who can be counted on to tackle problems head-on, and who buries his or her head in the sand. Knowing how people behave and fit into the big workplace picture will give you an edge by allowing you to align yourself with the right people, and to avoid the wrong ones.

CORPORATE CULTURE ISSUES

Did you ever work someplace where you felt you fit in perfectly with the other employees and had a lot in common with them? Again, it is probably corporate culture at work. The same thing can be said for those times when you felt out of place.

The makeup, backgrounds, and similarities of employees are a part of corporate culture. A company's culture could consist of a number of young, married parents of preschoolers that work with older employees who have grown children. In that culture, the older workers would not have the same needs as the younger ones who may want a company day care or to take time off to care for a sick child. The older workers would have little or no interest in the latest toys, child-care issues, booster shots, toddlers' eating habits, etc., as the young parents would. On the other hand, college tuition and retirement issues would not be as pressing for the younger workers as the older ones.

Issues involving corporate culture include (among others):

- How things are normally done
- Who does what task
- What attitudes are prevalent throughout the company
- Who holds what position

5

- Who holds the power
- Who is highly visible
- Who to avoid if possible
- How people gain recognition for their work
- How employees dress
- How people act
- How people communicate
- What everyone is expected to do
- What the basic mission statement is for the company

DO NOT BE SABOTAGED BY CORPORATE CULTURE

All companies have a culture, and when not all rules and policies are written, it may cause confusion, especially to a newly hired person.

Unfortunately, the corporate culture rules that prevail but are not written anywhere are not usually discussed when you are hired for a position. However, their existence can make your life miserable, or at the very least unpleasant. The best way not to sabotage yourself and your career is to observe the way employees perform tasks and how they normally do everything around the workplace, and then follow suit.

When beginning a new job, do not jump in and change things to your way of thinking before you have had a chance to observe what is going on and to figure out why things are done a particular way. Do not make waves.

Take the time to learn how to fit in with everyone else. If the workplace mode of dress is professional, do not wear khakis. If no one plays music, do not blast your desktop CD player. If certain people occupy the same seat every day in the lunchroom, or park in the same spot in the lot, respect their seniority.

Some organizations are informal to the point where employees call the boss by his or her first name, dress casually, and chat with coworkers throughout the day. Other organizations are highly formal places where titles of respect are used, bosses are not on a first-name basis with lower-ranking employees, people wear professional attire, and employees do not socialize during work hours. Some places allow employees to send e-mail jokes and place an occasional personal call. Others have a strict policy against personal e-mails and phone calls.

To be successful and "fit in" with other employees, it is crucial that you behave as expected. It will not help your career to call the boss "John" if everyone else calls him "Mr. Stone." He may think you are disrespectful, and the other employees may assume you are trying to befriend the boss so you will receive special treatment.

So how do you know what is expected of you if the rules are not written down or discussed? One way is to ask questions and listen closely to the answers. Another way is to observe what everyone else says and does. In your observations, learn who the people are you should avoid—the gossips, socializers, rulebreakers, complainers, idea stealers, and credit grabbers. Some employees are so desperate for attention and praise they will steal their coworker's idea or sabotage them in some way. Others complain from the time they arrive at work until they leave. Some never have a good word to say about anyone.

Learn which employees can be counted on to help, to get the job done, to lead, or to produce the most work. Get to know the experts, the thinkers, the confidants, and the high achievers.

Know who has the authority in the company. Even if you do not personally know the CEO, recognize the name in the event he or she telephones or corresponds with your boss. Obviously, the CEO's requests would be given top priority.

Figure out how you can advance in your position and what it will take to be recognized for your achievements by asking these questions. The answers should direct you toward the strong and weak members of the organization, enabling you to make positive choices.

In summary, observe what goes on, listen, and ask questions. Keep a low profile until you figure out what is acceptable. Table 5–1 is a corporate culture evaluation sheet to be used in evaluating a job.

DETERMINE CORPORATE CULTURE
(Continued)

- Which individuals do other employees respect?
- Which individuals do supervisors respect?
- Who are the people who steal ideas from others?
- Who deals with problems effectively?
- Who avoids dealing with problems?
- What do most employees wear?
- What do the high-level executives wear?
- Who can be counted on for support?
- Who is highly visible and seems to run the office?
- Who are the leaders?
- How do you gain recognition for achievements?
- Who can you count on for help?
- Who keeps confidences and who gossips?
- Who are the problem employees?
- What are the general policies regarding overtime, doctors' appointments, personal phone calls, e-mail and the Internet, socializing, breaks, etc.?
- Which employees and supervisors are the experts?
- Who are the thinkers and planners?
- Who are the rulebreakers?

5

TABLE 5–1

UNDERSTANDING AND EVALUATING CORPORATE CULTURE
CORPORATE CULTURE EVALUATION

Answer these questions to help determine the culture in a company.

- What is expected of me?

  _____

  _____

- Does my company have an open-door policy, or are things run in secret?

  _____

  _____

- Is it permissible to date a coworker?

  _____

  _____

- Am I permitted to eat or drink at my desk or workstation?

  _____

  _____

- How should I address my boss?

  _____

  _____

- When do I take breaks and for how long?

  _____

  _____

- What does "casual dress" mean to my supervisor?

  _____

  _____

- Where can employees smoke?

  _____

  _____

- Who are the leaders?

  _____

  _____

- Who does the training, speaking, and planning?

  _____

  _____

(Continued)

TABLE 5–1 (Continued)

• Which employees are difficult to work with, and which ones are supportive?

_____

_____

• Are employees permitted to use the Internet for personal business, such as sending e-mail jokes to coworkers?

_____

_____

• Who are the power people in the company?

_____

_____

• Who are the people who gossip and spread rumors?

_____

_____

• Which individuals do other employees respect?

_____

_____

• Which individuals do supervisors respect?

_____

_____

• Who are the people who steal ideas from others?

_____

_____

• Who deals with problems effectively?

_____

_____

• Who avoids dealing with problems?

_____

_____

• Who can be counted on for support?

_____

_____

5

EXERCISE 5-A

Observe people in your workplace or school to see if you can determine what the corporate culture is that prevails. On the lines provided, answer these questions during the observation:

Are you permitted to eat at your desk or workstation?

_____

_____

What is the typical dress for employees/students?

_____

_____

What is the typical dress for supervisors/teachers?

_____

_____

How many breaks are you entitled to during the day and for how long?

_____

_____

Can you identify the gossips?

_____

_____

Can you identify the people who are trustworthy?

_____

_____

Who can you go to for help?

_____

_____

Do you know the people you should avoid?

_____

_____

UNDERSTANDING BUSINESS ETHICS

Ethical behavior is legal, moral, and responsible conduct; therefore, **business ethics** refers to legal, moral, and responsible conduct in the workplace. Ethical individuals hold themselves accountable to high standards.

Many companies have developed a code of ethics they expect their employees to follow. These companies work hard to build and maintain an excellent public image and reputation. They hold employees to a high level of integrity, ethical behavior, and responsibility. Employees who do not abide by these standards are often disciplined and/or dismissed from employment.

People who are unethical often try to justify their actions, thereby fooling themselves into believing they are acting ethically. These people do not allow their consciences, regulations, or societal rules to guide them. They take no responsibility for their actions.

ETHICAL PROBLEMS

Some ethical choices are easy to deal with; others are difficult and/or confusing. Even when a company code of ethics is in place, employees may not be able to arrive at a clear-cut decision about what to do. There are thousands of situations that arise which may not exactly fit the code. Employees will need to rely on their personal judgment in these cases.

Violating any of the company's policies is unethical, including abusing drugs or alcohol while working, gossiping, showing favoritism, accepting gifts from customers against company rules, calling in sick when not ill, and taking credit for something a coworker did. There are far too many other unethical actions and situations to mention.

Even doing or saying nothing can be unethical in certain cases. This covers not speaking up when you know a coworker is stealing, using drugs or alcohol, operating equipment in an unsafe manner, and the like. A good rule of thumb is that if the behavior clearly cheats the employer, creates a **safety** hazard, or threatens the well-being of others, it should be reported to the appropriate person.

Employers expect employees to exhibit ethical behavior at all times. Individuals who develop reputations as trusted employees with high integrity are likely to build successful careers and maintain

5

positive work relationships. Those who are unethical may be dismissed or held back from promotions.

Stealing

Employees may find themselves in situations where it seems everyone is doing certain activities they feel are not right, such as taking pens and other small office supplies. If 50 employees each take a $1 pen and $1 or $2 in other supplies once a month, the costs quickly add up to a sizeable chunk of money. Companies with hundreds of employees face significantly higher office supply bills. Therefore, ethically speaking, employees should not even take a pen from their workplaces.

Stealing items from the company is, of course, unethical no matter how petty the theft. This includes taking money, postage, office supplies, merchandise, food, services, and so forth. Making personal copies on company equipment and using company phones and equipment for personal business also qualify as stealing.

Some employees give friends and relatives free company products and services without their employers' consent. This is stealing, no matter how you justify it. An attempt at justifying the action might be: "My friend doesn't have any money, but the company makes a fortune."

It does not matter how much the company makes or how little your friend has. It is not the company's responsibility to provide for your friend free of charge.

Cheating

Have you ever had a coworker take credit for something you did? As deceitful as that is, it happens. People who are willing to steal someone's praise and/or ideas have no moral compass to point them in the right direction. They either do not care or are unaware of the serious consequences that may follow, including losing a friend, being discovered by the supervisor and others, creating a reputation for dishonesty, allowing others to falsely think they are capable of producing work when they are not, and so forth. This and all forms of cheating are unethical.

Time Theft

"Time theft," which is stealing time from the employer by any of a number of means, is a big problem that many employees seem to think is all right. It involves having the employees cheat the employers out of time when they are supposed to be completing company work. Instead, they do personal work or in some way avoid doing their jobs.

Time theft includes habitually socializing with employees, faking illness and then claiming the time as sick days, making excessive personal phone calls, taking extended lunches and breaks, coming to work late and/or leaving early, using company time to do personal business, deliberately working slowly to get overtime, and the like. The huge time thefts of excessive absenteeism and lateness are widespread in many companies and cost them in profits, productivity, and customers. Another considerable theft of company time is conducting personal business during hours you are being paid to work and/or using company equipment and materials inappropriately.

Think about an employee who socializes approximately 15 minutes per day. Added together over the course of a month, these minutes turn into hours, and this employee costs the company thousands of dollars in lost wages and productivity.

Destroying or Damaging Property

You have an obligation to take reasonable care of company property. If damage occurs, report it immediately to the supervisor so as not to endanger others. Do not destroy or damage the property of coworkers.

EXERCISE 5-B

In the space provided, answer the following questions. When you are finished, discuss your answers with a trusted friend, and get his or her opinion on the decisions.

What action, if any, would you take if you saw a coworker who is a good friend give one of your company's products to someone for free?

_____

_____

_____

(Continued)

5

EXERCISE 5-B (Continued)

What would you do if you saw a coworker who is a friend operate a piece of equipment unsafely?

_____

_____

_____

What would you do if you saw a coworker you did not like operate a piece of equipment unsafely?

_____

_____

_____

Would you be justified in making copies on the office copier of a personal e-mail you wanted to share with friends if everyone else makes personal copies from time to time?

_____

_____

_____

How many personal phone calls do you think are appropriate to receive at work per week? Explain your answer.

_____

_____

_____

ETHICAL ISSUES IN BUSINESS

- ▶ Telling confidential information to others, including financial, customer, and employee data
- ▶ Taking longer breaks and lunches than provided
- ▶ Coming in late or leaving early
- ▶ Stealing from the company
- ▶ Socializing excessively with coworkers or friends at work

▶ Placing/taking excessive personal calls at work

▶ Abusing alcohol or drugs on the job

▶ Making personal photocopies on the office copier

▶ Using company postage machines to send personal mail

▶ Using company equipment for personal business

▶ Doing personal work on company time

▶ Operating another business on company time

▶ Violating company policies

▶ Not reporting a coworker who steals, operates equipment in an unsafe manner, or violates other company policies

▶ Giving away products, food, services, extra change, etc., to friends who do business with your company without the employer's consent

▶ Destroying or damaging coworkers' property and not admitting it

▶ Destroying or damaging company property and not admitting it

▶ Spreading untrue rumors

▶ Spreading untrue gossip about others

▶ Showing favoritism to certain employees

▶ Taking praise for someone else's work

▶ Abusing sick days

▶ Operating equipment and machinery in an unsafe manner

▶ Lying about others

▶ Cheating

▶ Adding untrue expenses to your expense account

5

❱ Accepting gifts from customers/clients when it is against company policy

❱ Blaming others for your mistakes

❱ Covering up mistakes

❱ Giving away company secrets

ETHICAL GUIDELINES

It seems obvious that you should avoid illegal behavior, especially if prosecution is a possibility. However, some employees will perform illegal activities anyway, if their supervisors instruct them to do so.

If an employer orders an employee to do something illegal, and he or she does it, those actions will not be excused by law enforcement officials if the employee is caught. The law does not recognize the excuse, "The boss made me do it." Therefore, base your decision to do something on its legality, not on whether or not it will cost you the job. Why would you want to work in a company where you could be hauled off to jail at any moment because of illegal activities?

Ethics involves more than avoiding criminal activities. Many things people do and say everyday are unethical in some way. Companies lose profits to unethical behavior, causing all employees to lose. Ethical behavior benefits you, your coworkers, and your company.

MAKING ETHICAL DECISIONS

To arrive at ethical decisions, think before you act. Ask yourself how you will feel about yourself if everyone you know finds out what you did. Ethical decisions that should be easy to make are those involving someone (including yourself) getting hurt physically or mentally. If you think an action you are about to take would be harmful or unfair, it probably is not ethically correct. Ethical decisions should be fair, although all persons involved may not benefit equally. What you need to do is consider everyone's best interests, weigh all the facts, and come up with a solution that is reasonably fair to all parties involved. Treat others as you want to be treated, and look at the situation from the other person's viewpoint. If, after weighing all the facts, you are still having trouble making a decision, talk things over with someone you trust.

DETERMINE ETHICAL BEHAVIOR

- Is the action legal?

- Can I be arrested and prosecuted if I take this action?

- Is it likely that I will be caught?

- Does this action cheat my employer out of time, money, goods, supplies, or services?

- Does this action involve the misuse of company equipment, tools, or supplies?

- Have I witnessed someone else violating ethics in the workplace?

- Have I reported others who have violated ethics in the workplace?

Answering questions regarding your integrity, like the ones posed here, should steer you in the right direction so you can make a decision with a clear conscience. As you can imagine, making unethical decisions may result in a guilty conscience, public humiliation, personal dishonor, demotion, job loss, exclusion, fines, and prosecution.

EXERCISE 5-C

Complete the ethical self-assessment in Table 5–2.

Table 5–2 SELF-ASSESSMENT: ETHICAL BEHAVIOR CHECKLIST

ETHICAL SELF-ASSESSMENT

Answer each of the questions on ethical behavior by checking the appropriate box.

	Yes	No
Would you always do what your boss tells you, even if you suspect it is illegal?		
Would you always do what your boss tells you, even if you suspect it is ethically questionable?		
Do you believe bringing home pens and/or paper from work for personal use is a benefit of working for the company?		
Do you take money, products, food, etc., from work without permission?		
Do you sometimes overlook safety rules when you need to finish a job quickly?		
Do you make excessive personal phone calls at work if they are not long-distance?		
Do you use the copier at work to make personal copies?		
Do you try to squeeze in an extra few minutes at breaks?		
Would you tell a customer what he or she wants to hear to avoid a confrontation, even if it is not true?		
Have you had someone punch your timecard in or out at work because you were running late or had to leave early?		
Do you excessively surf the Internet for personal business?		

Note: Ethically speaking, you should have answered "no" to all questions in Table 5–2. If you answered "yes" to any of the questions, go back and review the information on ethics.

ASK YOURSELF THESE QUESTIONS:

- Would you be proud of your actions and have respect for yourself?
- How do you think others will feel about you?
- How would you feel if what you did were broadcast on the evening news and your friends, family, and coworkers were watching?
- Would you still be proud of yourself?

5

EMPLOYER/COMPANY LOYALTY

Employees must remain loyal to their supervisors and their companies if they hope to have a successful career. Being loyal means you are committed to, and believe in, the company. A strong belief in the company's mission statement is a primary requirement for loyalty. The mission statement identifies the company's values and guides everything that the employees do.

How can an employee profess loyalty if he or she does not believe in what the company stands for or its mission statement?

Loyal employees are proud of their companies and the work they do. They strive toward fulfilling the company's mission by providing quality goods and services, and by conducting business in an ethical manner. They set a good example through their actions and speak positively about the company, products, services, employees, and work environment. They work hard to make their companies successful, and they determine to build their careers with those companies. They do not quit their jobs when things get difficult.

As a loyal employee, you should be positive. Looking on the bright side will keep you from getting discouraged. Do not complain about the tasks you must perform, but rather be glad to have the job and responsibilities.

Extend loyalty to your supervisor through a commitment to make his or job easier. Perform your tasks efficiently, offer as much support as possible to the supervisor, be respectful, and abide by his or her decisions. If you are having a difficult time working with the supervisor, either learn how to get along or find another job and someone with whom you can work. Keep confidential information to yourself.

Do not criticize your company or its employees when talking with coworkers, friends, customers, or anyone else. Avoid gossip and rumors.

No situation is perfect. If you do have a problem with the company, supervisors, coworkers, environment, guidelines, or policies, discuss it with the supervisor or an appropriate individual.

DISPLAY LOYALTY

▶ Commit to doing a good job.

▶ Set a positive example through your actions.

▶ Do not quit when things get difficult.

▶ Avoid gossip and negative criticism.

▶ Do not start or spread rumors.

▶ Be proud of your company and the work you do.

▶ Follow the company's mission statement.

▶ Speak positively of your company.

▶ Discuss problems with the supervisor.

▶ Maintain a positive attitude.

▶ Do not criticize the company, coworkers, or supervisors.

▶ Make your supervisor's job easier.

▶ Be respectful.

EXERCISE 5-D

On the lines provided, list several ways that you show your loyalty to your company or school.

_____

_____

_____

_____

In what additional ways can you express your loyalty?

_____

_____

_____

_____

● SAFETY IN THE WORKPLACE

Thousands of employees die every year from work-related accidents and toxic exposures. Millions more suffer from nonfatal illnesses and injuries. These deaths and injuries, which are devastating personal losses, cost companies billions.

Employers have a responsibility to provide appropriate protective equipment, accessories, and clothing. They must provide adequate training on equipment that employees are required to operate as part of their job duties. They must make sure tools and equipment are well-maintained. They must provide safety and health training, as well as information related to toxic substances, and they must advise trainees of any other safety procedures required for an employee's position.

You have a responsibility as an employee to learn the company's safety rules and procedures and to obey them. Many companies require employees to view safety videos and/or read safety manuals containing regulations, accident and illness avoidance, first aid procedures, etc. Thoroughly read all safety rules and regulations, and ask questions if you do not understand something. Your employer will expect you to work safely for your benefit and that of your coworkers.

Listen carefully when you are given instructions on the use of equipment and tools. Be sure you understand the proper operation and follow all guidelines. Wear the protective clothing, accessories, and equipment, if any are required for your position.

When operating equipment and tools that could cause injury, proceed with caution, avoid shortcuts, concentrate on the task, and avoid distractions such as talking with others. For additional guidance, observe how veteran workers do their jobs, ask their advice, and follow their lead. If you are in doubt about a procedure that involves a safety concern, check your manual or ask your supervisor about it.

If you feel you need additional training, request it. Find a mentor who will give you tips and assistance. Get proper rest and avoid alcohol and substances that impair judgment, including prescribed medication, while on the job. Use good judgment and common sense, and take precautions to prevent accidents. Safety is everyone's responsibility.

Take care of equipment and tools as instructed. For example, if equipment needs to be cleaned and oiled after each operation, make sure it is. Improperly cared for equipment may cause serious problems and injuries.

COMMON ACCIDENTS, INJURIES, AND ILLNESSES

▶ Falls

▶ Cuts, abrasions, and other injuries from equipment, tools, and machines

▶ Sprains and broken bones

▶ Stress

▶ Chemical and other burns

▶ Eye discomfort and loss of vision

▶ Toxic fumes and chemical sickness

▶ Puncture wounds

▶ Hearing damage and loss

▶ Permanent disability

AVOID ACCIDENTS AND INJURIES

Falls are common accidents that injure and disable thousands per year. To prevent falls, keep pathways and aisles clear. Do not stack piles of papers, boxes, or other items on floors, desks, file cabinets, and counters. Do not twist or bend backwards in chairs, as you may take a tumble.

Wear protective shoes or boots; do not wear sandals or open-toed shoes. Women should avoid spiked heels.

Avoid carrying things that obstruct your vision, especially near stairs. Keep stairs clear of debris. Do not walk around with uncovered mugs or cups, which can spill, causing slippery floors. Clean spills immediately.

File cabinets should be bolted to the wall to prevent them from toppling on someone. Open only one file drawer at a time to prevent the cabinet from tipping. Since all the weight is in the drawer, opening more than one drawer at a time can cause the cabinet to fall forward. Drawers should be kept closed when not in use so people will not trip over them or run into them, causing cuts and bruises. In addition, never position cabinets near doorways or in aisles.

Secure wires and extension cords and keep them out of walkways and high-traffic areas. Replace defective cords, and never expose them to water. Do not overload outlets. Repair damaged carpeting, furniture, and equipment.

To avoid puncture wounds, store sharp objects in a container, drawer, or other safe place. Protect yourself from back and neck sprains by lifting items properly and wearing a brace for heavy lifting. Keep objects and equipment away from the edges of desks and counters so they do not fall on anyone.

5

Repetitive stress injuries can occur when working with today's technology and equipment. These injuries result from the constant repetition of similar motions, such as typing, twisting, using the same finger(s) to operate equipment, etc. Follow proper operating instructions for all tools and equipment. Add ergonomic features (discussed later) whenever possible. These features are designed to prevent many of the repetitive stress injuries, and they add to the safety and comfort of the equipment operator.

Inexperienced, tired, or drug- and alcohol-impaired workers are a hazard to themselves and others, contributing to some of the millions of annual injuries. Those who rush too quickly are a hazard to themselves and others. As an employee, you should always be on the lookout for safety violations and hazards. If you see something wrong or have a suggestion for improvement, tell your supervisor or an appropriate person. Encourage people you work with to develop a safety mindset, too, as their unsafe actions could cause injury to you and others. Employers are obligated to correct any problems of which they are aware.

REPORTING ACCIDENTS

If you are injured at work, follow proper procedures, seek first aid or medical treatment, and inform the supervisor or proper person. Most companies require employees to fill out reports for work-related accidents, illnesses, or injuries. The report may be used by the company to investigate the incident and also be used by an insurance company to determine proper benefits and costs to both the employer and the employee.

If you witness an accident, follow proper procedures, administer first aid or seek medical attention, and inform the proper personnel. Witnesses may be required to fill out accident reports and/or give a statement about the incident.

If you see or smell smoke or a fire, notify company security and/or the fire department. If possible, activate the fire alarm. Follow the proper company procedures if you have been trained to use fire extinguishers or to disconnect equipment that is the cause of the fire or smoke. Always have an escape plan for fire, exposure, or other emergency situations.

EXERCISE 5-E

Research your company or school to find the following information, and then write your findings in the space provided:

Is there a company/school training manual for your job and/or the equipment you operate?

_____

_____

What are the company/school safety procedures?

_____

_____

_____

Do you know the company/school escape plan for fires or other emergencies? If not, how would you go about learning the proper procedures?

_____

_____

_____

Does your company/school have a procedure for reporting safety issues?

_____

_____

OCCUPATIONAL SAFETY AND HEALTH ADMINISTRATION

The Occupational Safety and Health Administration (**OSHA**) is an organization that sets and enforces standards for safety and health in the workplace. OSHA has various standards and compliance tools to help employees and employers develop and maintain a successful safety and health program. In 1970, Congress passed the Occupational Safety and Health Act (**OSH Act**) to require employers to provide safe and healthy working conditions for employees. OSHA oversees the OSH Act.

5

OSHA has various publications and assistance available to promote workplace safety and health. Check the OSHA Web site at (www.osha.gov) for publications, information, or advice.

Employers covered by OSHA guidelines must post OSHA posters that inform employees of their rights and responsibilities. Refer to the information if you feel health and/or safety violations are taking place in your company. If guidelines are not posted, refer to the OSHA Web site for helpful information. You have a right to work in a safe environment and to report violations without worry of employer retaliation.

You can ask an OSHA director to investigate a hazardous condition or safety violation. The director will inform you of his or her findings and make recommendations. If you file an OSHA complaint, you have the right to have your name withheld from your employer. It is illegal for your employer to punish you if he or she learns that you alerted OSHA.

Employers generally maintain records of work-related accidents, illnesses, injuries, and their causes. You, as an employee, have the right to review these records if your company keeps them. You may also review medical records related to harmful toxins that cause illnesses and injuries in your workplace.

Express concerns about safety to your supervisor. For example, if the company parking lot has no lighting and you leave work after dark, advise the supervisor that you believe lighting should be provided for your safety and well-being. A safe, well-lit parking lot is beneficial to everyone employed by the company.

Other private and government agencies have been established to promote safety. The Consumer Product Safety Commission, the National Highway Traffic Administration, the National Safety Council, and the Mine Safety and Health Administration are examples.

Stressed workers have a greater chance of developing emotional disorders and/or getting sick or injured. To reduce stress, take short breaks, get enough rest, talk things over with a trusted friend, manage your time, and get organized. Smile and look for the positives in situations. Go for a walk at lunchtime. For more information, review the stress-reducing tips provided in Chapter 4.

EXERCISE 5-F

Search the Internet for available agencies that deal with safety regulations. Choose one of the agencies and on the lines provided, answer these questions:

What is the agency's name?

_____

_____

What is the agency's special safety expertise?

_____

_____

What does the agency do to promote safety for employees?

_____

_____

What requirements does the agency issue to employers?

_____

_____

What pamphlets or brochures does the agency offer to the public on promoting safety?

_____

_____

What is the agency's contact information for filing complaints?

_____

_____

Tips & Tricks

Safety Tips

- Do not operate equipment without a safety guard.
- Use personal protective equipment and clothing if required.

(Continued)

Tips & Tricks (Continued)

- Do not operate equipment or dangerous machinery when tired.
- Do not operate equipment or dangerous machinery while intoxicated or drugged.
- Handle toxic substances properly.
- Do not goof off in the workplace.
- Be on the lookout for possible dangers in the workplace.
- Ask questions if you are unsure of how to properly operate equipment.
- Read all safety materials.
- Know emergency procedures.
- Do not carry liquids without a lid.
- Clean spills immediately.
- Pay attention to training and operation guidelines.
- Secure wires and cords.
- Replace damaged wires and cords.
- Close drawers and cabinets.
- Avoid stacking items.
- Keep aisles and doorways clear.
- Avoid carrying items that obstruct your view.
- Lift items properly.
- Avoid awkward reaches for tools.

EXERCISE 5-G

Research the career you are preparing to enter to determine what health and safety measures are generally implemented in that industry. For instance, if you plan to be a medical assistant, what health and safety measures might be implemented in your office?

All workplaces must implement general health and safety measures. Include these in your research.

Write a one-page report on your findings.

● ERGONOMICS

Ergonomics deals with making equipment, jobs, and the work environment safe for employees. Ergonomics takes into account lighting, noise, temperature, and color. It encompasses the design, adjustability, layout, and comfort of equipment, tools, and furnishings.

Ergonomics applies to tasks involving sitting, standing, lifting, pushing, pulling, twisting, moving fingers and hands, and squeezing.

The use of ergonomics can make jobs safer by preventing injuries and illnesses, and make tasks more efficient and pleasant.

Job design considerations include rest breaks, proper training, exercises, and job rotations that will help employees reduce stress physically and mentally. Proper job design can also minimize and/or prevent accidents and injuries.

Workstation design may include the design and comfort of chairs, height and dimensions of work surfaces and desks, layout of furnishings in the space, lighting, air quality, color, noise level, space, and the like.

Equipment design deals with the safety of equipment, including keyboards, screens, safety guards, etc. It also covers accessories such as tools that fit the hand properly, safety belts, wrist guards, equipment noise covers, earplugs, safety helmets and shoes, protective clothing, and the like.

Manufacturers are designing furniture, tools, equipment, and other workplace items for the safety, performance, and physical and mental comfort of operators. The work environment and everything employees use must suit their physical capabilities to help minimize or prevent injuries and accidents. As an example, if they must stretch, lift heavy objects, sit in cramped spaces, handle toxins, etc., employees should have the proper equipment, tools, information, and training. The application of ergonomics addresses many problem areas.

ERGONOMIC DESIGN

Ergonomics has become popular because companies are always looking for ways to reduce accidents, injuries, illnesses, and deaths. Some of the problem areas ergonomic design can eliminate or minimize include:

- Vision problems caused by improper lighting and computer screens
- Neck, shoulder, lower back, leg, and foot pain caused by improper chairs, furniture, equipment, and tools

5

- Respiratory illnesses caused by poor air quality
- Wrist, elbow, and hand injuries due to repetitive motions and/or improper tools and equipment
- Stress due to the work environment or job design
- Hearing loss due to excessive noise from equipment and machinery
- Broken bones due to improper design and layout of furniture, equipment, and tools or an unsafe environment

ERGONOMIC SOLUTIONS

Properly designed jobs, workspaces, and equipment can make a significant difference in how employees work and feel. Proper design can reduce illnesses, injuries, accidents, and boredom. It can increase productivity and efficiency.

Repeating a single motion over and over may cause problems. Repetition of limited actions causes fatigue, boredom, and repetitive stress injuries. To eliminate or minimize these problems, vary your actions and activities, or change your work procedure from time to time. Variety reduces boredom and the mental stress it creates. It also wards off repetitive stress injuries.

Muscle strain and fatigue can be caused by awkward posture and positions while improperly standing or sitting, lifting, twisting, slouching, etc. Poor posture can lead to lower-back and neck injuries. Sitting for long periods stiffens and tires muscles and reduces blood flow. Therefore, furniture design is very important to comfort and safety.

The more time you spend at your workstation, which includes your desk or work surface, chair, counters, etc., the more it should meet your needs. The height of chairs, desks, workspaces, counters, and equipment should be well thought-out for employees who must do their jobs in standing and sitting positions for long periods of time. Properly designed furniture can help prevent injuries to the neck, arms, elbows, hands, back, shoulders, legs, and feet.

An ergonomic chair is one that can be adjusted in a variety of positions to maintain proper posture and comfort. A properly adjusted ergonomic chair allows the user to place his or her feet flat on the floor. It also has a backrest that curves outward and can be adjusted up or down to support a sitting position. Sitting in an ergonomically designed chair should not place any pressure on the body. Avoid slouching, as that causes not only back problems, but also leg and neck problems. Footrests are available if needed or desired.

Poor hand posture leads to complaints about wrists, fingers, hands, elbows, necks, and shoulders. Wrist supports or rests help eliminate poor hand posture and the lack of support. They are easily attached to the front edge of equipment or table surfaces. A variety of supports are available, so be sure to try different ones for the best fit. Repetitive movements that involve fingers and hands may cause inflammation and injury.

In addition to support accessories, pay attention to the height and positions of desks, keyboards, monitors, and other equipment you operate. You should be able to sit or stand comfortably, depending on the task you are doing. Document holders improve posture and prevent leaning too far forward and looking down, which puts undue stress on the neck. An ergonomic mouse takes pressure off the index finger.

Light level is an ergonomic consideration since it affects vision, general health, and moods. A well-lit area can help prevent eye strain and falls, and induce upbeat moods, as can a cheery, sunlit area. However, too intense lighting, sunlight, and reflective surfaces cause eye strain, stress, and a glare on computer screens. To eliminate glare on computer screens, face them away from windows or tilt them. Depending on conditions, you may want to use indirect lighting and surface lamps.

Air quality is affected in many buildings where windows are sealed and cannot be opened. The air in these buildings can be re-circulated or purified, depending on how the company handles it. Sealed buildings can pose health problems when fumes are emitted from carpeting, drapes, furniture, chemicals, paint, and building materials. In addition, ink from copiers and printers can generate fumes. These pollutants cause headaches, dizziness, sinus conditions, and other health problems and discomforts. Therefore, care should be taken when selecting and installing building materials, carpeting, and ventilation systems. Copiers should be placed in well-ventilated areas away from employees.

5

Temperature affects employees' ability to work. If it is too cold and drafty, employees may become stiff or ill. If it is too hot and stuffy, employees may become lethargic or suffer the effects of heat exhaustion. Humidity should be controlled to prevent dampness, mold, and mildew. Comfortable temperatures and humidity levels improve moods and productivity.

Use sound panels, carpeting, drapes, and equipment covers to reduce noise. Playing soft background music helps mask irritating sounds. Wear protective ear coverings, if required for the tasks you perform, or if necessary for your comfort.

Color affects moods. Bright, bold colors stimulate and excite, whereas soft blues and greens are calming. Drab, dark colors are depressing, especially when the lighting is poor.

The layout and placement of furniture, equipment, and other furnishings has a significant impact on employees' ability to do their jobs. It is hard to maneuver and/or perform tasks and operate equipment properly in tight, cramped spaces. Allow for plenty of leg room under desks and counters. An open environment that allows for free movement and comfort will improve productivity, safety, and the general atmosphere. If your workplace does not take ergonomics into consideration, suggest the benefits of such designing.

Tips & Tricks

Ergonomics Tips

- Replace uncomfortable chairs.
- Adjust the height of your chair and desk.
- Make various chair adjustments periodically.
- Rest your eyes frequently by focusing on distant objects.
- Stand and stretch occasionally.
- Change positions often.
- Relax shoulders.
- Bend knees at no more than a 90 degree angle when sitting.
- Alternate tasks.
- Take deep breaths occasionally.
- Keep wrists aligned with forearms when operating equipment.
- Sit upright with feet flat on the floor; do not slouch.

(Continued)

Tips & Tricks (Continued)

- Use shades or blinds on widows.
- Adjust monitor screens to eliminate glare from windows and sunlight.
- Position monitors an arm's length in distance.
- Maintain a comfortable temperature.
- Dress comfortably for workplace temperatures.
- Reduce stress.
- Replace broken chairs or other furniture.
- Replace broken equipment and tools.
- Use noise-reducing accessories.

EXERCISE 5-H

Look around your workplace or school to determine the use of ergonomics. Briefly describe to what extent the items in Table 5–3 are ergonomically planned in your workplace or school.

Table 5–3 ERGONOMICS IN THE WORKPLACE

Desks/workstations	Accessories (computer, keyboard, mouse)
Lighting	Air quality
Temperature	Equipment/tools
Chairs	Placement of furniture and equipment
Color	Job design
Noise reduction	Protective clothing

● ADMITTING MISTAKES

No one is right all the time. We all make mistakes. The only people who do not make mistakes are the ones who do nothing. If you make a mistake, report it quickly. Taking personal responsibility for your actions is key to correcting a mistake and putting it behind you. Making excuses and blaming others for your mistakes detracts from your integrity. If you do not admit mistakes, you might find yourself defending inaccuracies just for the sake of saving face. It is important to admit the error and correct it. Not admitting errors could cause harm to, and lost income for, the company, and can result in lost customers.

5

If practical, offer to do whatever you can to correct mistakes by looking for acceptable solutions. Learn from mistakes so you do not repeat them; instead, gain knowledge and develop good judgment. In this way, you turn the mistake to your advantage.

Do not let the fear of making mistakes keep you from arriving at decisions or taking action. You will not get far in your career by being stagnant and fearful. If you try and fail, it is still better than not taking a chance, which limits your thinking and opportunities.

Once you have taken responsibility for a mistake and have resolved it, commit to not repeating the behavior. Do not dwell on it, but rather treat it as an experience from which you can learn and grow. Now you have more experience on which to base future decisions and develop good judgment. Move on with a positive outlook.

ACCEPTING CRITICISM

Making mistakes and accepting criticism often go hand in hand. It is likely your supervisor will criticize mistakes you make that cost the company time, money, and/or business. Accepting the criticism as a learning tool that turns the negative situation into a positive one will help you grow professionally. No one likes to hear he or she is incompetent, but looking at criticism as something you have done that needs improvement can be a deterrent to making future mistakes. Continually work on improving yourself.

Keep in mind the criticism is of your work or the mistake, not you personally. If constructive criticism were never given, you might never learn from mistakes or improve yourself and your work.

REPORTING MISTAKES

If a mistake affects others in an adverse way, admit it, apologize, help to fix it, and then put it behind you. Apologizing is difficult, which causes some people to gloss over their mistakes. However, sincerely admitting fault could remedy the situation and save relationships.

Follow the proper **chain of command** when you need to report a mistake. The chain of command is the order of employees from lowest to highest on the company's organization chart. For example, you report to your supervisor who reports to his or her supervisor and so on up the chain. If you can personally fix the problem, do so, and then inform your supervisor of what transpired. If you cannot solve it, advise your supervisor or other appropriate person. Do not jump over someone in the chain of command. To do so risks a breakdown in the team effort.

If someone else made the mistake, again follow the chain. For instance, if a coworker made a mistake that can easily be resolved, inform him or her. If it is something of which the supervisor should be notified, do so.

Oftentimes it is difficult to point out a coworker's mistake because of friendship or a desire to remain on good terms with the person. However, care must be taken for the safety and concern of everyone who is involved. You cannot ethically let friendship stand in the way when mistakes are made, especially if they are serious ones. Not advising the appropriate person of a critical act is dishonest and dangerous to everyone and could have dire consequences.

EXERCISE 5-1

On the lines provided, explain how you would handle each of these situations:

You are an office clerk who sent out an advertising mailer to 2,000 customers without weighing it, so insufficient postage was used. Several of the mailers have been returned due to the insufficient postage. You expect all of the mailers to be returned. What do you do?

_____

_____

_____

_____

You are a copier salesperson. You demonstrated your company's newest model copier, and then quoted the customer an incorrect price hundreds of dollars lower than the actual selling price. The customer accepted the deal before you realized your error. What do you do now?

_____

_____

_____

_____

5

REPORTING MISTAKES

▶ Admit that a mistake has occurred.

▶ Take responsibility for the mistake.

▶ Offer to help resolve the mistake.

▶ List available solutions.

▶ Chose a solution.

▶ Resolve the mistake.

▶ Learn from the mistake.

▶ Put the mistake behind you.

▶ Take care not to repeat the mistake.

UNDERSTANDING DISCRIMINATION AND HARASSMENT

Equal treatment is the law. All people must be treated fairly regardless of age, race, gender, sexual orientation, disability, religion, or national origin.

DISCRIMINATION

Discrimination, or differentiating between people in the workplace, is illegal. Prejudice and mistreatment cause professional and legal trouble, as does failure to report them. Never assume anyone's origin, appearance, or background indicates his or her capability to do the job.

Several laws govern fair treatment, including:

• Equal Employment Opportunity—employers cannot discriminate against people because of race, color, religion, sex, or national origin.

• Age Discrimination Act—prohibits discrimination against people 40–60.

• Americans with Disabilities Act—gives protection to those with physical and/or mental disabilities.

• Family and Medical Leave Act—employers with 50 or more employees must grant up to 12 weeks of unpaid leave per year to allow workers to care for a newborn or an ill family member.

- Affirmative Action—designed to correct past discrimination against minorities, women, people with disabilities, and Vietnam veterans.

The Equal Employment Opportunity Commission (**EEOC**) administers many of these laws. Employers are required to treat everyone equally and fairly and to hire the best person for the job regardless of origin. Employers must treat people fairly with regard to hiring, promoting, paying, providing benefits, firing, and all aspects of employment.

Favoritism is a form of discrimination and must be avoided in the workplace. Supervisors, especially, must adhere to the laws concerning discrimination and not show favoritism among employees.

TABLE 5–4

TYPES OF DISCRIMINATION

TYPES OF DISCRIMINATION	
• Race	• Color
• Age	• Religion
• Sexual orientation	• National origin
• Disability	• Minorities
• Women	• Vietnam veterans

HARASSMENT

Harassment is unwanted and unsolicited comments, gestures, physical contact, graphic material, or favors. Sexual harassment (discussed later) is imposing sexual attention on someone who is not in a position to refuse it. All harassment is illegal, including any acts that create an intimidating, hostile, or offensive workplace and/or adversely affect someone's promotion or progress within the company.

Some individuals do not think their actions constitute harassment; however, if they are told the behavior is offensive, they must stop it or face discipline. Most companies today have very specific harassment policies that comply with the laws.

5

DEALING WITH HARASSMENT

If you feel you are being harassed, confront the person and let him or her know what behavior you find objectionable. Keep a written, dated record of the harassment and any action you take in return. If the harassment continues, file a complaint with your personnel department. Some companies require that the grievance be filed within a certain time period from when the offense occurred. Your company should provide a grievance form for you to complete. If none is available, check the Internet or phone book for a local agency that can assist you. Usually the reported incident will be investigated and a meeting will be held to resolve the problem. If the problem is not mutually resolved, you have the right to contact an attorney and file a lawsuit.

SEXUAL HARASSMENT

Sexual harassment is any unwelcome sexual advance, physical contact of a sexual nature, or request for sexual favors. It can be physical, such as unwanted touching, patting, kissing, assaulting, etc., or visual, such as obscene gestures, or displays of sexually explicit pictures, materials, and cartoons. Verbal sexual harassment includes innuendos, lewd comments, and any request for sexual favors.

Sexual harassment is illegal when employees believe they must put up with the behavior to keep their jobs, advance, or receive pay raises. Be careful not to tell and/or circulate jokes that may offend even one person.

DISCRIMINATION AND HARASSMENT PROCEDURES

Learn your company's procedures for dealing with the unfair employment practices of discrimination and harassment. If you feel you have been a victim of these unfair practices, follow proper company procedures according to discrimination and harassment guidelines. If your company does not have a specific policy, report the incident to your supervisor or union representative. You can also contact agencies that deal with these violations. Consult your telephone book or the Internet for names and addresses of appropriate agencies.

In all cases, keep a detailed record of violations, your reporting of them and to whom, and what, if anything, was done to resolve the issue.

EXERCISE 5-J

Research the Internet for examples of lawsuits on discrimination and harassment. On the lines provided, write down three incidents or examples that you find, including whether or not the issue was resolved and how.

_____

_____

_____

_____

_____

_____

_____

_____

_____

_____

END OF CHAPTER WORK

CASE STUDIES

● **ADMITTING MISTAKES CASE STUDY**

Bob works in a small company where he does accounts payable. One day he received an invoice for a company bill that was a month late. He should have paid the bill. He checked his records and found that he wrote the check for the original invoice last month but forgot to mail the payment. Now the company must pay a late charge. Bob is hesitant to tell his employer, because he is afraid that he will be reprimanded or possibly fired.

Questions to Ask Yourself

1. Should Bob pay the bill with the late charge and keep quiet about it?

   _____

   _____

5

2. Do you think telling the employer about his mistake would jeopardize Bob's job?

_____

_____

Things to Consider

Employers value honesty and integrity. Chances are Bob's employer would be far more upset to learn that he tried to cover up a mistake rather than admit the error, even if it meant a reprimand. Dishonesty is a breech of ethics. People in the accounting department must maintain the highest level of integrity.

It is unlikely Bob would be terminated if he admitted to an error. However, if he had made many errors in the past, especially of the same type, he could be facing stiff consequences. If he has not made a lot of errors, he would be expected to learn from this one and be careful not to repeat it in the future. Double-checking work will eliminate many errors. Perhaps Bob needs to take a look at his procedures and put a safety net in place that will eliminate future problems of this nature.

● EMPLOYER LOYALTY CASE STUDY

Jennifer complained to Niki about her supervisor. "I don't even know how he became a boss," Jennifer said. "He doesn't have a clue what goes on around here. If you ask me, all bosses are clueless." She then asked Niki if her supervisor was incompetent.

Sometimes Niki became irritated with her supervisor, but she had no intention of telling Jennifer. Niki and her supervisor were a team, and she refused to gossip about him.

Question to Ask Yourself

1. How could Niki disengage from Jennifer's complaint session?

_____

_____

2. What suggestions could Niki make to help Jennifer build a better relationship with her own supervisor?

_____

_____

Things to Consider

Niki was right to remain loyal to her supervisor. Being a team player with him will ensure that she has a good working relationship.

In an effort to end the complaining, Niki should tell Jennifer that she has work to do, or else she could change the subject. Niki should not encourage Jennifer's complaints, nor should she agree with her. By remaining noncommittal, Niki does not give Jennifer the chance to mislead other people into thinking Niki agrees with her.

Niki could suggest that Jennifer sit down with her supervisor and discuss the problems she is having. She could point out the benefits of working harmoniously with her supervisor versus the upheaval Jennifer now faces.

Niki could also suggest some stress-relieving tips to Jennifer, letting her know that reducing her stress might improve her mood and the atmosphere around her office.

● **ETHICAL CASE STUDY**

Gerred worked in the accounting department of a home remodeling business. The owner sometimes installed used furnishings and materials but charged the customers full price. This is an illegal practice. He asked Gerred to adjust the invoices and other paperwork to reflect the changes. Gerred knew it was illegal to charge customers for new materials when the materials were actually used, but he made the changes the boss requested. Gerred felt he would lose his job if he did not comply.

Questions to Ask Yourself

1. Do you think it was all right for Gerred to change the figures to the illegal numbers in order to keep his job?

   _____

   _____

2. What recourse does Gerred have if he refuses to do as the boss asks?

   _____

   _____

5

Things to Consider

Gerred should refuse his supervisor's request. It is never a good idea to perform illegal activities, even if a superior tells you to do so.

If the company gets caught committing the illegal acts, most likely everyone involved would be prosecuted, including Gerred. Although he might feel he will lose his job if he refuses, Gerred will knowingly break the law if he takes part in and then covers up the illegal actions. The courts would not accept his excuse that he would have been fired.

If Gerred believed the company was doing something illegal, he would do well to find another job in a company where he agreed with its principles and moral code.

● ETHICAL CASE STUDY

Madison attended a business meeting in a city near her office. After the meeting, Madison decided to drive to a grocery store a few miles away to purchase items for dinner. When she returned to the office and turned in her hours, she included the time it took to drive to the grocery store and the time spent there, which was 45 minutes. She gets paid by the hour. Madison also turned in her mileage and included the miles to and from the store.

Questions to Ask Yourself

1. Was Madison entitled to payment for the extra time and mileage?

   _____

   _____

2. Why or why not?

   _____

   _____

Things to Consider

Madison should only submit hours for work she actually did or business she participated in for the company. The same is true for mileage. Charging the company for extra expenses is called "padding expenses" and is stealing. It also dishonestly and unethically takes advantage of the employer.

Madison should reserve her personal shopping for after work hours. However, if she feels the need to do errands during company time, she should not expect the company to pay for her time and mileage.

● CORPORATE CULTURE CASE STUDY

Mikaila was hired as a paralegal at a large city law office. On her first day, she arrived ten minutes early in her new, fine-quality navy blue suit. Mikaila was well-groomed and her hair was conservatively cut and styled.

Mikaila greeted everyone she met with a smile, handshake, and her name. Later, when the lawyer that she was to assist called her in his office, she grabbed a pen and notebook from her briefcase. When the lawyer gave her directions for researching a brief he was preparing for a client, Mikaila took detailed notes.

Questions to Ask Yourself

1. What impression do you suppose Mikaila made on the law office employees?

   _____

   _____

2. What positive things did Mikaila do that will help her in her career?

   _____

   _____

Things to Consider

Mikaila did a number of positive things that should make a great first impression on the law office employees. Dressing the part of a successful individual and being well-groomed shows everyone that she is ready for business and wants to maintain the company's image. Arriving early and taking the initiative to greet everyone shows her determination to fit in and be part of the team. Being prepared upon her arrival and taking notes in the meeting with the lawyer conveys she is responsible and dependable.

Overall, Mikaila did everything she could to show she is ready for a career in the legal field.

5

● REPORTING MISTAKES CASE STUDY

Blaine worked as a travel agent in a small agency. The other people employed at the agency were another travel agent, an accountant, a receptionist, and the office manager/owner.

Blaine shared an office with Hannah, the other agent. He became frustrated with Hannah because she would never pick up the phone if Blaine was available to answer it. When she did answer calls, Hannah often misquoted prices to the clients. When the weekly and monthly reports needed to be compiled, Hannah was no where to be found, leaving Blaine to do them himself.

On many days Blaine went home with a headache, because he held his resentment toward Hannah inside.

Questions to Ask Yourself

1. What can Blaine do to get Hannah to do her share of the work?

   _____

   _____

2. What can Blaine do to relieve his stress?

   _____

   _____

Things to Consider

The first thing Blaine should do is objectively look at the situation to determine if he is indeed doing the majority of work or if he is operating under a false perception.

If he is actually doing more than his share of the work, Blaine could sit down with Hannah and explain how her behavior makes him feel. He could tell her the situation is the cause of frequent tension headaches. He needs to emphasize his feelings and not create a hostile environment by blaming or accusing Hannah.

As a friendly gesture, Blaine could tactfully mention that Hannah has misquoted some prices and then offer to help her locate correct information.

If Hannah is unreasonable or takes offense and does not improve, Blaine may have to approach the owner if he intends to continue working for the agency. However, things will go more smoothly if he can work out a solution with Hannah instead of involving the owner.

To relieve his stress, Blaine could concentrate on the positive aspects of his job, occasionally take deep breaths and short breaks, get proper rest, manage his time, and take walks at lunchtime.

END OF CHAPTER QUESTIONS

1. What are four kinds of safety problems you could encounter in the workplace?

2. How would you handle a coworker who operates equipment unsafely?

3. What are four types of discrimination employees could face?

4. Why is it so important to follow safety practices daily?

5. Define corporate culture.

6. List five observations you should make about the corporate culture of your particular company.

7. How could corporate culture sabotage your career?

8. Define ethics.

9. Why is ergonomics important to your safety in the workplace?

10. What are three things you can do to ergonomically improve your workstation?

11. What are three things you can do to ergonomically improve your work environment?

12. Name two ethical situations you could face on the job.

13. What are two guidelines to consider when facing ethical decisions?

14. List three ways you can eliminate stress.

15. What should you do if you are sexually harassed in the workplace?

16. What agency oversees the safety and health of employees in the workplace?

17. Name four ways you can make your work environment safer.

18. List two things you can do to avoid injury in the workplace.

19. Define time theft and give two examples of it.

20. Do you find it difficult to admit mistakes when you make them? Why or why not?

5

Success Beyond Your Externship

CHAPTER 6

Finding a Permanent Position

LEARNING OBJECTIVES

After completing this chapter, you should be able to:

1. Search for a permanent position in your field.
2. Use the externship as a stepping-stone to a permanent position.
3. Find job leads.
4. Determine the benefits of a job fair.
5. Develop network contacts from the externship.
6. Update your resume, reference sheet, and portfolio.
7. Create personal business cards.

Chapter 6 will guide you in updating your resume, reference sheet, and portfolio when you have finished your externship and are ready to begin your career. Information is provided on how to find job leads and contacts, and learning to use your externship to your advantage when searching for that permanent position.

KEY TERMS

business cards
job fair

Civil Service Exam
job leads

employment agency
recommendation
letter

6

INTRODUCTION

Chapter 2 dealt with a number of ways to search for an externship position. These methods are appropriate to use when searching for a permanent position as well. A summary of these methods include:

JOB SEARCH SUMMARY

- Newspaper want ads
- Applying directly
- Using telephone books
- Networking
- Joining a professional organization
- College, hospital, and company bulletin boards
- Internet searches

TURNING YOUR EXTERNSHIP INTO A PERMANENT POSITION

Permanent positions within companies are often filled with qualified externs. Company personnel evaluate externs during the externship period to determine their suitability for future employment with the company. These externs may or may not have worked in the open positions before being hired full time. For instance, an extern may have performed well in a position within a company before another opening occurs. It may be a position the extern held, or may be something completely different.

Because the extern has familiarized himself or herself with company policies, procedures, equipment, and employees, he or she becomes a likely candidate when job openings occur.

To be sure you will be considered for a permanent job with your externship company, complete your assignments with the utmost professionalism. Follow all company guidelines, including arriving on time every day and working until the assigned quitting time. Come back from lunch and breaks in a timely manner. Perform your tasks as directed to the best of your ability, quickly and accurately. Double-check work and ask questions when appropriate. Give the company the agreed upon hours. Avoid doing personal work, socializing unnecessarily with other employees, making personal phone calls, playing on the Internet, gossiping, and the like.

Maintain the highest integrity and work ethics as discussed in Chapters 1 and 2. Show the employer you are serious about your work and will be an asset to the company if hired permanently.

Oftentimes, employers will help their externs find suitable full-time positions elsewhere if there are no available openings in their own company.

FINDING OTHER JOB LEADS

Job leads are comprised of hints and information gathered about positions in the workplace. Remember, before accepting a position where you will spend most of your waking hours, take the time to match yourself to it. Review Chapter 1 and the self-assessments you completed. With a bit of planning and an in-depth look at yourself, you will be in a better position to find a job that is right for you. Then the work hours you put in will be enjoyable. If you enjoy what you do, you will look forward to going to your job, and you will want to do your best when you get there. The more you like about your job, the more satisfied and happy you will be.

In Chapter 2 you learned of ways to find an externship position. Review that material when you are preparing to search for a full-time position. All of the methods discussed pertain to landing a full-time job as well as an externship. In addition, other ideas are discussed here, including the hidden job market.

THE INTERNET

As mentioned in Chapter 2, the Internet provides access to hundreds of newspapers. In addition to searching the classifieds, job seekers can use the Internet as a powerful job-search tool. Thousands of openings are posted on a variety of job sites, and most of these sites are updated on a daily basis.

There are sites for general employment (for example, Career Mosaic), which list all occupations, and other sites designed for specialized fields. Some sites (for example, Careerlink) allow job seekers

6

to submit resumes on-line and wait for employers to contact them. Some sites (Monster) attempt to match resumes with open positions and also provide on-line applications for various companies.

Thousands of companies have Web sites. A number of these are interactive job sites that help users format resumes, research employment opportunities and topics of interest, and prepare for interviews. They post job descriptions, titles, salaries, and benefits.

Many companies encourage applicants to apply on-line and attach their resumes and cover letters to the applications. Some companies do all or most of their hiring and recruiting on-line.

When looking for jobs on-line, search for specific companies. If you cannot find a particular company's Web site, call and ask if they have one. If they do, get the Web address.

With Internet access, job seekers can hunt for employment opportunities 24 hours a day, 7 days a week if they so desire, rather than waiting for the classifieds in their local papers, or contacting various companies in person or by telephone. Internet searches can be local or worldwide, giving job seekers a look at companies to which they would not normally have access. Resumes posted on these sites reach their destination in minutes instead of days. An Internet search can be less expensive than placing long-distance phone calls, buying several newspapers, or driving from company to company to drop off resumes.

NEWSPAPER WANT ADS

Read the classifieds in local daily and Sunday papers and on the Internet. Now that you have completed your externship, apply for openings that require moderate work experience. Your externship may give you an edge over other candidates who have no work experience in the field.

Think in broad terms when searching for positions. If you want a job as an administrative assistant, look under the headings "administrative assistant," "executive assistant," "office manager," "secretary," "word processing specialist," etc. The broader you make your search, the more jobs to which you will be exposed. Table 2–3 in Chapter 2 lists several abbreviations used in want ads. Use this list for hard-to-understand abbreviations you encounter.

In addition to individual company ads, you will find ads from employment agencies in the want ads. Agencies have access to a variety of jobs and employers.

SIGN UP WITH A TEMPORARY AGENCY

Temporary agencies (temp agencies) employ thousands of people in all fields of work for all types of positions. Temporary agency employees (temps) are hired to work on special projects and to assist regular employees when the workloads are heavy. Temps also fill in when regular employees are sick, on vacation or leave, or quit. The temp agencies place people with companies for short- or long-term assignments. They have daily contact with employers and have access to a significant number of jobs. Most temp agencies have conveniently located offices.

Many agencies have details on temp-to-hire positions, where an employer can try you out on a temporary basis to see if you will fit the requirements for the position before they actually put you on their payroll. Working for a temp agency is a great way to keep a high profile with companies, because people who like your work may request you from the agency. Some companies do all their hiring through these agencies, and you will have the opportunity to showcase your skills by working for them.

On the other hand, you will have the opportunity to try out different employers to see whether or not you would like working for them. An added advantage to working as a temp is that you can also brush up on your skills in order to meet future career goals.

Research the Agencies

Details, procedures, and policies vary from one temporary agency to another, so check with several in your area before making a decision as to which one(s) to use. There are agencies that offer good wages, benefits, and free training—where you can learn a new skill or improve on an old one. Ask friends for recommendations before choosing an agency to represent you. Obtain references from the agency.

Learn what types of jobs the agency handles and if you will be required to pay a fee for their services. Some positions in which temp agencies place people require that a fee be paid. This fee varies and could be paid by the job seeker, the employer, or be split between the two of them. Be sure to read the fine print of any contracts you sign.

You can sign up with several agencies if you wish. After you have worked on an assignment for the temp agency, ask for feedback on your job performance.

6

EXERCISE 6-A

Look in the yellow pages of your local phone book under "employment" and list the temporary agencies in your area in Table 6–1.

Include the names, addresses, Web sites, and telephone numbers of the agencies. If the agency has an ad that lists the kinds of jobs it specializes in, write down that information as well.

Table 6–1 POTENTIAL TEMPORARY AGENCIES CONTACT LIST

MY LIST OF POSSIBLE TEMPORARY AGENCIES TO CONTACT			
Company Name	Address	Telephone No.	Contact if Available

SIGN UP WITH STATE EMPLOYMENT AGENCIES

States have public employment offices to aid in your job search. These offices have daily contact with hundreds of employers, maintain multiple locations, and do not charge fees. State employment agencies offer free job counseling and training. Employment counselors at the agencies interview people who sign with them to determine their interests and qualifications. They offer help with resumes, filling out applications, searching for jobs, and interviewing. Some companies only hire through state employment services.

Check your phone book government pages, with your school placement office, or on the Internet for locations of agencies in your area. State and federal agencies do not charge a fee to find you a job.

Civil Service Exam

You might want to take the **Civil Service Exam**, which is a specific test required to work in government positions, in order to increase your job opportunities. Civil service jobs are located in cities and counties all over various states. The federal and local governments need a variety of employees. Check phone books and the Internet for locations where you can take the exam.

SIGN UP WITH PRIVATE EMPLOYMENT AGENCIES

Private employment agencies place people in jobs, but for a fee. The majority of these jobs are full-time, permanent positions. As with temp agencies, fees vary and could be paid by the job seeker, the employer, or be split between the two of them. Be sure to read carefully any contracts you sign.

Many private agencies will also help with resume and interview preparation for a fee. Check phone books and the Internet for agency locations in your area.

JOB FAIRS

Many cities and colleges put together **job fair**s that cater to general job seekers or fairs that are meant to attract specifically skilled individuals. These fairs give job seekers the opportunity to submit resumes to a number of businesses that are actively recruiting. Both the job seekers and employers benefit from job fairs because they can make lots of contacts in a single day at one location.

Be assertive when you attend a job fair. Gather company literature and find out what job skills and education are required at those companies. Contact as many employers as possible, sell your skills and personal traits through conversations, and schedule interviews. Keep a record of the names and titles of employers you speak with, and collect their **business cards**.

Of course, you will want to dress in your interview suit and carry your portfolio with several copies of your resume and reference sheet. Be sure to have plenty of business cards with you and hand them out to everyone with whom you talk. Act mature and professional in all ways.

6

RADIO AND TELEVISION ADVERTISEMENTS

Some companies advertise via local radio and television stations. Check your local listings for program times. In addition, commercials give valuable information about products and services that are selling, the current buying trends, and companies that make the products. Successful companies always need good employees.

SPECIALIZED MAGAZINES

Trade magazines and journals that are written for specialized industries often advertise for jobs in those fields. They also spotlight companies and their employees. You can also place a personal ad for a job in these publications.

Check with your school or local library for copies of trade magazines in your targeted career.

Hidden Jobs

Jobs that are not advertised to the public are called "hidden" or "invisible" jobs because it takes some searching to find them. If a job is available and an employer wants to fill it, why would he or she not advertise it to the public? Employers may choose not to advertise publicly for a number of reasons, including (1) they do not want to deal with the countless applicants a job advertisement draws, (2) they intend to go through applications they already have on file, (3) they may be using the services of an **employment agency** (a business that helps individuals find jobs and/or companies find employees), (4) they may be evaluating resumes from people who apply directly to the company, or (5) they may be soliciting referrals from current employees.

Your placement department may know of jobs not advertised to the public. As mentioned, employment agencies have job contacts not available to the public. Applying directly and sending resumes may uncover hidden jobs.

RESEARCHING THE COMPANY

To find out what an employer looks for in employees, research the company. Researching a company lets you know if your background meets company requirements. It also prepares you to give intelligent comments throughout an interview and positions you to ask good questions of your own. Researching shows that you are truly interested in working for a particular company and meeting the employer's needs.

Contact Companies

To obtain information, write or call the company and ask the receptionist to send an annual report or brochures on products and services. If the company has a newsletter, request one. It may give clues as to what company personnel are involved in and their interests, what is happening in the company, and trends in the industry. Check for a company Web site, where details on all aspects of the company and its employees might be mentioned. If possible, talk with people currently employed with the company.

The information you obtain may let you know what the company expects of its employees and how the company treats them. The company's mission statement should tell you whether your values align with those of the company.

Research is the key to formulating your career plans. Interviewers today expect job candidates to know something about their companies and products, especially since information is easier than ever to find. Learning something about the company shows a candidate is well prepared, which sets him or her apart from those who do not research.

WHEN CONDUCTING RESEARCH, FIND OUT THE FOLLOWING:

- What is the location of the company, and how many other locations does the company have?
- How many employees does the company have?
- What products and services are offered?
- What is the projected growth of the company?
- What are some of the job descriptions?
- Who are the executives in the company?
- What can you learn about the company's history?
- What is the company's mission statement?
- What are the company's policies and procedures?
- Is the company publicly or privately owned?
- What are the educational requirements for a position in the company?
- Is the company active in the community?
- Does the company encourage employees to be active in their communities?
- What is the company's reputation in the community?

Contact School Career Centers

If your school has a career center, take advantage of the resources it has available for researching companies. Career centers generally have information about industry trends and outlooks, local companies, specific job openings, salary, job descriptions, skills required for a position, and related Web sites.

Libraries

Check the reference section of your local library for publications, trade journals, and Web sites for the industry in which you want to

6

work. A few references are the *Occupational Outlook Handbook*, *Moody's Manual*, and *Thomas's Register*. In addition, some magazines and trade journals rate the top best companies for which to work.

Your library and school career center may also have sources for special job-seeking candidates, such as people of color, those who are disabled or have other special needs, the economically disadvantaged, women, those under the age of 21, and so forth.

EXERCISE 6-B

Select a company of interest to you and research the answers to the following questions. Write your answers in the space provided.

• Where is the company located?

_____

_____

• How many locations does the company have?

_____

_____

• How many employees work for the company?

_____

_____

• What products and services does this company offer?

_____

_____

• How long has this company been in business?

_____

_____

(Continued)

EXERCISE 6-B (Continued)

• What is this company's mission statement?

_____

_____

• Does this company have current job openings?

_____

_____

• Is the company publicly or privately owned?

_____

_____

• What are the educational requirements for positions in the company?

_____

_____

• What are some typical job descriptions for positions in the company?

_____

_____

• Does the company have a good reputation in the community?

_____

_____

• What is the projected growth of this company?

_____

_____

• How well is the company performing now?

_____

_____

• Who are the top executives?

_____

_____

6

NETWORKING CONTACTS AT THE EXTERNSHIP

Some ways you can find hidden jobs are through networking with friends and relatives. The externship position also opens new networking opportunities for you. Tell everyone you are looking for full-time work when you complete your externship. Ask your supervisor for guidance in updating your resume, answering interview questions, and searching for jobs.

Review the networking tips from Chapter 2.

INFORMATIONAL INTERVIEWS

Informational interviews can help you gain knowledge about various industries, job openings, and careers in a particular field. Conducting an informational interview with the right person can provide you with a wealth of company facts, as well as an understanding of what employers want. You may want to talk with an interviewer, or to another professional who is performing the duties you would like to do.

If you are not sure of the career path you want to take, conduct informational interviews in several different fields.

Be Prepared

Although an informational interview is not a formal job interview, prepare for it as if it were. Dress professionally and carry your portfolio with copies of your resume and reference sheet. Have a pen and paper for taking notes and a list of pertinent questions ready to ask.

Conduct an Informational Interview

Arrive a few minutes early, conduct yourself in a professional manner, and be respectful of the person you are interviewing and his or her time.

Ask the questions you have prepared, focusing on the positive aspect of the job/industry. Be an active listener by concentrating on the speaker's words and letting the speaker answer your questions without interruption. Maintain eye contact throughout the conversation, although it is all right to take notes. If you want to tape the interview, you must obtain permission.

At the end of the interview, ask questions about any confusing points you need to clarify or if something was said that you would like the speaker to expand upon. Then ask if there is anything he or she would like to add aside from your questions.

Ask the person you interviewed if he or she would mind looking through your portfolio to see if you have included adequate examples of your skills. Also ask him or her to read and critique your resume. Note any suggested changes and, if appropriate, implement them later.

Thank the person for his or her time and ask for a business card. Follow up by sending a thank-you letter or card within a day or two.

Informational Interview Questions

1. Are there new industry trends I should be aware of in this field?
2. What kinds of opportunities are there in this field? In this company?
3. What is the most challenging part of your job?
4. What advice would you give me about searching for information in this field?
5. What are the advantages and disadvantages in this field?
6. What specific advice do you have for me to advance in my career?
7. Who are the top professionals in this industry?
8. What professional organizations should I join?
9. What helped you the most when you applied for this job?
10. What kind of training would a new hire receive at your company?
11. How long is a typical interview?
12. What do you look for when interviewing candidates?
13. What else can I do to better prepare for a position in this industry?
14. How can a job candidate make a good impression in an interview?
15. Could you give me some sample interview questions?
16. Where can I find more information about this industry?
17. What skills and experience are required for a position such as yours?
18. What personal qualities are important in a job such as yours?
19. What are your specific duties?
20. Do you have a sample application I can have?

EXERCISE 6-C

Arrange and conduct an informational interview in your field of interest. Fill out the informational questionnaire in Figure 6–A, and be sure to also take note of the bulleted items that follow.

Figure 6–A SAMPLE QUESTIONS TO ASK AT AN INFORMATION
INTERVIEW

INFORMATIONAL INTERVIEW QUESTIONS

Name of Company _____   Date _____

Person Interviewed _____   Job Title _____

1. Are there new industry trends I should be aware in this field?

   _____

   _____

2. What kinds of opportunities are there in this field? In this company?

   _____

   _____

3. What is the most challenging part of your job?

   _____

   _____

4. What advice would you give me about searching for information in this field?

   _____

   _____

5. What are the advantages and disadvantages of working in this field?

   _____

   _____

6. What specific advice do you have for me to advance in my career?

   _____

   _____

(Continued)

FIGURE 6-A (Continued)

7. Who are the top professionals in this industry?

_____

_____

8. What professional organizations should I join?

_____

_____

9. What helped you the most when you applied for this job?

_____

_____

10. What kind of training would a new hire receive at your company?

_____

_____

11. How long is a typical interview in this company?

_____

_____

12. What do you look for when interviewing candidates?

_____

_____

13. What else can I do to better prepare for a position in this industry?

_____

_____

14. How can a job candidate make a good impression in an interview?

_____

_____

15. Could you give me some sample interview questions?

_____

_____

(Continued)

6

FIGURE 6-A (Continued)

16. Where can I find more information about this industry?

_____

_____

17. What skills and experience are required for a position such as yours?

_____

_____

18. What personal qualities are important in a job such as yours?

_____

_____

19. What are your specific duties?

_____

_____

20. Do you have a sample application I can have?

_____

_____

Tips & Tricks

- Take a list of questions such as the ones provided in this chapter or some of your own.
- Carry a portfolio and resume.
- Take a pen and paper.
- Dress professionally.
- Conduct yourself in a professional manner.
- Arrive on time.
- Respect the interviewer's time.
- Ask for a business card.
- Ask for a referral—someone else with whom it might be helpful to talk.
- Follow up by sending a thank-you note or card.

WHERE TO LOCATE INFORMATION ON COMPANIES

▶ Talk to employees.

▶ Call or write the company.

▶ Search the Internet.

▶ Look through catalogs.

▶ Contact the local Chamber of Commerce.

▶ Read *Standard and Poor's*.

▶ Talk with network contacts.

▶ Read annual reports.

▶ Read newsletters.

▶ Contact the Small Business Administration.

▶ Read *Moody's Industrial Journal*.

▶ Research at the library.

WHAT TO KNOW ABOUT A COMPANY

▶ Location(s).

▶ Products and services currently offered.

▶ Future plans.

▶ Job openings.

▶ Names of top-level employees.

▶ Number of employees.

▶ Company profitability.

▶ New products and services the company plans to offer in the future.

▶ Company mission statement.

▶ Years the company has been in business.

▶ Educational requirements for jobs.

6

❱ Whether the company is publicly or privately owned

❱ Job descriptions

❱ The company's reputation in the community

❱ What the company looks for in its employees

UPDATING YOUR INTERVIEW SKILLS

Hopefully, the externship experience will increase your self-confidence and communication skills as you learned how to conduct yourself in a professional manner. You should be able to transfer these traits to the interview by greeting the interviewer with a self-assured smile and handshake, direct eye contact, and confident answers.

After observing professionals in the externship workplace, you should have a good idea of appropriate dress. For an interview, a suit is appropriate for both men and women. You will want to dress a step above regular workplace attire for your field. Pay attention to details, including shoes, accessories, hygiene, and hair.

Prepare yourself for questions (such as those listed in Chapter 2) by thinking about your education and work backgrounds, skills, abilities, and the externship. Be honest and straightforward, answering with enthusiasm. Discuss research you have done on the company. Update your portfolio and look for an opening to present it. Review the interview tips in Chapter 2. Send a thank-you letter as soon as possible.

LEARNING TO SELL YOURSELF

Prepare yourself for the interview mentally by researching the company and thinking about answers to questions you may be asked. Prepare yourself physically by getting plenty of rest, avoiding stress, dressing professionally, and having the right tools. These tools include your resume, reference sheet, application, portfolio, and business cards.

FILLING OUT AN APPLICATION

Add your externship to the experience section when filling out an application. Generally, this will be the first experience listed. The procedure for filling out an application was discussed in Chapter 2. Review the procedure.

Include the name, address, and phone number of your externship company, as well as the dates of employment, duties performed, and responsibilities. Supervisors may be added to the reference section. For the position held, indicate externship and/or the name of the position.

Look over the tips for filling out applications in Chapter 2.

UPDATING YOUR RESUME

Update your resume by adding the externship position under work experience. Because employers are interested in a current, successful work history, list the externship experience first. Include the company name, address, and telephone number. Pay particular attention to job duties and responsibilities, listing them in detail. You may list a supervisor's name in the work experience section, or else list it on the reference sheet.

You will need to update your reference sheet to reflect any references you would like to use from your externship. These references may include your supervisor, others for whom you did work, and coworkers.

Review the information in the section on writing the resume and reference sheet in Chapter 2 when you are ready to update.

UPDATING YOUR PORTFOLIO

Update your portfolio with your externship information. Include a current resume, reference sheet, any employment awards, seminar participation certificates, and anything else you feel will assist you in getting a job. In addition, ask your externship supervisor for a **recommendation letter**. Employers often write recommendation letters for individuals who have performed well on the job. These letters are an asset to the job seekers' portfolio, as they may attest to his or her abilities, character traits, and employability. Ask your

6

externship supervisor and/or employer to write you a letter of recommendation when you leave an externship or job. Perspective employers look favorably on such letters when they vouch for your ability, skills, and work ethic.

If possible, include sample documents of the types of software you used and the work you did during the externship, such as documents in Word, spreadsheets in Excel, and PowerPoint presentations. Be sure to ask permission from your externship supervisor if you wish to include any documents from there.

Carry the portfolio to every interview; be alert for an opportunity to show the portfolio to the interviewer. Check Chapter 2 for a list of items to include in the portfolio.

PREPARING BUSINESS CARDS

All professionals should carry business cards. Therefore, have business cards printed with your contact information, and carry them with you at all times. Exchange cards with people you meet that you would like to have in your network. This gives individuals a permanent record of your name, address, and phone number, and you will have theirs as well. After you have been given a business card, take the time later to jot down on the back of the card where and when you met. Add any other pertinent information such as mutual interests and ideas you share.

Business cards should look professional. Use easy-to-read fonts and a good quality card stock. Arrange information in a simple format, and avoid cutesy pictures and sayings. Include your name, address, telephone number, and your title or profession. Optional information includes fax and cell phone numbers, and an e-mail or Website address. Most people today, however, do include e-mail addresses on their cards.

Always carry a notebook, pen, and business cards with you. After you meet people, record information you have received, as well as information about the person who provided it. Once you have gathered names, business cards, and information through networking, set up a system to organize everything. Use a flexible, easy system.

Figure 6–B

SAMPLE BUSINESS CARDS

BUSINESS CARDS

💻 Arletta Oberlindy
Accountant

9995 River Road, South
Pittsburgh, PA 15223
412-223-8767
aoberlindy@net.com

✈ Arletta Oberlindy
Travel Agent

9995 River Road, South, Pittsburgh, PA 15223
412-223-8767   aoberlindy@net.com

EXERCISE 6-D

Design a business card for yourself. Include your name, address, telephone number (including area code), e-mail address, and title or type of work desired. You may include a cell phone number, a fax number, and a professional-looking logo.

If possible, type and print your business cards, or have a professional business card company design and print them.

END OF CHAPTER WORK

CASE STUDY

● EXTERNSHIP NETWORKING CASE STUDY

Maria did an externship at a small medical supply company, where she was an administrative assistant. Three weeks before Maria's externship was to end, her supervisor told her of a position that had recently opened in another department. Maria wanted the position, but was not sure how to go about getting it.

6

Questions to Ask Yourself

1. Should Maria ask her supervisor for advice?

     _____

     _____

2. Should Maria simply submit an application on her own?

     _____

     _____

Things to Consider

Since Maria's supervisor told her about the position, Maria would be wise to seek her assistance in applying for the job. The supervisor must have thought Maria would be suited to the position if she mentioned the job to her. Maria should definitely inform the supervisor that she is interested in the position.

Maria could seek the supervisor's help in updating her resume to reflect her externship responsibilities and in updating her portfolio. She could ask if there is anything extra she should do to obtain the position.

END OF CHAPTER QUESTIONS

1. Why is it a good idea to ask for a recommendation letter from your externship supervisor?

2. How should you update your resume after you have finished your externship?

3. What should you include on your business card?

4. What information should be listed on the application with regard to the externship?

5. Why might an employer prefer to hire an extern?

6. Is it appropriate to take copies of tasks you completed for the company you are working for, to include them in your portfolio?

7. How could you benefit from a job fair?

8. Name three places where you can find job leads for a permanent position.

9. Who would be an important network contact from an externship experience?

10. What are two advantages of finding a job through a temporary agency?

6

CHAPTER 7

Achieving Professional Success

LEARNING OBJECTIVES

After completing this chapter, you should be able to:

1. Create a positive professional image.
2. Dress professionally.
3. Identify and use professional language.
4. Maintain a positive attitude.
5. Work cooperatively with supervisors.
6. Work cooperatively with coworkers.
7. Create a positive work environment.
8. Solve problems through critical thinking.
9. Research where to learn new skills.
10. Set goals and motivate yourself.
11. Create an action plan for attaining goals.

Chapter 7 discusses how you can develop a positive professional image and maintain success in the workplace. Ideas are presented on dealing with supervisors and coworkers, creating a positive environment, and developing professionalism. You will also learn how to set goals and create an action plan that will help you meet those goals.

KEY TERMS

action plan	casual business dress	lifelong learning
attitude	critical thinking	professional attire
career goals	dress code	professional image
career plan	judgment errors	professional language

INTRODUCTION

Working in a satisfying position doing enjoyable tasks in a company with an ethical mission statement brings success. Working in a company that has a positive image in the community, maintains good relationships with its customers, and employs professional people increases your chances of achieving professional success. A number of other things will ensure your professional success, including (1) setting goals, (2) maintaining a positive **attitude** or manner, (3) dressing and behaving in a professional manner, (4) using business language, (5) dealing positively with supervisors and coworkers, and (6) learning new skills and technology.

MAP OUT A CAREER PLAN

A road map guides you along your journey, helping you to reach your destination in a timely, efficient manner. Similarly, a **career plan** guides you in finding the right job, helping you to secure a position that allows you to enjoy career success. With some direction and guidance, you can match yourself to a job that encourages you to use your strengths.

EXERCISE 7-A

In Chapter 1 you completed several self-assessments to gain an in-depth knowledge of your likes and dislikes, strengths and weaknesses, skills, knowledge, and personality traits. Taking these self-assessments into account, answer the following questions in the space provided. Thoughtful, specific answers will assure that your career plan map will put you on the right track.

1. What is your concept of an ideal job?

_____

_____

_____

(Continued)

EXERCISE 7-A (Continued)

2. What is most important to you in a job?

_____

_____

_____

3. Who do you feel are the ideal coworkers?

_____

_____

_____

4. What is the perfect work environment for you?

_____

_____

_____

5. How much time do you expect to commit to your ideal job?

_____

_____

_____

6. What are your strengths? Weaknesses?

_____

_____

_____

7. What tasks would you enjoy performing?

_____

_____

_____

8. Where do you see yourself in five years?

_____

_____

_____

(Continued)

EXERCISE 7-A (Continued)

9. Do you need more training or education for your ideal job?

_____

_____

_____

10. For which are you looking, a job or a career?

_____

_____

_____

TYPES OF GOALS

After you have answered the questions about the job, tasks, environment, and coworkers you are looking for, you are positioned to set **career goals** and map your route to success. Setting goals will help you focus your time and energy in the right direction. Without goals to give you direction, you might wander aimlessly and accomplish little.

Goals should be challenging enough so that you will put forth your best effort to attain them, but not so difficult that they are unreachable.

Defining and setting main goals, secondary goals, personal goals, and career goals are covered in this chapter. It is important to set goals in each of these categories.

Main Goals

Main goals are the basic ones that you set for much of your life. You will find yourself continuously striving toward the achievement of these goals, as they will be what you desire most in life and what you constantly work toward achieving.

Main goals might include these among others: (1) attain a career, (2) obtain a degree, (3) get married, (4) buy a sports car, and/or (5) purchase a house. It may take years of determination to satisfy your main goals.

Secondary Goals

Secondary goals are more flexible than main ones and may change according to your wants and needs. They may be revised or eliminated as you change and grow. Therefore, secondary goals may be important to you one day, but not the next. For example, you might set a career in travel as a secondary goal. While you are working toward a travel degree, let us assume you take a part-time job as a salesperson and have to travel a good bit. After traveling for a year, you decide you would rather settle down in one place and spend more time at home with your family. As a result, you change your goal of a travel career. In this case, your goal of attaining a degree in travel will subsequently end, too.

Just because secondary goals may change, you should not fail to give those goals the action they deserve. They were important to you when you set them, and they may never change.

Personal Goals

Personal goals indicate what you want out of life. They represent the standards you hold for yourself, such as maintaining integrity. Personal goals include things like the type of person you hope to become and the kind of legacy you want to leave behind. They may include career goals but will encompass not only career skills but also customer service skills.

Career Goals

As the name implies, career goals are those you hope to attain throughout your work experiences. These goals include what position you want, what tasks you want to do, and a step-by-step plan for advancing in your career. Career goals may include a desire for higher wages, a prestigious position, challenging duties, and good benefits.

Some career goals will be set for you by people at work, such as having a certain sales quota you must reach. Others you will set for yourself, such as those regarding the pay, benefits, and advancement you will accept.

The career goals you set will affect your ability to find a job you like and advance in it.

7

EXERCISE 7-B

On the lines provided, answer these questions:

• Where do you see yourself in a year?

_____

_____

• Where do you see yourself in 5 years?

_____

_____

• What are your long-term career objectives?

_____

_____

• What is most important to you in a career?

_____

_____

• How much do you expect to earn in 5 years?

_____

_____

• What position do you aspire to attain during your career?

_____

_____

• How do you plan to achieve your goals?

_____

_____

DETERMINE GOALS

Along with setting goals, you will need to list the steps you must take in order to reach them. Set short-term (days, weeks, months), intermediate (1–5 years), and long-term goals (5 years or longer). Goals must be specific, tangible, and measurable.

State specifically what you hope to achieve. For example, "find a job" is too vague a statement. Instead state, "I will send out ten resumes a week." Make the goal specific so you will know just how to focus your energy and time. It is difficult to know how to go about arriving at a vague goal, because you are not sure what it is you are going after in the first place.

Attach a timeframe to goals. Having a target date will encourage you to take the time necessary to work on goals. Otherwise, too much time could pass without your having achieved anything at all.

Goals must be measurable so you will know how far you have come, how much farther you must go, and whether you have reached them. "I will send out ten resumes a week" is a goal that is specific and has a timeframe. It is also measurable, because you will know if and when you reach it. If possible, keep a written record of your progress.

Create both short- and long-term goals, and state them in positive language. To increase your chances of success, write goals down. Written goals create realism, and you are more likely to go after and attain them.

Take into consideration your skills and abilities to make goals attainable. If you have little or no chance of reaching goals, you set yourself up for defeat before you start. Goals should be something you really want; do some serious contemplating and be honest with yourself. The more you want a goal, the harder you will work toward it, and the faster it will materialize.

SET GOALS

Before setting career goals, refer to your personal assessments from Chapter 1. Match your interests, skills, abilities, and education to a potential career so you have a likelihood of succeeding.

EXERCISE 7-C

Answer these questions on the lines provided.

• What are you willing to do to reach your career goals?

_____

_____

(Continued)

7

EXERCISE 7-C (Continued)

- How much time and energy are you willing to spend on attaining career goals?

  _____

  _____

- How do your career goals relate to your values?

  _____

  _____

- How long do you estimate it will take to reach your career goals?

  _____

  _____

- Do your career goals reflect your interests?

  _____

  _____

- Do your career goals reflect your abilities?

  _____

  _____

EXERCISE 7-D

Refer to your answers for Exercises 7-C and 7-D to determine a short-term and a long-term goal. Fill in these goals in Figure 7–1. Create additional forms if you would like to set more goals.

FIGURE 7–1

SETTING GOALS SHEET

Short-term Goal

_____

_____

Begin date _____

End date _____

(Continued)

FIGURE 7–1 (Continued)

Long-term Goal _____

_____

_____

Begin date _____

End date _____

CREATE AN ACTION PLAN

An **action plan** is a map that charts a path toward a goal. Looking at a large, time-consuming task is daunting and so can working toward goals be. Therefore, it is much easier to reach goals when they are broken down into steps or tasks. Think in terms of a step-by-step plan of action. Make each step a reasonable action you can complete. Ask yourself what one step you can take right now to get started reaching your goals.

A series of steps, arranged in logical order, should be prepared for each goal. Finding something you can do every day to move toward the goal will keep you on target.

Take into consideration your strengths, preferences, and personality by creating a plan you will be able to follow. There is no benefit to designing an elaborate plan that requires strict discipline if you are an undisciplined person who most likely will not carry through. Make a plan that will work for you by building on your strengths.

PRIORITIZE

After you have determined your goals and set up an action plan, prioritize. Begin with the goal that is most important to you and work on it. Look at the steps you have recorded for attaining the goal and arrange them in the most effective order. Then, take the first step on your action plan. Work your way through the steps as time and energy permit, completing each until your goal is reached. It is fine to work on more than one goal at a time if you prefer, but do not set an overwhelming number of them.

7

EXERCISE 7-E

In Figure 7–2 create an action plan for each of the goals you wrote down in Figure 7–1. Be sure to take your strengths and personality traits into consideration.

FIGURE 7–2

ACTION PLAN SHEET

Action plan

Goal _____

_____

Begin Date _____

End Date _____

Steps to achieve

1. _____

2. _____

3. _____

4. _____

Action plan

Goal _____

_____

Begin Date _____

End Date _____

Steps to achieve

1. _____

2. _____

3. _____

4. _____

FOCUS ON GOALS

Staying focused on goals keeps them embedded in your mind. Taking steps toward them every day brings them closer to reality. Through persistence and enthusiasm, all realistic goals can be reached. Create a clear picture in your mind of what you want to accomplish. When visualizing a goal, bring as many of your senses as possible into play by asking: What does the goal look like? What does it feel like? Does it have a smell? Does it have a sound? How will it feel when you achieve the goal?

Never let setbacks and frustration keep you from achieving success. Many people fall short of goals because they lack the stamina necessary to eliminate obstacles. Knowing how goals benefit you and others gives them importance and creates the desire to work toward attainment. How will reaching your goals benefit you? How will reaching them benefit others?

Picture yourself reaching your goals, tell yourself you have achieved them, and believe that you have. Reward yourself when you accomplish a goal.

Be Flexible

If a goal no longer meets your needs, change it or eliminate it. This is not to say you should give up on a goal that is hard to conquer. Sometimes, though, life situations make goals obsolete or no longer desirable, as pointed out in the discussion about the travel career in the section on secondary goals.

Be flexible, and periodically re-examine your goals. Adjust them as you change and grow. Goals should reflect your beliefs and values, which also may change with time and circumstances.

Be Positive

Taking the right steps and remaining positive lead to goal success. Never let self-defeating thoughts keep you from setting and reaching your goals. Posting goals where they can be seen daily keeps them solidly in mind. To use this valuable technique, write your goals on sticky notes or 3 × 5" cards and post them where you will see them. Repeat goals to yourself often, and believe hard work and dedication will achieve them.

If you hit a roadblock or have a setback, refocus and do what you can do to eliminate the problem. Keep the vision of your completed goal firmly in your mind.

7

EXERCISE 7-F

On the lines provided, answer these questions to arrive at suitable goals.

1. What do you want to do most in life?

_____

_____

2. Is it possible for you to do this?

_____

_____

3. If it is possible, when do you hope to be doing this?

_____

_____

4. What is most important to you in life?

_____

_____

5. What is most important to you in a career?

_____

_____

6. Are you prepared for this career?

_____

_____

7. Why did you choose the career path or course that you chose?

_____

_____

8. How are you preparing for this career?

_____

_____

(Continued)

EXERCISE 7-F (Continued)

9. Do you need additional skills and education for the career?

_____

_____

10. Have you developed a plan for achieving your goals?

_____

_____

11. Did you set career goals?

_____

_____

12. Do you know what the first step is that you will take to reach your goal?

_____

_____

13. Can you take this step now?

_____

_____

14. Do you have a timeframe for achieving your goal?

_____

_____

15. Are you fully committed to your goals?

_____

_____

PROFESSIONAL IMAGE

Professionals are self-confident experts who handle tasks in a competent, efficient manner. They know what needs to be done and do it in a timely, accurate manner. Professionals keep up-to-date on technology and industry changes while continuously looking for

7

ways to do things more effectively. They constantly work on improving their skills, developing good judgment, dressing impeccably, and maintaining positive personal traits. Professionals think critically and creatively to solve problems and complete their tasks. They can work independently or on a team and are able to assume leadership roles when necessary. Professionals possess excellent written, oral, and listening communication skills, and they help others attain professionalism. The combination of all these traits is what creates a professional image. This image impacts dealings with customers, coworkers, and supervisors in a positive way. Therefore, companies strive to hire and keep people who maintain a **professional image**.

This chapter gives pointers on creating and continuing a professional image that will take you far in your career. Information is given on dress, behavior, **critical thinking**, goal setting, and keeping skills and education up-to-date. Putting forth the effort to become the best you can be requires self-discipline and hard work, two qualities of the professional. Displaying these qualities pays big dividends.

Chapter 1 discussed the personal characteristics that generate success. Review these; you will need to develop them in order to create a professional image. Chapter 3 provided information on becoming a better communicator, which is a trait of all professionals.

Although it takes time and energy to build a positive professional image, it can easily be destroyed with one negative incident. Protect your image by doing and saying the right things at all times.

POSITIVE ATTITUDE

Your attitude will determine your success or failure in life and throughout your career. It affects your thoughts, behavior, and interactions with others, and it determines the way everyone views you. Because your attitude is such a driving force, it is extremely important to cultivate the right attitude, which is a positive one.

A positive attitude makes tasks enjoyable, draws customers and coworkers to you, and creates a pleasant working environment. It gives you more energy and sees you through stressful, demanding times. It would be difficult to keep on going if you were negative. A positive attitude will impact your career as you continuously strive to improve yourself, perform your tasks well, increase your knowledge, and interact with others.

Positive individuals are sincere, helpful, dependable, loyal, and genuinely interested in helping others and making them feel important. Positive individuals take the initiative and perform their duties whether someone is watching or not. They look for the good in others and do not make negative comments about supervisors, coworkers, or the company. Positive individuals feel good about themselves, their jobs, and other people; their eagerness and enthusiasm show. People are drawn to, and enjoy being around, those who are positive.

BUILD A POSITIVE ATTITUDE

How can you create a positive attitude that will bring you success? One way is to use positive self-talk to build self-esteem and self-confidence. That is, tell yourself you can do whatever it is you need to do (i.e., your job duties) and that you are a worthwhile individual.

Concentrate on your talents, reminding yourself that you have many. If your skills are limited, you can always learn new ones (additional information on that in the Leaning New Skills section).

Another way to remain positive is to be grateful. Appreciating what you have gives you an optimistic outlook. Make a list of all the things you have to be thankful for and review it periodically. No matter what situation we find ourselves in, all of us can list many things.

In addition, do the things you enjoy such as socializing with friends, laughing, working on a hobby, watching uplifting movies, reading motivational books, eating healthy, exercising, being flexible, meeting challenges, communicating, playing with children and pets, and the like. Even while working or cleaning, you can listen to your favorite music, repeat positive sayings to yourself, or take mental breaks. Listen to motivational tapes while driving and plan your day to reduce stress. Take the time to create the right mental atmosphere.

7

EXERCISE 7-G

Fill out the attitude evaluation in Table 7–1.

Table 7–1   SELF-EVALUATION: PROFESSIONAL ATTITUDES AT WORK

ANSWER THE FOLLOWING QUESTIONS ABOUT YOUR ATTITUDE:	Yes	No
• Do you remain positive at work?		
• Do you remain positive while performing your tasks?		
• Do you face challenging situations with a positive attitude?		
• Do you put difficult situations in perspective?		
• Do you look for additional ways to be more effective at putting difficult situations in perspective?		
• Do you make the best of situations?		
• Do you look for the good in others?		
• Does your attitude affect your mood in a positive way?		
• Does your attitude affect your coworkers in a positive way?		
• Do you relate well to others?		
• Do you remain positive whenever you have a task to do that you dislike?		
• Do you do your part to create a pleasant atmosphere?		

Note: If you checked *no* to any of the questions, research ways to improve yourself in those areas.

AVOID NEGATIVISM

A negative attitude repels others, creates a hostile work environment, and makes a drudgery out of completing tasks. A negative attitude drains energy from you and those around you, creates stress, and leaves you feeling frustrated. Avoid negativism.

EXERCISE 7-H

Think of someone who is a positive individual. How do you suppose this person maintains a positive attitude? Write your answer in the space provided.

_____

_____

_____

Talk to this person (or another positive person). Ask for pointers to help you maintain a positive attitude. What did you learn? Write your answer in the space provided.

_____

_____

_____

MAINTAIN A POSITIVE ATTITUDE

Attitude awareness gives you a sense of your feelings and moods. Be aware of the kind of attitude you carry around with you—positive or negative—and how it affects other people. Because our moods change, it is a good idea to re-examine our attitudes from time to time and adjust them as needed.

Oftentimes it takes work to maintain a positive attitude, especially if you are exposed to a negative environment, coworkers, or supervisors. Poor communication and misunderstandings can damage work relationships and create an undesirable situation. If communications seem strained, sit down and talk things over with the person involved. Refrain from assuming the worst; rather, hear the other person out and be open to a compromise.

If your attitude sags, lift it by focusing on the positives in life. Looking at the bright side is preferable to complaining and staying in

7

a rut. Read and listen to motivational materials, and repeat positive sayings to yourself such as, "I enjoy my job and concentrate on my tasks fully, shutting out any negativity." Avoid negative people as much as possible. Take the time to relax on weekends and socialize with friends. When you are away from the office, put the place out of your mind.

Stress and deadlines are draining. To reduce stress, manage your time and be flexible. Take mind breaks, where you visualize a pleasant place like the beach. If possible, bring a personal item or two (a picture or plant) to the office that will give you a boost when you need one.

It is difficult to remain positive when suffering from poor health. Therefore, take time to relax, get enough sleep, exercise, and eat right. Spend time enjoying family, friends, hobbies, and whatever makes you happy. Expose your mind to uplifting situations, people, and material to keep it positive. Avoid snacks that give you a quick burst of energy, followed by a quick drop.

Boredom can be depressing. To prevent the routine of a daily job from becoming boring, challenge yourself and look for interesting ways to perform tasks.

By focusing on the positive aspects of your job, you can appreciate it and your company. There are many things you can do to stay positive as shown in the Maintain a Positive Attitude tips list.

Tips & Tricks

Maintain a Positive Attitude

- Examine your attitude periodically.
- Focus on the positive aspects of your job.
- Keep the lines of communication open between employees and supervisors.
- Accept change and be flexible.
- Look for ways to keep your job challenging.
- Smile and laugh often.
- Maintain your health.
- Relax on weekends.

(Continued)

Tips & Tricks (Continued)

- Read positive, motivational books and articles.
- Repeat positive sayings to yourself.
- Look for the good in others.
- Look at the bright side of situations.
- Focus on life's positives.
- Enjoy a hobby.
- Watch uplifting movies.
- Socialize with friends.
- Exercise.

EXERCISE 7-I

On the lines provided, make a list of the things you currently do to maintain a positive attitude.

_____

_____

_____

_____

Are the things you currently do enough to keep you in a positive frame of mind the majority of the time?

_____

What else can you do to be more positive?

_____

_____

_____

_____

7

CREATE A POSITIVE ENVIRONMENT

Working in a positive environment is certainly preferable to working in a negative one. An upbeat environment makes for pleasant working relationships and conditions, where people actually enjoy being at work. One negative person can spoil the environment, so everyone must do his or her part to create a positive environment by cultivating beneficial working relationships with others. Petty arguments, gossip, and rumors do not belong in the workplace and tend to escalate over time.

Be cooperative and keep the lines of communication open in order to exchange information and ideas, solve problems, and attain your personal goals and the company's goals. Look for the best in everyone, and treat people courteously. Avoid arguments, ignore little daily irritations, and be an active member of the company team. Friendly greetings and smiles go a long way toward creating a pleasurable setting.

Refrain from taking sides in coworker arguments. Do not join in gossip sessions, especially when it ruins reputations and causes hard feelings. Maintain a distance from people who have negative attitudes that bring everyone down. If it is impossible to avoid them, draw on your own positive attitude whenever they are near.

Creating a pleasant work environment requires people to respect one another's space and property. Do not encroach on people's workspace, take their things without permission, or go through their drawers and cabinets. Clean up after yourself in the areas you share, such as the employees' lounge and lunchroom. Do not leave your belongings lying around. Be considerate with equipment you share such as copiers, printers, and fax machines.

PROFESSIONAL ATTIRE

Professional attire includes suits, dress slacks and jackets, and coordinated outfits. Imagine how the CEO of a company, the head of a nonprofit agency, a politician giving a speech, and a lawyer arguing a case in court would dress. Quite likely you will picture these people dressed in professional attire. Of course, clothing should be clean, pressed, and well-fitted.

Professionally attired individuals consider their total look, paying attention to details such as shoes, purses, and other accessories. To complete their look, these individuals opt for neat, attractive haircuts.

Planning what to wear to work is an important decision because your appearance speaks volumes about you. People judge you by your appearance. They form an impression of your appearance in face-to-face contact that will run through their minds in all dealings with you.

A neat, orderly appearance conveys that a person is confident, efficient, well-organized, and capable. A sloppy, casual dress may give the impression the person's work is sloppy. Dressing too casually may imply that an individual is not career-minded or even that they are careless.

Companies have an image they expect their employees to uphold, and they may have a particular **dress code** in place which dictates what the proper attire is for that particular workplace. If the company has a dress code, everyone is expected to follow it. If there is no dress code, ask about appropriate attire. Every employee should present a neat, clean appearance daily, whether there is a written dress code or not.

If you aspire to advance in a company, dress in clothes that mean business. Dressing professionally gives you a greater chance to move up in the organization. If you want to fit in and advance, you must look the part and send the right message.

> **ASK YOURSELF THESE QUESTIONS:**
> - What does your clothing say about you?
> - Do you convey the message you want?
> - How should you dress to maintain a professional appearance?

LOOK THE PART

A professional is well-groomed and dressed in quality, conservative clothing. For a clearer picture of the professional, imagine how you would expect a top CEO or the president of a large company to dress. Chances are these individuals dress conservatively in well-tailored, well-pressed business attire. In general, professionals present the ultimate image.

Professional dress includes well-pressed suits or jackets with white blouses or shirts; coordinated outfits; tailored slacks, skirts, dresses, and/or other fashionable clothing styles; polished shoes; and matching accessories.

Men should wear blue, gray, or black solid or pin-stripe suits with white or pale-colored shirts. Coordinate ties with shirts and jackets. Stripes and solid colors are best for ties. Wear dress socks that cover the calf in a color that matches trousers and shoes. Remove rings and other jewelry from facial piercings. Men should not wear earrings.

7

Women should limit the number of accessories they wear (i.e., one pair of earrings and one ring on each hand, unless it is a wedding band set). Do not wear flashy, bright jewelry that interferes with the performance of tasks. Remove rings and other jewelry from facial piercings. Scarves should match the outfit, and shoes and hosiery should be the color of the hem of slacks or skirts, or else a lighter shade.

Women should wear moderate makeup, keeping in mind that daytime makeup should be applied with a lighter touch than that for evening wear. Hair should be neatly cut and styled.

Choose quality accessories and leather belts and briefcases. Wear appropriate clothing that covers tattoos and body piercings.

CASUAL BUSINESS DRESS

If other employees do not wear suits and ties, you will not have to either. Many companies have a **casual business dress** code, which means employees do not wear suits; however, they do wear good quality dress slacks, blouses, shirts, skirts, sweaters, and jackets. Business casual should not be confused with the more relaxed dress of jeans and t-shirts.

Companies have different degrees of casual business attire. One company's business casual may be as strict as another's regular dress code; another's might include golf shirts and khakis. In general, business casual may mean a jacket with slacks or a skirt, shirts and blouses, sweaters, knit tops, khakis, and polo shirts. As with professional dress, all casual clothing should be clean, well-pressed, well-fitted, and fashionable.

Most business offices do not permit jeans and t-shirts as acceptable attire. If t-shirts are permitted, they should not be sloppy, dirty, torn, or display any controversial sayings.

Wear well-maintained, well-heeled shoes that show you pay attention to details. Polish shoes often, and coordinate them with outfits. Women should not wear spiked heels, opened-toed shoes, tennis shoes, or sandals. Men should not wear tennis shoes or sandals.

DRESS UP

Dress a step above the position that you currently hold if you hope to advance. Take a look at the people whose jobs you would like to have or those who are in higher-level positions within the company. What are they wearing? Suits and ties? Better quality casual wear? Model their dress and behavior, but avoid standing out too much from the other company personnel.

Some company decision-makers will not promote employees who are not professionally dressed, even if they have the skills and knowledge to advance. It is often all about the image you project.

FOLLOW THE COMPANY DRESS CODE

Many companies have dress code rules that govern acceptable attire for their employees. This dress code may be written or unwritten. If there is a written dress code, follow it. In a professional business office, you will be expected to dress in accordance with the policy. If you do not, you may be sent home, or a warning may be placed in your file.

If there is no written dress code, observe what others wear. Do employees wear business suits or sweaters and khaki slacks? Observing both men's and women's dress habits will give you an idea of how formal or casual the company's dress code is. If uncertain, it is better to overdress than to underdress. Attempt to fit in with the group, but dress tastefully.

Different types of jobs require different styles of clothing. If employed in a large city law firm, you may be required to wear suits. If you work in a factory, you may be permitted to wear jeans. Companies that have several locations may have different dress requirements for each location. For instance, a company's plant in a rural area may have a lax dress code, whereas that same company's city headquarters may have a professional one.

Take note of how employees dress when they attend meetings with customers or go on business trips or to conventions. Even on casual dress days, it is important to dress professionally for meetings with customers so they feel you are competent. If you have several meetings or VIP appointments, you should upgrade your dress for the day to leave a favorable impression. If you do not feel confident with the way you are dressed, change into something more suitable.

UNIFORMS

If you work in a service industry such as a restaurant or hotel, you may be required to wear a uniform. If other employees in your company wear uniforms, you will probably be required to wear one, too. When you wear uniforms, be sure to keep them clean, in good repair, and well-pressed. A uniform does not give you an excuse to be careless in your dress.

7

CLOTHING GUIDELINES

Buy clothing suited for the work you do. A factory worker, an office manager, a banker, and an accountant will dress differently. The factory worker would be foolish to wear a suit, for it would be ruined. If the banker wore coveralls on the job, he or she would not seem very trustworthy or professional.

Clothes should fit well and feel comfortable. Choose fabrics that are easy to care for and are durable, such as linen, cotton, wool, and silk. Select colors that compliment you, but avoid bold, overly bright colors and patterns. Think conservatively for business offices. Blues, grays, and black are good choices. Dry-clean or wash and press clothes after each wearing.

Think of clothing as an investment in your career, and choose wisely. Purchase basic items that you can mix and match and around which you can build your wardrobe. These items may include black or navy dress slacks and skirts, white or pale-colored shirts and blouses, and jackets in conservative colors. Match colors and designs properly; do not mix stripes and plaids.

When shopping for clothing on a limited budget, watch for sales at department stores on quality clothing that is fashionable. Also, check secondhand shops, which often have gently worn outfits for a fraction of the original price. Check Web sites for bargains and for nonprofit organizations that help low-income individuals.

There are many books on fashion, professional dress, and color that will be helpful when you are planning your career wardrobe. The Internet is also a source of information on workplace clothing styles.

PROPER HYGIENE

In all cases, you will be expected to wear appropriate attire, be well groomed, and use good hygiene in the workplace. Wear deodorant or antiperspirant; do not offend others by giving off offensive odors. Keep hair, body, teeth, and fingernails clean. Dry-clean or wash clothing after each wear.

Trim nails, beards, and mustaches. Wear hairstyles that suit your job. Cooks and servers may be required to wear their hair off the face and in a hairnet. Employment in a conservative business office means that quality haircuts and styles are in order.

Use perfume and aftershave sparingly, being aware that others may have allergies or sensitivities to them. The same applies to scented hair products and hand creams.

EXERCISE 7-J

Check several Web sites for pictures of CEOs and other high-level company professionals. Pay attention to how they dress and wear their hair. In the space provided, list the details that stand out to make them look professional.

_____

_____

_____

Make a list of things you can do to enhance your own appearance to fit the workforce you intend to enter.

_____

_____

_____

Tips & Tricks

Proper Business Dress

- Suits and coordinated outfits
- Polished shoes
- Fashionable, flattering clothing
- Conservative makeup
- Accessories coordinated with outfits
- Adherence to company dress code
- Tasteful clothing
- Conservative, flattering colors
- Cleaned and pressed clothing
- Comfortable, well-fitting clothing
- Easy-to-care-for fabrics
- Conservative jewelry
- Quality briefcases

7

Tips & Tricks

Grooming/Hygiene Tips

- Bathe/shower daily
- Shampoo hair often
- Style hair daily
- Brush teeth and use mouthwash
- Wear deodorant or antiperspirant
- Manicure nails
- Trim beards and mustaches
- Use perfume/aftershave sparingly
- Cover tattoos and body piercings
- Wear moderate makeup
- Use scented hair products sparingly

EXERCISE 7-K

Check your dress and grooming by evaluating yourself. Answer the following questions in the space provided:

- Do you dress appropriately?

_____

_____

- Do you bathe/shower daily and wear deodorant?

_____

_____

- Is your hair clean and styled?

_____

_____

- Do you brush your teeth daily and use mouthwash?

_____

_____

(Continued)

EXERCISE 7-K (Continued)

• Do you clean your clothes after each wear?

_____

_____

• Do you press clothing before each wear?

_____

_____

• Do you keep your shoes shined and in good repair?

_____

_____

• Do you keep your nails clean and manicured?

_____

_____

• Do you apply makeup conservatively?

_____

_____

• Do you cover tattoos and body piercings in the workplace?

_____

_____

• Do you limit the amount of jewelry you wear?

_____

_____

Note: You should have answered _yes_ to all of these questions. If you did not, implement a proper grooming/hygiene program.

7

EXERCISE 7-L

Look over your current wardrobe. On the lines provided, make a list of the clothing that is suitable for business attire. Do the same with accessories, shoes, and jewelry. After taking inventory, determine how many outfits you have available to wear to work. Make a list of future items you will need to purchase (when you are in a position to buy them) that will enhance your wardrobe.

_____

_____

_____

_____

_____

_____

_____

_____

_____

_____

EXERCISE 7-M

Search for pictures of clothing in catalogs and on-line that would be suitable for the workplace that you intend to enter. On a poster board, make a collage of the appropriate pictures.

USING PROFESSIONAL LANGUAGE

Professional language consists of speaking correctly, using appropriate words in a proficient manner. Using correct grammar leaves a positive impression, as it indicates the speaker is educated and language conscious. Applying grammar rules to oral and written communications sends clear messages that an individual is competent. Brush up on your grammar rules if necessary so you will be able to communicate properly. Consult reference books when in doubt.

Although academic terms express your knowledge, they do not necessarily convey your messages in the best way, as some people will not understand them. Business words get your message across clearly and at the same time label you a professional. Become familiar with standard business terms that most professionals use. Improve your vocabulary by adding new words on a regular basis. Check the meaning of unfamiliar words and add them to your vocabulary. It is also vital to pronounce words correctly so the listener interprets the message the way you intended.

EXERCISE 7-N

Table 7–2 contains a sampling of standard business terms. On a separate sheet of paper, define the words and be able to use them in sentences.

Table 7–2 LIST OF STANDARD BUSINESS TERMS

STANDARD BUSINESS TERMS		
Reimburse	Authority	Delegate
Performance	Exempt	Compensation
Strategy	Critical	Requisition
Convenience	Alternatives	Achievement
Influence	Decision making	Communication
Projections	Advertisement	Electronic mail (e-mail)
Advantageous	Discipline	Manageable
Correspondence	Facilitate	Prominent
Documentation	Integrity	Serviceable
Advise	Ethical	Opportunity
Agreement	Transferable	Occasionally
Analysis	Auxiliary	Campaign
Thoroughly	Procedure	Minimum

(Continued)

7

TABLE 7–2 (Continued)

STANDARD BUSINESS TERMS		
Conscientious	Responsibility	Productivity
Interpersonal	Incentive	Cooperation
Evaluation	Tendency	Punctuality

CHARACTERISTICS OF A PROFESSIONAL

▶ Self-confident
▶ Expert in his or her field
▶ Impeccably dressed
▶ Excellent communicator
▶ Continuously improves self
▶ Helps others become professionals
▶ Competent and efficient
▶ Keeps up-to-date on technology and industry trends
▶ Skilled
▶ Uses good judgment
▶ Problem solver
▶ Works independently
▶ Educated
▶ Maintains a positive attitude
▶ Flexible
▶ Deals positively with change
▶ Welcomes challenges
▶ Dressed for success
▶ Well groomed
▶ Goal oriented
▶ Critical thinker
▶ Decision maker
▶ Team player

EXERCISE 7-O

Fill out the evaluation in Table 7–3 to determine if you display professionalism.

Table 7–3 SELF-EVALUATION: PROFESSIONAL ATTITUDES AT WORK

ANSWER THE FOLLOWING QUESTIONS ABOUT YOUR ATTITUDE:	Yes	No
• Are you generally positive at work?		
• Are you positive while performing your tasks?		
• Do you face challenging situations with a positive attitude?		
• Can you put difficult situations into perspective?		
• Can you find additional ways to be more effective at putting difficult situations into perspective?		
• Do you make the best of situations?		
• Do you look for the good in others?		
• Does your attitude affect your mood in a positive way?		
• Does your attitude affect your coworkers in a positive way?		
• Do you relate well to others?		
• Do you remain positive whenever you have a task to do that you dislike?		
• Do you do your part to create a pleasant atmosphere?		

LEARNING NEW SKILLS

Employers want employees who are willing to improve themselves and keep their skills up-to-date. In today's workplace it is important to commit to developing your skills to the fullest and to add new skills that will keep you competitive (i.e. meeting the latest technological advancements). Because change is inevitable, the employee

7

who refuses to keep up with technology and current industry trends will quickly become obsolete and of little value to the employer.

One of the best things you can do to make sure you remain employable and valuable is to upgrade your skills and expand your knowledge. Learn everything you can about your industry and your position. Employers are more likely to keep employees who improve their skills over those who do not.

We are in an age where **lifelong learning** is a requirement to stay competitive in the job market. That means you can never stop learning, whether it is in a formal classroom, at seminars, in company training programs, or through reading materials.

When deciding what skills you should develop or which new ones to learn, build on your strengths and interests. If you have abilities in certain areas, it will be easy to turn them into useful, workable skills. For instance, effective communication skills are always in demand. If English and writing are two of your strengths, perhaps you could look into courses in journalism or editing and take a position at a newspaper, magazine, or book publisher. Learn something you would enjoy doing, as having an interest in a subject makes it easier to excel.

Instead of concentrating on a particular job opening, prepare yourself to be a highly employable person. Learn skills and gain education in areas where there are ample jobs, such as health care, accounting, computer operations, etc. This provides an edge because you will be able to take your skills from job to job, adapting them to each position as needed.

Check to see if your company has a tuition reimbursement program. Employers look favorably on employees who further their education.

You can gain education and skills in a variety of ways, many of which are free or inexpensive. These include company training programs, seminars, and workshops; observing other workers; finding a mentor; volunteering in organizations where you can develop new skills; attending professional organization workshops; and reading journals and other materials.

If you can afford to pay for your education, a number of colleges and schools offer a wide variety of courses. Keep up-to-date with technology, since computer software programs and technology are always changing. Become familiar with current information and computer applications so you will be in a position to remain competitive with other job candidates. The more you learn, the more confident you will become.

Tips & Tricks

Where to Learn

- College credit and noncredit courses and seminars
- On-the-job training programs
- Programs offered by professional organizations
- Reading about subjects
- Completing projects
- Observing others
- Volunteering
- On-line classes
- Workshops sponsored by professional organizations
- Conventions for the industry

EXERCISE 7-P

Review the skills self-assessment evaluation you took in Chapter 1 and determine what skills you need to develop further, or which new ones you should learn. Check into possible ways of attaining these skills.

SOLVING PROBLEMS THROUGH CRITICAL THINKING

Critical-thinking and decision-making skills will be required throughout your career. You will need to see problems clearly to arrive at sound decisions. Analyze problems by gathering all the facts, looking at them objectively, considering them from different angles, and then questioning everything.

Suspend judgments, perceptions, and personal opinions while you gather and examine the facts, so you get a true picture. Weigh the facts and then list steps you could take to solve the problem. What do you know about the problem? Think about the pros and cons, and write them down.

Take a creative approach to problem solving by challenging ordinary solutions and exploring new ideas. Process the information you have gathered by applying logical reasoning to find available options. List these in the best possible order, and select the most appropriate one.

Once a solution has been agreed upon, implement it. After a suitable time period, evaluate the solution. If it is not working, go back to your list of options and select another. Implement and then evaluate the new solution.

Critical thinkers challenge the norm, dig deep into the facts, remain objective, and use their imaginations to come up with workable solutions. They raise questions, brainstorm ideas alone or with others, list the options, assess each option carefully, and make logical decisions based on all of this information. Creative thinkers disregard their personal opinions, use good judgment based on past experiences, and arrive at decisions objectively and fairly.

JUDGMENT ERRORS

Judgment errors occur when incorrect personal opinions, stereotyping, generalizations, assumptions, and perceptions cause an individual to be ineffective at making decisions. Errors are often made when options and solutions are arrived at before they have been researched thoroughly.

FACE CHALLENGES

When positive professional individuals run into problems, they look for ways to solve them, treating them as challenges. Learn to look at problems from the right viewpoint.

All of us face difficult situations periodically that we would prefer to ignore. However, that seldom works. Instead, treat a problem as a challenge, and search for ways to solve it. Write down the facts, determine some options, and choose a solution. If the solution does not work, go through the list of options again and implement another one. Focus on solutions to overcome the problem.

ASK YOURSELF THESE QUESTIONS:

- What is the problem?
- Have I researched the problem?
- Where can I research the problem?
- What steps can I take to solve the problem?
- What solution options are available for the problem?
- Have I eliminated errors in judgment?
- Is my attitude positive toward solving this problem?
- Have I explored all options?
- Have I analyzed the problem?
- Have I analyzed the possible solutions?
- Have I chosen a solution?
- How can I implement my solution?

TAKE STEPS TO SOLVE PROBLEMS

Oftentimes the major problem is difficult to define because minor problems are disguising it. The facts may not be clear, or they may not directly relate to the major problem. In addition, it may be difficult to look at the facts objectively because of personal feelings. In such cases, you may want to consult a coworker or supervisor. Get others involved in the process of solving the problem by having them brainstorm ideas with you. Take action and accept responsibility for the problem and solutions you implement.

When looking for solutions, answer the question: "What is the problem?" State the problem in clear language, defining what you know and what you need to determine. Search for additional information you will need in order to make an informed decision by considering (1) the main problem, (2) the pertinent facts, (3) any disguised minor problems, and (4) possible solutions.

Break down the problem into steps so it is manageable. Apply logical reasoning to each step as you work to solve it. Use all the information you have obtained to create a workable plan. Develop a strategy, implement a solution, and evaluate the outcome.

Take the time necessary to arrive at an effective solution. Your first or even second attempt to solve a problem may fail, requiring that you try again.

If the problem is not satisfactorily resolved for some reason, repeat the problem-solving steps. Keep trying until you find the correct solution. Thinking of the problem as a challenge that can be overcome will help you discover workable strategies.

EXERCISE 7-Q

Think of a major problem you have recently solved or one you are working toward solving. What steps did you take to solve the problem? Write your answers in the space provided.

_____

_____

_____

_____

Were you able to resolve the problem?

_____

7

Tips & Tricks

Tips for Solving Problems

- Clearly state the problem.
- List all pertinent facts.
- Ask questions to clarify.
- Gather information through research.
- Analyze the facts.
- Choose possible strategies.
- List options.
- Assess each option.
- Choose an option.
- Implement a solution.
- Anticipate the outcome.
- Evaluate the outcome.
- If necessary, select another option and implement it.

EXERCISE 7-R

Think of a problem you tried to solve, but the solution you chose did not work. Answer the questions in the space provided.

- Do you believe you made an error in judgment?

_____

_____

- If so, what did you learn from the situation?

_____

_____

- If there was no error in judgment, why do you think the solution failed?

_____

_____

● WORKING WITH THE SUPERVISOR

You can work *for* a supervisor or *with* a supervisor. Your attitude and the way you approach the supervisor makes the difference. Working *with* a supervisor is applying a team player approach to this all-important relationship. Working *for* a supervisor gives you a sense of having the supervisor dictate what you are to do.

Working with someone means you stay in close contact with him or her when determining daily and long-term priorities, and you keep the lines of communication open. If something happens that the supervisor should know about, provide complete, timely details, but do not waste time on petty incidents.

When working with a supervisor, keep confidential information to yourself and never betray him or her. Maintain loyalty by following directives, policies, and decisions. In general, make the supervisor's work life easier by doing your part to keep everything running smoothly. Be considerate of the supervisor's time by limiting your messages and questions to brief, but complete, facts.

To maintain a good working relationship, display the positive work ethics discussed in Chapter 2—report to work every day, and put in an honest day's work by completing your duties accurately and efficiently. Do not pass blame, criticize the supervisor to others, or undermine him or her in any way.

Learning as much as you can about your supervisor's position in the company, responsibilities, and background will help you determine how you can help him or her reach goals. Find out how your position fits with the company in relation to your supervisor's.

It is imperative to get along with your supervisor in order to complete your individual tasks and the team's tasks effectively. Do the best job you can, and look for ways to increase your productivity while being cooperative. Ask for directions if you are unsure of how to complete a task.

ACCEPTING CRITICISM FROM YOUR SUPERVISOR

After observing you, the supervisor may offer criticisms or suggestions for improving your work and productivity. Do not take offense. The supervisor does have a right to expect you to complete work accurately and efficiently according to company requirements. Therefore, accept the suggestions and consider them an opportunity to improve yourself.

7

When you have a problem with the supervisor, sit down and discuss it, rather than telling someone in a higher position about it or complaining to others. Negative talk is destructive and counterproductive, and going to your supervisor's superior is disloyal. It will aggravate the situation and portray you in an unfavorable light.

COOPERATING WITH COWORKERS

Getting along with others is extremely important. A majority of people who get fired do so because they cannot get along. Therefore, employees must find a way to cooperate with one another in the workplace.

You do not have to be best friends or even a friend at all to your coworkers. However, you do have to be able to complete all your tasks, work with anyone when you are assigned to do a job, and refrain from causing workplace strife. Put negative personal feelings aside when it comes to coworkers and supervisors; cooperate.

If you do not have an amicable relationship with a particular worker, ask yourself what you can do to foster one. Poor working relationships cause low employee morale, which creates unfriendly and rude attitudes, excessive absenteeism, high turnovers, and low productivity.

Find a way to deal with everyday frustrations and irritations so they do not escalate into major problems. Do not overreact to anger; keep everything in proper perspective. Remember, anything you say could be repeated. If you do not want information to become common knowledge, keep it to yourself. When you hear negative comments, look beyond the words to the motives of the one speaking. Rumors are often distorted by people who add their opinions as they pass them along to others.

Accept responsibility for your actions. If you make a mistake, admit it and work on finding a satisfactory resolution. Do your share of work, complete assignments to the best of your ability, and follow the rules. Company rules are for all employees. If certain employees do not abide by the rules, they send a message that they are better than everyone else. Follow company rules to show you are a team player.

Everyone must take orders from employees who have more seniority and/or who are in supervisory positions. Learn to do as you are told by willingly accepting assignments.

Showing an interest in coworkers and their jobs, encouraging them, smiling, and being friendly will greatly enhance your workplace relationships. Pitch in when coworkers need help.

Tips & Tricks

Things You Can Do to Get Along with Supervisors and Coworkers

- Avoid gossip and rumors.
- Do not bad mouth anyone.
- Remain professional.
- Deal positively with daily irritations.
- Keep things in perspective.
- Accept responsibility for your actions.
- Admit mistakes.
- Show courtesy.
- Hold up your end of the team.
- Work quickly and accurately.
- Maintain a positive work ethic.
- Maintain a positive attitude.
- Discuss problems and complaints.
- Keep your emotions in check.
- Keep confidential information to yourself.
- Do your share of team-related responsibilities.
- Have a genuine interest in others.
- Pitch in and help whenever you can.
- Remember that angry words can come back to haunt you.
- Learn about your boss's background and position.
- Support your boss and team members.

END OF CHAPTER WORK

CASE STUDIES

● COWORKER CASE STUDY

Shelly and Jill work in a customer service center, where they take calls for eight hours a day. Shelly noticed that Jill let the phone ring whenever there was someone else available to answer it. When everyone was busy with other calls, Jill would answer the phone, although she let it ring several times. When she answered

7

the calls, Jill said "Hello" with an abrupt tone. Jill also told Shelly over and over how she hated the customers.

Although Shelly reminded her that it was their job to answer the phones and help customers, Jill continued to complain. Shelly reached the point where she wanted to tell Jill to go work somewhere else if she was so unhappy.

Shelly debated with herself about whether to inform the supervisor of Jill's attitude. She did not want to continue doing Jill's share of the work whenever she ignored the ringing phone. She also knew the company might lose customers because of Jill's negative attitude. On the other hand, Shelly did not want to cause friction with a coworker, especially when they worked in such close quarters.

Questions to Ask Yourself

1. What could you tell your supervisor about Jill's attitude?

   _____

   _____

2. What would you say to Jill when she complained about customers?

   _____

   _____

Things to Consider

Telling a supervisor about negative actions of a coworker may put you in a compromising situation. You could gain an enemy (the coworker) and create problems for yourself if the coworker brands you a traitor and then turns others against you. The supervisor may be grateful for the information and consider you a loyal employee. The reverse may also be true. The supervisor could already know what is going on and label you a troublemaker and immature for tattling on a coworker.

If possible, Shelly could talk to Jill about ways in which she could gain a better attitude or else explain what she does to maintain her own positive attitude. Another thing Shelly might do is to inform Jill that she feels she is taking more than her share of calls, and it is creating a stressful situation. Shelly should not accuse Jill of slacking but rather state her feelings of being overwhelmed with work.

PROFESSIONAL IMAGE CASE STUDY

Moranda is the supervisor for a large billing firm. She dresses impeccably, works efficiently, and treats everyone fairly and respectfully. Her personal assistant Jarin loves working with her.

Moranda has one habit, however, that ruins her professional image. She frequently uses the word *crap* in her speech. Jarin wants to tell Moranda the word is a detriment to her image, but she does not know how to approach her about it without hurting her feelings or their working relationship.

Questions to Ask Yourself

1. Do you think Jarin is correct in thinking Moranda's word choice is detrimental to her image?

   _____

   _____

2. How would you handle the situation if you were Jarin?

   _____

   _____

Things to Consider

Moranda's word choice is definitely a detriment to her professional image, since it is a tasteless slang word. She may think that using such a word is preferable to swearing, but it is just as tactless. Jarin would be doing Moranda a favor if she could find a diplomatic way of telling her that she should eliminate the word from her vocabulary. If Jarin has a very good working relationship with Moranda, she may be able to open a conversation by saying something like, "You are the most professional person I know. That is why I'm surprised you would use the word *crap*. It is so out of character for you."

If Jarin does not want to confront Moranda directly, perhaps she could say a customer took offense to the word or nonverbally communicated that it was in poor taste.

LEARNING NEW SKILLS CASE STUDY

Alex works for an accounting firm. His supervisor wants him to attend a series of seminars, which will be held twice a week for one month. The seminars will teach employees a new accounting software that will be implemented companywide. Alex has been complaining ever since he learned about the seminar. Although he can attend during work hours, he does not want to drive out of his way to get to the seminar or upset his daily routine. Another complaint is that he will have to study and then spend time practicing the software.

Questions to Ask Yourself

1. Why should Alex welcome the opportunity to attend the seminar?

   _____

   _____

2. Would you be willing to attend company seminars like the one Alex must attend? Explain your answer.

   _____

   _____

Things to Consider

We are in the age of lifelong learning, and technology is one ever-changing area that will require constant updating. Alex should look at the seminars as a learning opportunity that will make him a more valuable employee, and he should welcome the chance. In addition, knowledge of the new software will give Alex another skill he can take elsewhere should he lose his job.

Employees should take advantage of every prospect to gain skills and/or knowledge. Learning at the company's expense is a big plus since courses and seminars tend to be expensive. Another advantage in Alex's case is having the opportunity to take classes during work hours. Everyone should be prepared to embrace lifelong learning in order to stay competitive on the job, as well as in the job market.

● **GOAL-SETTING CASE STUDY**

Courtney started her first full-time job and wanted to buy a new car. She lives with her parents, who do not charge her rent. She has a school loan from college and will need money to pay for car insurance. Courtney is considering a vehicle that is fairly expensive for her starting salary, but she believes she can afford the payments if she saves a $2,000 down payment.

Questions to Ask

1. Is it likely Courtney could save $2,000 in a reasonable amount of time given her circumstances?

   _____

   _____

2. If Courtney sets a goal of saving $2,000, what steps should she take to reach the goal?

   _____

   _____

Things to Consider

If Courtney sets a goal of saving $2,000, she should draw up a budget so she will know how much money she will have coming in and how much she will have going out on expenses. That will give her an idea of what she can afford to save. Then she needs to set a timeframe for her goal. For instance, if she wants to save $2,000 in one year, she should save $167 per month. If she prefers a different timeframe, she must divide the $2,000 by the number of months she wants to save.

Since Courtney is living with her parents, it seems like the right time to save money. She should be careful, though, not to overspend or get herself too deep in debt. Building a separate savings/emergency fund will help Courtney meet unexpected future expenses.

● **ATTITUDE CASE STUDY**

Shavan enjoys his job and happily hums to himself while he works. Since he works in an isolated area, his humming does not bother anyone. At lunchtime, Shavan smiles and cheerfully greets his coworkers.

Bob, one of the coworkers, makes negative comments when he is greeted. He hates the job and dislikes several of the other workers. Lately, Shavan has been internalizing the negative comments and feels his own attitude slipping.

Questions to Ask Yourself

1. What can Shavan do to maintain his positive attitude?

   _____

   _____

7

2. Should Shavan try to change Bob's attitude?

_____

_____

Things to Consider

There are many things Shavan can do to maintain his positive attitude, including focusing on the reasons he enjoys his job, repeating uplifting sayings to himself, being flexible, and socializing with people who share his enthusiasm.

Shavan will not be able to avoid Bob, so he should find a way to ignore the comments and stop internalizing them. Shavan needs to accept the fact that there will always be people who will try to make everyone else as miserable as they are. In addition, he should sit with coworkers he enjoys.

Since it is unlikely that Shavan will change Bob, he should work on keeping himself positive. Perhaps in time, Shavan's positive attitude will rub off on Bob.

● PROFESSIONAL DRESS CASE STUDY

Maddie works at a large city law firm. She has been warned twice about wearing unsuitable clothing in the office. Later, Maddie complained to a friend, "I guess I'll have to look for another job. They're too strict."

"But doesn't that job pay well?" her friend asked.

"Yeah, but they want me to wear old-lady skirts below my knees and black or navy suits. They even want me to pull my hair back."

Questions to Ask Yourself

1. Do you think Maddie has a satisfactory reason for quitting her job?

_____

_____

2. Is there some way she could compromise to keep the job?

_____

_____

Things to Consider

Maddie needs to exam her goals and decide what she wants from a career. If she decides to remain employed in the legal field, she must abide by the conservative dress of that industry.

There are many styles a young woman can wear that do not look frumpy or that will not outdate her. Maddie should go to a better department or clothing store and ask for a consultation. In addition, she could check on-line fashion sites and consult with friends who are in similar positions. Reading current fashion magazines and attending fashion shows will also give Maddie choices. If she decides to abide by the law firm's dress code, she can express her bolder side when she goes out in the evenings and on weekends.

● **SOLVING PROBLEMS CASE STUDY**

A customer called Scott, a supervisor, complaining about a shipment that arrived badly damaged. He told Scott that he had called one of the company's shipping clerks several days earlier to report the problem. The clerk promised to check into the matter and call him, but he never did.

Questions to Ask

1. How should Scott resolve the customer's problem?

   _____

   _____

2. What should Scott do about the shipping clerk who did not return the customer's call?

   _____

   _____

Things to Consider

Scott should calm the customer by reassuring him that he will resolve the problem. Scott should write down the details, clarify information he is unsure of, and research the problem. He should get back to the customer in a timely manner. After gathering all the facts, Scott should suggest options to the customer.

7

Once the customer's problem has been resolved, Scott should look into the incident with the shipping clerk. He could meet with the clerk and listen to his side of the story. Then Scott can determine the best course of action, which may include a warning, retraining, or disciplinary action. The shipping clerk must be made aware that the customer's satisfaction is a priority.

END OF CHAPTER QUESTIONS

1. Define professionalism.
2. How will your attitude determine your success or failure throughout your career?
3. Name five things you can do to maintain a positive attitude.
4. Describe an outfit that is acceptable as professional dress.
5. Describe an outfit that is acceptable business casual dress.
6. Name three things you can do to increase your professionalism.
7. Why is it important to set goals?
8. What are the characteristics of a goal?
9. Where can you learn new skills in your community?
10. What are three steps you can take to solve problems?
11. What types of goals could you set for your career?
12. Why is it so important to maintain outstanding business ethics?
13. What are three things you can do to ensure a positive work environment?
14. What are three things you can do to maintain a positive work experience with your coworkers?
15. How can you learn background information on your supervisor?
16. How can you improve your language skills?

17. If your company does not have a dress code, how can you learn how to properly dress for your job?

18. What are some things you should consider when buying clothing for the workplace?

19. What is critical thinking?

20. What are the steps to solving problems?

7

PERSONAL INFORMATION

Name _____

Address _____

City _____ State _____ Zip _____

If at this address less than 2 years:

Previous Address

City _____ State _____ Zip _____

Phone number (h)   (_____) _____ - _____

                (w)   (_____) _____ - _____

Date of birth _____/_____/_____
              mo   day   year

Place of birth City _____ State _____

U.S. citizen Yes _____ No _____

Social Security number _____-_____-_____

If not a U.S. citizen:

Visa number _____ Visa type _____

PROFESSIONAL EXPERIENCE

EMPLOYER 1

Name _____

Address _____

City _____ State _____ Zip _____

Phone number (w)   (_____) _____-_____

Job title _____

Reported to _____

Dates of employment   From _____/_____/_____ To _____/_____/_____
                             mo   day   year   mo   day   year

Reason for leaving position

_____

_____

Recommendation available   Yes _____ No _____

1. Contact name _____

   Contact title _____

2. Contact name _____

   Contact title _____

Duties and responsibilities

1. _____

_____

2. _____

_____

3. _____

_____

4. _____

_____

5. _____

_____

Technology used (software, telecommunication systems)

_____

_____

_____

_____

Equipment used (tools, machinery, hardware)

_____

_____

_____

_____

Accomplishments (qualify in terms of concrete employer-related benefits)

1. _____

_____

2. _____

_____

3. _____

_____

4. _____

_____

5. _____

_____

PROFESSIONAL EXPERIENCE

EMPLOYER 2

Name _____

Address _____

City _____ State _____ Zip _____

Phone number (w)   (_____) _____ - _____

Job title _____

Reported to _____

Dates of employment   From _____/_____/_____ To _____/_____/_____
                            mo   day   year   mo   day   year

Reason for leaving position

_____

_____

Recommendation available   Yes _____ No _____

1. Contact name _____

   Contact title _____

2. Contact name _____

   Contact title _____

Duties and responsibilities

1. _____

_____

2. _____

_____

3. _____

_____

4. _____

_____

5. _____

_____

Technology used (software, telecommunication systems)

_____

_____

_____

_____

Equipment used (tools, machinery, hardware)

_____

_____

_____

_____

Accomplishments (qualify in terms of concrete employer-related benefits)

1. _____

_____

2. _____

_____

3. _____

_____

4. _____

_____

5. _____

_____

PROFESSIONAL EXPERIENCE

EMPLOYER 3

Name _____

Address _____

City _____ State _____ Zip _____

Phone number (w)   (_____) _____-_____

Job title _____

Reported to _____

Dates of employment   From _____/_____/_____ To _____/_____/_____
                           mo   day   year   mo   day   year

Reason for leaving position

_____

_____

Recommendation available   Yes _____ No _____

1. Contact name _____

   Contact title _____

2. Contact name _____

   Contact title _____

Duties and responsibilities

1. _____

_____

2. _____

_____

3. _____

_____

4. _____

_____

5. _____

_____

Technology used (software, telecommunication systems)

_____

_____

_____

_____

_____

Equipment used (tools, machinery, hardware)

_____

_____

_____

_____

_____

Accomplishments (qualify in terms of concrete employer-related benefits)

1. _____

_____

2. _____

_____

3. _____

_____

4. _____

_____

5. _____

_____

PROFESSIONAL EXPERIENCE

EMPLOYER 4

Name _____

Address _____

City _____ State _____ Zip _____

Phone number (w)   (_____) _____ - _____

Job title _____

Reported to _____

Dates of employment   From _____/_____/_____ To _____/_____/_____
                      mo   day   year   mo   day   year

Reason for leaving position

_____

_____

Recommendation available   Yes _____ No _____

1. Contact name _____

   Contact title _____

2. Contact name _____

   Contact title _____

Duties and responsibilities

1. _____

   _____

2. _____

   _____

3. _____

   _____

4. _____

_____

5. _____

_____

Technology used (software, telecommunication systems)

_____

_____

_____

_____

_____

Equipment used (tools, machinery, hardware)

_____

_____

_____

_____

_____

Accomplishments (qualify in terms of concrete employer-related benefits)

1. _____

_____

2. _____

_____

3. _____

_____

4. _____

_____

5. _____

_____

EXTERNSHIP EXPERIENCE

Name _____

Address _____

City _____ State _____ Zip _____

Job title _____

Reported to _____

Dates of employment   From _____/_____/_____ To _____/_____/_____
                              mo   day   year   mo   day   year

Reason for leaving position

_____

_____

Recommendation available   Yes _____ No _____

1. Contact name _____

    Contact title _____

2. Contact name _____

    Contact title _____

Duties and responsibilities

1. _____

_____

2. _____

_____

3. _____

_____

4. _____

_____

5. _____

_____

Technology used (software, telecommunication systems)

_____

_____

_____

_____

_____

Equipment used (tools, machinery, hardware)

_____

_____

_____

_____

_____

Accomplishments (qualify in terms of concrete employer-related benefits)

1. _____

_____

2. _____

_____

3. _____

_____

4. _____

_____

5. _____

_____

EXTERNSHIP EXPERIENCE

Name _____

Address _____

City _____ State _____ Zip _____

Job title _____

Reported to _____

Dates of employment   From _____/_____/_____ To _____/_____/_____
                            mo   day   year   mo   day   year

Reason for leaving position

_____

_____

Recommendation available   Yes _____ No _____

1. Contact name _____

   Contact title _____

2. Contact name _____

   Contact title _____

Duties and responsibilities

1. _____

_____

2. _____

_____

3. _____

_____

4. _____

_____

5. _____

_____

Technology used (software, telecommunication systems)

_____

_____

_____

_____

_____

Equipment used (tools, machinery, hardware)

_____

_____

_____

_____

_____

Accomplishments (qualify in terms of concrete employer-related benefits)

1. _____

_____

2. _____

_____

3. _____

_____

4. _____

_____

5. _____

_____

VOLUNTEER EXPERIENCE

Name _____

Address _____

City _____ State _____ Zip _____

Job title _____

Reported to _____

Dates of employment   From _____/_____/_____ To _____/_____/_____
                             mo   day   year   mo   day   year

Reason for leaving position

_____

_____

Recommendation available   Yes _____ No _____

1. Contact name _____

   Contact title _____

2. Contact name _____

   Contact title _____

Duties and responsibilities

1. _____

_____

2. _____

_____

3. _____

_____

4. _____

_____

5. _____

_____

Technology used (software, telecommunication systems)

_____

_____

_____

_____

_____

Equipment used (tools, machinery, hardware)

_____

_____

_____

_____

_____

Accomplishments (qualify in terms of concrete employer-related benefits)

1. _____

_____

2. _____

_____

3. _____

_____

4. _____

_____

5. _____

_____

VOLUNTEER EXPERIENCE

Association/Organization name _____

Address _____

City _____ State _____ Zip _____

Job title _____

Reported to _____

Dates of employment From _____/_____/_____ To _____/_____/_____
                              mo   day   year   mo   day   year

Reason for leaving position

_____

_____

Recommendation available   Yes _____   No _____

1. Contact name _____

   Contact title _____

2. Contact name _____

   Contact title _____

Duties and responsibilities

1. _____

_____

2. _____

_____

3. _____

_____

4. _____

_____

5. _____

_____

Technology used (software, telecommunication systems)

_____

_____

_____

_____

_____

Equipment used (tools, machinery, hardware)

_____

_____

_____

_____

Accomplishments (qualify in terms of concrete employer-related benefits)

1. _____

_____

2. _____

_____

3. _____

_____

4. _____

_____

5. _____

_____

MILITARY EXPERIENCE

Branch of Service _____

Service Number _____

Armed Forces Code _____

Service Number _____

Honorable discharge Yes _____ No _____

Registered with Selective Service Yes _____ No _____

Vietnam Era veteran Yes _____ No _____

Disabled veteran Yes _____ No _____

Recommendation available Yes _____ No _____

1. Contact name _____

   Contact title _____

2. Contact name _____

   Contact title _____

Duties and responsibilities

1. _____

_____

2. _____

_____

3. _____

_____

4. _____

_____

5. _____

_____

Technology used (software, telecommunication systems)

_____

_____

_____

_____

_____

Equipment used (tools, machinery, hardware)

_____

_____

_____

_____

_____

Accomplishments (qualify in terms of concrete employer-related benefits)

1. _____

_____

2. _____

_____

3. _____

_____

4. _____

_____

5. _____

_____

EDUCATION AND

PROGRAM	INSTITUTION	FROM		TO	
		MO.	YR.	MO.	YR.
High School	Name: _____ _____ Address: _____ _____ City _____ State ____ Zip _____ Phone number (school) (_____) _____ - _____				
College	Name: _____ _____ Address: _____ _____ City _____ State ____ Zip _____ Phone number (college) (_____) _____ - _____				
Other	Name: _____ _____ Address: _____ _____ City _____ State ____ Zip _____ Phone number (_____) _____ - _____				
Other	Name: _____ _____ Address: _____ _____ City _____ State ____ Zip _____ Phone number _____				
GED	Date Received _____ / _____ mo. yr.				

VOCATIONAL TRAINING

AREA OF STUDY	CREDIT HOURS COMPLETED	DIPLOMA/ DEGREE/ CERTIFICATE	DATE GRANTED		GRADE POINT AVERAGE
			MO.	YR.	
Major: Minor:					
Major: Minor:					
Major: Minor:					
Major: Minor:					

City _____ State _____

CAREER OBJECTIVES

Job title 1. _____

Job title 2. _____

Preferred salary $_____

Start date _____/_____/_____
           mo   day   year

Preferred schedule   Mon.–Fri. _____

                    Other _____

Weekends Yes _____ No _____

Holidays   Yes _____ No _____

Overtime   Yes _____ No _____

Relocation Yes _____ No _____

Preferred locations 1. _____

                       2. _____

                       3. _____

Professional Memberships

Organization name _____

Organization name _____

Professional Certifications/Licenses

Type _____   exp. date _____

Type _____   exp. date _____

Personal interests (hobbies, leisure activities)

1. _____

_____

2. _____

_____

3. _____

_____

4. _____

_____

5. _____

_____

PERSONAL REFERENCES

REFERENCE 1

Name _____

Address _____

City _____ State _____ Zip _____

Phone (w) _____ phone (h) _____

Relationship _____ Number of years known _____

Received resume or work history? Yes ____ No ____

REFERENCE 2

Name _____

Address _____

City _____ State _____ Zip _____

Phone (w) _____ phone (h) _____

Relationship _____ Number of years known _____

Received resume or work history? Yes ____ No ____

REFERENCE 3

Name _____

Address _____

City_____ State _____ Zip _____

Phone (w) _____ phone (h) _____

Relationship _____ Number of years known _____

Received resume or work history? Yes ____ No ____

PROFESSIONAL REFERENCES

REFERENCE 1

Name _____

Title _____

Company name _____

Address _____

City _____ State _____ Zip _____

Phone _____ ext. _____

Received resume or work history? Yes____ No____

REFERENCE 2

Name _____

Title _____

Company name _____

Address _____

City _____ State _____ Zip _____

Phone _____ ext. _____

Received resume or work history? Yes ____ No ____

REFERENCE 3

Name _____

Title _____

Company name _____

Address _____

City _____ State _____ Zip _____

Phone _____ ext. _____

Received resume or work history? Yes ___ No ___

REFERENCE 4

Name _____

Title _____

Company name _____

Address _____

City _____ State _____ Zip _____

Phone _____ ext. _____

Received resume or work history? Yes ___ No ___

REFERENCE 5

Name _____

Title _____

Company name _____

Address _____

City _____ State _____ Zip _____

Phone _____ ext. _____

Received resume or work history? Yes ___ No ___

FREQUENTLY ASKED INTERVIEW QUESTIONS

- Why are you interested in working for us?
- Tell me about yourself.
- What are your strengths?
- What is your major weakness?
- What interests you most about this job?
- Do you work better alone or in a group?
- What do you know about our organization?
- What do you like to do in your spare time?
- How would you describe your personality?
- Which of your accomplishments have given you the greatest satisfaction?
- How would you define your long-range career goals?
- Why are you leaving your present job?
- Do you have any questions for me?

QUESTIONS YOU SHOULD ASK

Asking questions demonstrates your interest in the position.

- What do you like and dislike most about the organization?
- How do you see your organization developing over the next few years?
- What would be the highest priority for me to accomplish if you hired me?
- If you were to offer me the job, where could I expect to be five years from now?

ADDITIONAL QUESTIONS YOU WISH TO ASK

1. _____

   _____

2. _____

   _____

3. _____

   _____

4. _____

   _____

5. _____
   _____

6. _____
   _____

7. _____
   _____

8. _____
   _____

9. _____
   _____

10. _____
    _____
    _____

WHEN YOU ARE LEAVING THE INTERVIEW

- Offer a firm handshake while expressing your thanks to the interviewer.
- Mention that you are eagerly looking forward to hearing from him or her.
- Always be courteous to the secretary or assistant upon leaving the office.

FOLLOW UP AFTER THE INTERVIEW

- Send a thank-you letter.
- Start with a courteous thank you for the interview.
- End with a reiteration of why you want the job and what you can do for the organization.
- One week after the interview, follow up with a phone call.
- If you do not get the job, ask the interviewer for some constructive criticism on your interview technique.

INTERVIEW INFORMATION

Date of interview _____

Company name _____

Company address _____

Interviewer's name _____

Interviewer's title _____

Date of interview _____

Company name _____

Company address _____

Interviewer's name _____

Interviewer's title _____

Date of interview _____

Company name _____

Company address _____

Interviewer's name _____

Interviewer's title _____

Date of interview _____

Company name _____

Company address _____

Interviewer's name _____

Interviewer's title _____

Date of interview _____

Company name _____

Company address _____

Interviewer's name _____

Interviewer's title _____

INTERVIEW INFORMATION

Date of interview   _____

Company name   _____

Company address   _____

Interviewer's name _____

Interviewer's title   _____

Date of interview   _____

Company name   _____

Company address   _____

Interviewer's name _____

Interviewer's title   _____

Date of interview   _____

Company name   _____

Company address   _____

Interviewer's name _____

Interviewer's title   _____

Date of interview   _____

Company name   _____

Company address   _____

Interviewer's name _____

Interviewer's title   _____

Date of interview _____

Company name _____

Company address _____

Interviewer's name _____

Interviewer's title _____

INTERVIEW INFORMATION

Date of interview   _____

Company name   _____

Company address   _____

Interviewer's name   _____

Interviewer's title   _____

Date of interview   _____

Company name   _____

Company address   _____

Interviewer's name   _____

Interviewer's title   _____

Date of interview   _____

Company name   _____

Company address   _____

Interviewer's name   _____

Interviewer's title   _____

Date of interview   _____

Company name   _____

Company address   _____

Interviewer's name   _____

Interviewer's title   _____

Date of interview _____

Company name _____

Company address _____

Interviewer's name _____

Interviewer's title _____

INTERVIEW INFORMATION

Date of interview _____

Company name _____

Company address _____

Interviewer's name _____

Interviewer's title _____

Date of interview _____

Company name _____

Company address _____

Interviewer's name _____

Interviewer's title _____

Date of interview _____

Company name _____

Company address _____

Interviewer's name _____

Interviewer's title _____

Date of interview _____

Company name _____

Company address _____

Interviewer's name _____

Interviewer's title _____

Date of interview _____

Company name _____

Company address _____

Interviewer's name _____

Interviewer's title _____

NOTES

NOTES

Glossary

CHAPTER ONE

attributes mannerisms and characteristics, such as dependability and loyalty

career job or occupation

career center a special department, usually at a school, that provides assistance in finding a suitable job

competencies abilities and areas of expertise

evaluate to examine and explore all options

inventory an account of one's abilities, skills, and education

life experience accumulation of knowledge and skills gained by living

life skills abilities and talents accumulated through every day living

life stages different periods in one's life, including childhood, young adulthood, adulthood, parenthood, school/college student, spouse, and employee, etc.

personal assets a talent, abilities, and or character traits

self-assessment an evaluation of one's interests, goals, skills, and education

values beliefs

CHAPTER TWO

application a form used by companies to request your background information for a job opening

cover letter a letter that accompanies a resume

externship a position within a company that allows you to hone your skills while learning on the job and using your education

group interview held with two or more interviewees

illegal question laws prohibit interviewers from asking certain questions that may discriminate against people

informational interview when a person interviews someone in the workplace to learn about a particular career and/or company

integrity honesty; honor

Internet site a specific place on the Internet that displays information

job objective a main career goal

job shadow going to a workplace and following an employee to learn what he or she does on the job

networking making contacts and taking advantage of support from others who encourage, motivate, and offer help in developing a career

portfolio a collection of documents used during an interview to impress a prospective employer

professional organization a group or association in a particular industry or field

punctuality consistently arriving on time

reference sheet a listing of people who will recommend a job seeker by vouching for his or her work, education, and personal traits

resume a professional summary of your background information

screening interview when an interviewer is checking to see if the candidate is qualified; it may be conducted by phone or in person

structured interview follows a set question–answer format, where the interviewer determines if the candidate has sufficient skills and experience to do the job and a personality that will fit well with other employees

team player someone who gets along with and works well with others

work ethic the moral code by which you operate in the workplace, such as attendance record, honesty, maintaining confidences, and the like

CHAPTER THREE

articulation pronunciation

concrete words words that are specific; see Table 3–1 for examples

empathy putting yourself in the other person's place; showing understanding and compassion

feedback reactions and responses

inflection raising and lowering the volume of your voice

jargon words, terms, and phrases specific to an industry or field of study that may be confusing to the average person

listening barriers obstacles that could sabotage a speaker or listener, such as the audience talking, attendee lateness, background noise, monotone voice, speaking too softly, etc.

monotone a flat, boring voice

nonverbal communication body language (gestures, nodding, eye contact, smiling, etc.), appearance (dress and grooming), and the like

oral communication the use of spoken words to exchange or convey information

paraphrase to restate or summarize something in one's own words

tone how you say something and the feeling—positive or negative—it conveys

visual aids handouts, products, samples, equipment, slides, DVDs, wall charts, blackboards, and the like

voice mail recorded verbal messages, generally by telephone

CHAPTER FOUR

biases personal opinions, stereotyping, and judgments

cultural differences the diversity in the beliefs and values people from different countries hold, as well their customs, actions, thoughts, feelings, etc.

customer loyalty occurs when customers faithfully use a company's products and services, returning again and again

customer service attitude an attitude that encompasses product knowledge, personal appearance, and positive customer contact

goodwill the feeling created by displaying a helpful, friendly, concerned attitude

open-ended questions questions that require an explanation, not a simple yes-or-no answer

perception an individual view or opinion based on individual backgrounds, experiences, education, and life situations

product knowledge encompasses learning all you can about your company's current products and striving to learn about new ones that are being developed

professionalism includes expertise, level-headedness, and competence

rapport the positive feeling one gets when he or she "connects" with someone by finding something in common; displaying an interest in another person and being genuinely likeable

CHAPTER FIVE

business ethics refers to legal, moral, and responsible conduct in the workplace

chain of command the order of employees ranked from lowest to highest on the company's organization chart

corporate culture pertains to employee dress, attitude, performance, interaction with customers, overall knowledge, communication, facilities, furnishings, etc.

discrimination differentiating between people in the workplace, using favoritism, and displaying prejudice and inequity

EOC the Equal Employment Opportunity Commission, which administers many of the laws dealing with discrimination

ergonomics deals with making equipment, jobs, and the work environment safe for employees; it includes lighting, noise, temperature, color, and the design, adjustability, layout, and comfort of equipment, tools, and furnishings

harassment unwanted and unsolicited comments, gestures, physical contact, graphic material, or solicited favors

norms are informal, unwritten rules that cover acceptable conduct for employees, conveying various values, traditions, cultures, and rules of behavior for companies

OSHA the Occupational Safety and Health Administration, an organization that sets and enforces standards for safety and health in the workplace

OSH Act is the Occupational Safety and Health Act, which requires employers to provide safe and healthy working conditions for employees

repetitive stress injuries injuries resulting from the constant repetition of similar motions, such as typing, twisting, using the same finger(s) to operate equipment, etc.

safety security and protection from hazard or anything that threatens the well-being of others

CHAPTER SIX

business cards cards that include name, address, phone number, and other contact information useful in a business situation

Civil Service Exam a specific test required to work in government positions

employment agency a business that helps individuals find jobs and/or assists companies in finding employees

job fairs gatherings of many employers meant to attract specifically skilled individuals by providing the opportunity to submit a number of resumes in one location within a specific time period

job leads hints and information gathered about positions in the workplace

recommendation letters letters employers write for individuals who have performed well on the job, recommending them for other employment opportunities

CHAPTER SEVEN

action plan a map that charts a path toward a goal and success

attitude a way of thinking; thoughts and feelings

career goals job-related objectives or targets

career plan a guide to help find the right job or to secure a position that leads to career success and enjoyment

casual business dress good quality dress slacks, blouses, shirts, skirts, sweaters, and jackets; it does not include jeans and t-shirts; it also does not include suits or formal attire

critical thinking analyzing situations and problems while suspending judgments, perceptions, and personal opinions while gathering and examining the facts

dress code a policy that dictates what the proper attire is for a particular workplace

judgment errors mistakes brought on by incorrect personal opinions, stereotyping, generalizations, assumptions, and perceptions, causing an individual to be ineffective at making decisions

lifelong learning learning that continues throughout life, whether it is in a formal classroom, at seminars, in company training programs, or through reading materials

professional attire suits, dress slacks and jackets, and coordinated outfits

professional image the way someone is seen by others when he/she possesses excellent written, oral, and listening communication skills

professional language correct, appropriate words spoken in a proficient manner

Index